Praise for *Mag...*

'It's a magical, true story of the friendship between an impoverished young boy and a famous opera star in 1950s Dublin' – *Irish Independent*

'*Maggie's Breakfast* is an honest tale of optimism and humour, and one the remains with you for a long time. Highly recommended' – *Woman's Way*

'An astonishing memoir of redemption' – *Irish Examiner*

'A heart-warming story of an extraordinary life' – *Evening Echo*

'The story of friendship and opportunity could only come from a movie script' – *The Sunday World*

'*Maggie's Breakfast* is an entertaining, witty and often surprising account of a poor Dublin childhood' – *Bord Gáis Energy Book Club*

'A fascinating story of the old times in Dublin' – Gay Byrne, *Lyric FM*

'Reads like the plot of a rags-to-riches movie' – *Irish Daily Mail*

'A remarkable story' – TV3's *Ireland AM*

Maggie's Breakfast

GABRIEL WALSH

POOLBEG

Published 2012
by Poolbeg Books Ltd
123 Grange Hill, Baldoyle
Dublin 13, Ireland
E-mail: poolbeg@poolbeg.com
www.poolbeg.com

1

A catalogue record for this book is available from the British Library.

ISBN 978-1-84223-531-7

Typeset by Patricia Hope in Sabon
Printed and bound by CPI Group (UK) Ltd, Croydon, CR0 4YY

About the author

Gabriel Walsh was born in Dublin. He later went on to study in America and France. Gabriel has lectured at colleges in Los Angeles and Cork and was a staff writer for Universal Pictures in Hollywood. He has worked on different occasions with actors such as Jack Nicholson, Gene Wilder and Robert Redford. He wrote the original screenplay *Quackser Fortune Has a Cousin in the Bronx* which received a Writers Guild of America nomination. He also wrote the film *Night Flowers* which received an ecumenical award at the Montréal World Film Festival.

Acknowledgements

There are times, when I look up at the sky, I see mingled among the stars faces of people with whom I shared some of my hopes, joy and pain. Often these faces appear brighter than their adjacent celestial neighbours. In wonderment and awe I see my parents Paddy and Molly, they who deposited me here on earth. I see the shadow of my sister Rita and the silhouette of the kind nun at Goldenbridge Convent, both of whom had the religion of love. In another part of the vast infinity I see Maggie Sheridan and hear the arias she sang on the operatic stage; and I remember gratefully how she pointed me in a direction that took me to many defining destinations. I also see the face of Sally Faile, a friend who helped keep me afloat when I was sinking and floundering in the confusion of my youth. In another illumination I see the face of Melanie Cain, a partner in pursuit of fantasy and art, and also the mother of my beloved daughter Juliana, who became and is the Supernova of my existence.

Gabriel Walsh

Dublin

During the First World War thousands of sixteen and seventeen-year-old boys in Ireland enlisted in the British army. To facilitate this and because of the need for bodies in the trenches, the English conveniently ignored age requirements at the time of enlistment. No one, it seemed, was too young or too old to die for the Crown. Many Irish who enlisted did so because of the dismal poverty in their own country. There weren't many alternatives to "taking the king's shilling". Countless Irishmen chose to die on the battlefields of France and Belgium instead of in the poorhouse in Dublin and elsewhere in Ireland.

At the time of the 'Great War' my father, Paddy Walsh, was one of the thousands of young Irish boys who joined up. At the age of seventeen, Paddy Walsh survived the carnage without a scratch on his body and remained a soldier in the British army for several years more than he might have originally intended. Paddy experienced first-hand in the Great War

GABRIEL WALSH

what most people would not want to see or remember. His prolonged stay in the army doubtless had something to do with the sense that he had no place to return to. It is more than likely that his reason for leaving Ireland had been to do with the fact that as the second son he felt unwanted at home. Second sons didn't inherit from their fathers and were generally considered to be akin to the dog that slept in the yard rather than the one who got to sleep in the house. For my father the reality and pain of abandonment at home overwhelmed the images of the death-trenches that awaited him on the battlefields in France when he decided he wanted to be a soldier.

One summer he was made aware that his father back in Ireland had taken ill and, with the same determination that had impelled him to leave home in the first place, he decided to return to County Kildare and revisit his past. When he returned there wasn't anybody to greet him at the isolated railroad station that served the crossroads of the village he came from, Maganey near Athy. After standing alone at the station and maybe even wondering if he should go home or not, Paddy Walsh picked up his bag and started walking to the cottage where he was born and where, before he left, he lived with his father, sister and two brothers. While crossing the field towards it, he heard several rifle shots and bullets went whizzing by his head. When he made his way to the rear of the cottage and looked in the back window he saw his older brother John, heir to the small farm, rifle in hand, still trying to find his target. Within seconds John was outside and the brothers were in a fistfight but my father with his military agility separated John from the rifle. The two brothers eventually retreated back to the cottage where my Uncle John wanted to burn the English army uniform my father wore

2

but Paddy would have none of it. The uniform was a symbol of freedom for him. It meant travel, adventure and in an odd but obvious way it meant identity.

For a week or so, while my grandfather recuperated from his undiagnosed ailment, my father spent his days at home and his nights at the local Three Counties pub (named because of its proximity to the counties of Laois and Carlow) talking about the differences between England and Ireland and the Irish and the English. Under the influence of a few pints, the subject was civilly accepted.

The day my father was set to leave his father's cottage and rejoin his army outfit in England, he came across Molly MacDonald, an attractive twenty-year-old country girl. When he saw her washing the windows at the railroad station he couldn't resist the urge to talk to her and he did so unhesitatingly. For Paddy at age twenty-three, Molly might have been the most beautiful woman he had seen in a long time, although at the pub he did boast about seeing and meeting beautiful women while serving in France and Egypt. I often wondered what he said on that day to my mother, who as it turned out was a package of pain and penance wrapped in a natural rural beauty.

Uncle John was as distrustful of the MacDonald clan as he was resentful of his brother wearing the English army uniform and he unwisely advised my father to stay away from Molly. In his narrow mind the MacDonalds were way down the scale on the social ladder. Uncle John made it clear to my father that he would never approach a MacDonald if they owned all the cows and grass in the county. John rarely ventured out of the realm of the attitudes and values of the small Irish village he lived in.

With a certain kind of rebellion towards his father and brother and a display of romantic adventure, Paddy fell in love. With a soldier's impatience on short leave, he proposed to Molly and spent his army salary on a gold wedding ring: the most expensive thing he had ever purchased and the most beautiful item my mother had ever seen. From my father's side of the family, marrying a MacDonald was a greater sacrilege than joining the English army. This rejection left Paddy with a great sense of detachment that was to distinguish him in his dealings with my mother, his growing family and just about everything and everybody else he encountered in his daily life.

* * *

Against all opposition, Paddy married Molly MacDonald and they escaped to Dublin. They arrived at a pivotal time in Irish history, when the Civil War was breaking out.

In July 1921 the War of Independence had ended in a truce and in December 1921 Michael Collins and other members of the revolutionary *Dáil Éireann* ('Assembly of Ireland') had signed an agreement with the British government that gave independence to twenty-six of the thirty-two counties that comprised the Island of Ireland. Presumably Collins and his negotiating team accepted this as a stepping-stone that would eventually lead to the unification of the entire island. Collins and his negotiators also accepted the most contentious aspect of the entire agreement: an unpopular proviso in the document required swearing an oath to the English Crown. This was no doubt accepted with the intention of eventually doing away with it, once the new Irish Republic was established. It was considered by those in power in England that the notion of not swearing allegiance to the Crown would spread to other parts of the Empire and might eventually contribute to the diminution of England's global influence. Lloyd George, the English Prime Minister from the Liberal party, bowed to the insistence of the Conservative party in opposition to him at the time, that the oath be part of the agreement. Also, a young Winston Churchill, a member of Lloyd George's cabinet, advocated that the Irish government of the new Free State should swear allegiance to the Crown.

The man who led the faction that rejected the taking of the oath to the English Crown was Éamon de Valera, the then leader of *Dáil Éireann* and President of the notional Republic of Ireland. De Valera went against Collins and a majority of the Irish people who voted and accepted the treaty at the time. The consequence of de Valera's decision led to a split in the ranks of those who sought and dreamed of separation from England. The result of the break-up led to the Civil War and the carnage that ensued. The war ended in May 1923 in a defeat for de Valera and his faction.

Paddy had been drawn to the Pro-Treaty side led by Michael Collins and, doffing his British uniform at last, for a short time wore the uniform of the army of the Irish Free State.

It might not have been more than a year or two into the marriage when Molly and Paddy began to drift from each other: if not in body certainly in spirit. He fought for the Free State; she in her ignorance and innocence had sided with those in favour of rejecting the negotiated treaty. She might have taken this stand to exert a sense of independence of her own.

Their flight to Dublin from the countryside coincided with a harsh and impoverished period in the history of Dublin. With money as scarce as sunshine at the end of the Civil War, the population of Dublin resembled the poor and impoverished masses of some cities in India. For my mother, frequent pregnancies and a growing family underlined the pain.

* * *

When they got undressed to go to bed at night my mother Molly would moan, groan and complain about how she felt about my father Paddy. With the zeal of a religious missionary, she consistently and proudly reminded him about her humble beginnings, as if they were a badge and a symbol of her suffering.

"If we picked potatoes we planted them ourselves in our own bit of ground. Didn't your own flesh and blood let you leave home without a penny? Disinherited like a lame dog in the back yard! Your brother John got everything when your father died, God rest his soul! I'm tellin' no lie. That's as true as the Crucified Jesus. Sure didn't you run away from home yourself when you was a young fella? Didn't ya join up with the British army and leave your own mother and father? The MacDonalds were decent people. Didn't we own our own cottage in Maganey? That MacDonald cottage is still standin'. I've never heard a good word spoken about the Walshes. The Walshes thought they were too good for any MacDonald. Well, they weren't! Some people said you were disowned because you married me, a MacDonald. I wouldn't believe that for a minute! Me mother and father were decent people, I tell you no lie! They always did an honest day's work. I was a clean and proper girl when you met me. I was scrubbin' floors and cold marble steps since I was fourteen!"

When finished with her diatribe Molly would watch and wait for Paddy to defend himself. Silence and stillness would follow and as such it encouraged my mother to feel she had succeeded in her assault on my father. Molly would wait like a satisfied cat with a mouse in its paws for Paddy to break into a rage.

As he'd pull the bed-sheet over his head he'd give out one blast, in a voice both aggressive and pained: "Ditch-livin'

MacDonalds! They couldn't afford a roof over their heads and didn't have a penny to buy a potato!"

The Walshes and the MacDonalds not only hailed from the same county in Ireland but from the same village as well, but the way my parents behaved towards each other, the families might easily have come from different planets.

For generations the Walshes of the small town of Athy made saddles, harnesses, reins and straps and anything leather for things equestrian. Rumour also had it that the Walsh reputation as saddlers, in the distant past, had extended to England where at one time members of the royal family, including the king and queen, squatted their fat arses on a Walsh saddle. For some unknown reason, the aptitude and occupation of saddle-making vanished from the Walshes' way of life. It might have been that more than one character of royal blood fell out of a Walsh saddle. Or maybe because of political changes things Irish weren't embraced or accepted in England as they were in the past.

More than a few people bragged that Arthur Wellesley, the Duke of Wellington, had in another century lived in the area and was once a neighbour. Sadly, this rumour often encouraged young men to follow in the Duke's footsteps and travel to England in search of fame and fortune. Several families in the locale even boasted of being related to the duke. There might also have been a grain of truth in the gossip that some of my ancestors had a relationship with his horse. Whether any of this motivated my father to enlist and leave home, he never disclosed.

Molly had something of a spiritual impatience and appeared to be consistently regretful for having to dwell on earth too long when she believed that there was a better life to be lived in the next world. Her path to paradise had to be paved with suffering and, whether by design or coincidence, she was living in a place where suffering was not only in abundance but honoured as though it was the key that opened the door to salvation. Molly's involvement with living in the present was so minimal that she often appeared to be a ghost that had lost its way on the road to redemption. My mother lived as if she was in competition to win an award for suffering more than anyone else. Neighbours who came in contact with her considered her saintly and definitely heaven-bound. Night-time seemed to be her enemy because it reminded her that she hadn't died during the day and gone to heaven.

The ritual of Paddy and Molly getting into bed at night was not unlike that of two strangers finding themselves next to each other on a crowded bus. Indifference, separateness and isolation were practised. Yet no matter how determined they were to avoid touching, the sagging hollow in the centre of the bed obliged them to slide towards each other anyway. When Paddy and Molly did make contact they didn't complain. Perhaps because there was still a morsel of power left in the sacrament of marriage and back-to-back touching was a secret wish both shared but neither would ever admit to. The pleasure of sleeping with her back to my father was not something my mother would ever talk about. For my father Paddy, lying next to my mother might well have been his definition of Limbo. For Molly, pleasure, affection and optimism seemed to be three of the Seven Deadly Sins. Friendship, encouragement, inspiration and support were the other four. The bed Paddy and Molly slept in was held together by strings of rusty coiled wire, though the size and weight of the thing, with its strong firm legs and shiny rail-knobs, gave the impression that it had been made to last. Parts of the bed's railings still had bits and layers of brass that told of another era. When the bed was new it might have belonged to a prosperous family and might even have been the nest where somebody rich and famous was conceived. It probably saw its share of departing souls as well. Still, even a bed of such pedigree was vulnerable to the wounds of use and abuse. During daylight hours, when it was not being utilised, it looked like an abandoned boat floating on a calm sea, indifferent to dreams, snores and nightmares. In some respects it was now more of a memorial to what it promised when my parents first got married. The iron ribs on each side of it resembled two black horses standing side by side waiting for a funeral to commence. Yet something about the contraption still gave it an air of pride and importance. Like everything else in our home the bed was a second-hand purchase. My father bought it in a pawnshop shortly after he and Molly arrived in Dublin in the 1920's. Indeed, by the time the bed came into my family's possession it might well have been tenth or twelfth hand. Often the centre had to be repaired and replaced with strands of wire that held the thing together. When the wire holding the spring up gave way, it was neither unusual nor infrequent for my parents to end up on the floor next to the communal portable urinal that in itself was second-hand.

My parents' bedroom was like a museum for religious statues. Statues and portraits of saints of every size and colour littered the place. A small statue of the Infant of Prague on the small table next to my parents' bed was a favourite of Molly's. What it had to do with Prague I never knew. The statue had a gold crown on its head and was wearing a red cloak. It also held a gold stick in its hand. Several holy pictures in the bedroom were of the suffering Spanish or French saints that Molly often prayed to. Facing the wall were two other very small statues that my mother had won in a church raffle. They

9

were from Romania but she didn't pay much attention to them. I think it was because they were not the same kind of Catholic saints she had been brought up praying to. In my mother's eyes saints were judged by their suffering. Molly often said that Spanish saints were more like Irish ones. Mrs. Whelan, a neighbour from across the street who went around the church at Mass with a straw basket collecting money for the church, had a different opinion. She said the saints who suffered the most were French and that the French changed their religion many times and were tortured twice as much as any in Ireland or Spain – or Italy for that matter. But for some reason or other my mother had a reverence for martyrs from Spain.

* * *

Saint Stephen's Green in the centre of Dublin and the surrounding area is a combination of Ireland's past, present and future rolled into one. Lord Iveagh, the man who had a hand in inventing the pint of Guinness, named after his family, founded the little green oasis. It's also been said he insisted that the park be closed two hours before the pubs stopped serving the last mug of Guinness. His foresight in this instance may be the reason that the park is in such pristine condition and a jewel in Dublin's tilted crown.

At least twice a week my father would walk to Stephen's Green and sit on a bench near the Eblana monument and retreat into his reminiscences of his time as a soldier in the British Army. Sitting there, he would mumble out loud: "I didn't give a shite what was said about me when I came back in the English army uniform. Who raised the British flag in every piss-hole place on the globe? Who? Me! Paddy Walsh and a lot of fellas like me! Wasn't we the men who conquered the plains of India for England?"

The Royal Dublin Fusiliers' arch at the entrance to Stephen's Green was erected in 1907, a time when England and Ireland were less foreign to each other. The memorial was named 'Eblana' because some ancient scholar said it was Dublin's first name before it was named Dublin. Many of the Anglo-Irish accepted the arch as an edifice of affection that reflected the historical bond between the two countries at an earlier time. Irishmen who had served in the British army held the arch in high esteem. As a tribute it memorialises those of the Dublin Fusiliers who fell in the Boer War. For the most part, few in Dublin stopped to read the inscriptions on the arch because the names of the dead were inscribed on the inside of the arch and you had to contort your head backward to read the dedications. More than a few Dubliners chose to walk around it rather than under it and there were many voices that called for its destruction and referred to it as the "Traitors' Gate".

If anyone in Stephen's Green slowed down to listen to Paddy Walsh, he or she was likely to hear him continue with: "Did you know I was guarding the Jews in Palestine and nothin' to drink but camel piss? A double-breasted brass-button glory I was! What did ya want of me? What did ya want me ta do? Wasn't half of Ireland in the British army? Isn't that what made the British army? Irishmen fighting for a shilling a day! Didn't we beat Napoleon in the Peninsula and didn't we beat him at Waterloo?" Depending on how many pints of Guinness he had consumed on the day of his dole payment, Paddy would also be inclined to break into song.

"Oh, when the war was on we had rashers in the pan!
Now that it's all over, we've only bread and jam!
Oh right you are, right you are!
Right you are, me jolly good soldier, right you are!"

When pedestrians walked by Paddy he was unlikely to see or hear anyone. The world of his country, his city and his family were more like orbiting moons spinning about in the distant sky above and they were as detached from him as he was from them – except when he chose to look up which was rare indeed.

* * *

One day, after Paddy received his dole payment and while reminiscing in Stephen's Green, he heard from a man sitting on a bench opposite him that there was a vacancy for a porter's job in a big house on Ely Place. The position also provided living quarters in the large attic on the top floor. Ely Place was only a stone's throw from Saint Stephen's Green. With little hesitation Paddy Walsh went to the address and applied for the job. To his delight he became a house porter for the Knights of Columbanus.

The Knights of Columbanus, a conservative Catholic lay organisation founded in Belfast in 1915, advised and assisted Catholic institutions throughout the world. Their patron, Saint Columbanus, was a sixth-century Irish monk who founded many monasteries in Europe in his time. It was said by some and refuted by others that Columbanus preferred Easter to Christmas, the Resurrection to the Nativity, and besides that idiosyncrasy had trouble convincing the religious orders in France at the time that they had their calendars wrong. He was following the Celtic calendar which had a different date for Easter. When Columbanus informed the higher-ups in France about this he was thrown out of the country so he went to Italy where he got on better with the natives.

Paddy's first serious bit of employment since he left the British army and located to Dublin transformed him. He, my

12

mother and a family of nine moved into the attic at Number 7, Ely Place. By any standard it was a posh part of Dublin. Paddy's job required him to polish doorknobs and keep the front steps of the club free and clear of debris. Inside he swept the carpets and cleaned the windows. After a few months on the job he appeared to be the happiest man in the world. It was as if he had returned to his youth. He was so content with his work as a hall porter he went out of his way to boastfully tell anyone who would listen about his time as a seventeen-year-old soldier in the British Army. Paddy Walsh was a bit of entertainment for the strictly orthodox Knights of Columbanus. When he opened the door for the club members he was greeted with a smile and encouraged to talk about his past, which he did unhesitatingly.

The job afforded my father a comfort he'd probably never had. Comfort, on the other hand, seemed to frighten my mother Molly. She believed, with just about everyone else in Ireland at the time, that pleasure and happiness didn't get one into Heaven. And the more she witnessed Paddy basking in the joy of his employment the more she withdrew from him and the rest of the family. Almost every day she'd call to my father and demand he do something about his children running wild about the place. At the time my two oldest sisters Mary and Rita were frequenting the local dance halls and were being escorted home by young men they met during the course of the evening. Their loitering in the hallway late at night and making audible romantic sounds would send Molly into a frenzy. What she was hearing might as well have been the Devil screaming. Such was the effect on her, she'd stop praying and run down the stairway and chase my sisters' escorts out into the street in dismay and shock. In an effort to avoid any future occurrences, Molly did her best to prevent my sisters from wearing lipstick or nylon stockings. To her, these accoutrements were an invitation to commit sin. In order to avoid my mother's wrath, my sisters hid their make-up and nylon stockings anywhere they could. Sometimes they were stashed away in cooking pots and in the oven. On at least one occasion we had cooked nylon stocking and melted lipstick for dinner. Added to my mother's crusade and woes was my oldest brother Nicholas. He was about twelve at the time and was constantly stealing apples and pears from the orchard in the back of the large house. This didn't go down well with the Knights when their cook wanted to make stewed pear and apples for dessert.

When Paddy was outside the building polishing the brass doorknobs, Molly would approach him and complain that the family was out of control and he was too busy to do anything about it – or worse, didn't care what they did. When he did his best to ignore her or retreat into silence Molly would yell at him. She purposely did this, hoping to disturb the club members who were conducting their religious rituals or playing cards in the main meeting room. Paddy didn't like Molly yelling at him whether it was inside or outside the building and might have even wished he hadn't taken the job in the first place. When it was in the attic he'd lower his voice so as not to disturb the members of the club who were conducting their meetings downstairs in the main hall. When Molly accosted him outside the premises he'd tell her to go upstairs and mind her own business.

There was definitely something about my mother that prevented her from embracing comfort and happiness. She appeared to be even more disturbed if she witnessed her children and my father being content and relaxed. It wouldn't be an exaggeration to say that Molly practised being the image of Jesus on the cross. It was likely she saw herself as Christ and my father as the cross. With the family war going on in the attic and with fewer and fewer peaceful intervals, the Knights of Columbanus might easily have thought that they were living in the Middle Ages and that the crusades were being fought all over again. Nativity and resurrection was one thing for the Knights but they weren't prepared to endure another crucifixion and in spite of their orthodox beliefs one man on a cross was enough.

* * *

On a rare sunny morning a voice from outside on the street yelled out, "There's a scabby epidemic!" Then came a banging on the front door. The noise woke me up. My father rushed to open the door and was immediately confronted by a woman who was dressed in white from head to toe.

"I'm a nurse and all the children in the vicinity are to be brought to the hospital dispensary." The disturbance brought my mother and the rest of us downstairs.

When Molly saw the woman in white, she screamed out at the top of her voice. "Ah, Mother of Jesus, don't tell me we're all goin' to die!"

A second or two later the door to where the Knights were conducting their meeting opened and two men stepped out. One man, fuming with anger, stepped forward and took hold of my father's elbow. "What is going on?" he asked.

Before my father had a chance to answer the woman in white repeated her call. "A scabby plague!" She then reached out and pulled me towards her. "Look at your children's skin for red sores!" She lifted up my shirt and looked at my body and sure enough I was covered with tiny little red spots. They were all over me.

"They'll all have to be disinfected. Every last child!" the nurse said in a much calmer voice.

The two club members, who up to this point had stood mystified, rushed back to their meeting room and slammed the door fast and furious behind them.

My father then threw his duster against the wall and yelled out: "This won't help me! It won't help, I'm tellin' ya that!"

Molly then grabbed me back from the nurse and inspected me even more closely. "Holy Mother of God, look! Spots! Spots! Spots!"

They were in my mouth, in my ears, and in my nose. Everywhere there was skin, the scabies were. My mother began to cry. I was so frightened I didn't even notice my brothers and sisters being examined.

At any rate, within a few minutes I was marched off alone to Hume Street dispensary where I joined a lot of other young boys. The girls must have been taken to a different location. Another woman dressed in white instructed us to strip naked. Quickly all the young boys shed their clothes. After that we were marched into a big room. The room was crowded with even more naked boys scratching the skin off their bodies. Half were crying, a few were laughing.

After we'd stood naked for half the morning another nurse came by. "When sprayed keep moving and go out into the other room and don't touch yourselves or anything. You've another treatment after that before you're to go home!"

Then a man came by with a huge paintbrush and we were painted white. "Don't touch this until it hardens on ya! It'll become like plaster. Don't touch it till it does."

My body burned as if the man had put a match to it.

Some of the boys were comparing the heat from the white-wash to the heat in Hell.

"In Hell it's twenty million times hotter than this," one boy said.

Another called out, "It's a hundred million times hotter in Hell than this! If you have any mortal sins on your soul you'll be burnt!"

After that we were told to move out to make room for the next batch of children with itchy skin. Outside in the hallway we stood in the long corridor and waited for the white powdery paint to dry. A woman dressed in white came by carrying a small bucket and a paintbrush. She told us to line up against the wall and said she had to inspect us before we were released.

As she went from boy to boy she called out: "What's this? Ya left this out? It's not covered!" Some of our mickies hadn't got splattered with the white paint. She swiped at my groin area with the paintbrush.

One boy asked, "How am I goin' to pee?"

"If it falls off ya, ya won't be able to pee either, will ya now? Never mind whether ya can pee or not!" With that she slapped another gob of whitewash on him.

* * *

The seemingly constant noise of my sisters' nocturnal behaviour as well as the rest of the family running up and down the stairs during the day soon impacted on the peaceful order of the Knights of Columbanus. They felt under siege and were determined to do something about it.

Paddy was asked to explain the screams coming from the attic during the course of the day as well as the ructions between my mother and my sisters late at night. He could only offer the excuse that it was my mother's raised voice when saying the rosary. Among other complaints, the idea of the girls being courted in the hallway in the late evenings certainly wasn't what the Knights had bargained for when they hired my father. Having the Walsh family living in the building was akin to a replay of the Battle of Tours for the Knights. The intrusion and imposition of children yelling in the hallway while they were praying just didn't fit. The idea of conflict so close to home was a direct threat to their charitable instincts and agenda. Prayers and hymns didn't blend with screams and yells. Not to mention the odd profanity contributed by my sisters' escorts.

The decision to defend themselves was made and my father was soon called before the tribunal. Paddy's plea to keep his job only went so far and a Senior Knight informed him that his position would be terminated. Being fired from the only job he was ever likely to find was the last straw for him.

Rather than offering sympathy or concern when informed of the situation, my mother retreated to praying again – but this time very silently. In some ways her prayers had been answered. Paddy's happiness was a threat and Molly's proclivity for suffering was enhanced by the thought that she'd have to find a place to live and start all over, destitute again.

The next day my father was given two weeks' notice to find other accommodation. A week later Molly filed for a new place to live with the city housing department. Shortly thereafter the Walshes were relocated to Inchicore.

––◁◯▷––

Other than being about three miles north-west from the centre of Dublin, Inchicore had almost nothing to be said for it. Few people seemed to know or care if it was north or south of anything. The place had no statues of English generals on horses or memorials to soldiers who fought in far-off military campaigns. What it did have was smokestacks and an ironworks foundry belonging to C.I.E. where practically the entire male population of the neighbourhood worked. Whenever a bus or a train broke down in Dublin, or in any other part of Ireland for that matter, it was hauled to the foundry, repaired and put back in use.

Every morning and evening in Inchicore the factory horn assaulted people's ears and reminded just about every family in the area where their bread and butter was coming from.

At half seven in the morning the horn would bellow out, shake the windows of the small red-brick houses and wake everybody up. Wives and mothers would leap out of bed, rush down the small wooden stairs to their cold sculleries and heat up water for tea. They'd also slap gobs of margarine on slices of stale bread. A basin of cold water, set out the night before with a bar of industrial soap would be on a small table next to the fireplace. The little remaining heat from the ashes of the previous night's fire would help expel the chill from the small room. Before the water boiled on the stove the women would run back up to the bedrooms to shake husbands and sons out of their slumber. Groggy and still half-asleep, the men would roll out of bed and place their feet on the cold wooden floor and piss in the chamber-pots that were strategically placed near the bed. Years of practice had perfected their aim and rarely did any pee land on the floor. After a few minutes the women would return to the bedrooms, pick up the overflowing chamber-pots and retreat back down the stairs to empty the contents in an outhouse in the back yard. At the same time the men would pick up their shirts and overalls from the floor and get dressed for work at the foundry. They'd come down the creaking staircase buttoning their overalls and without stopping would scoop up a handful of cold water from the basin and splash their faces with it. Fathers and sons then sat down for a cup of tea with bread and margarine. Two bites into the bread they'd moan and grimace because the margarine on the bread tasted like foundry grease. Within ten minutes or so the men would get up from the small kitchen tables and place worn and greasy caps on their heads. They'd then wrap shredded scarves around their necks, the scarves smelling of a combination of hair oil and foundry grease. A man's neck was a good indicator of how often he'd avoided taking a bath. If it was a mixture of green and black it had been at least a week since he washed. If it reflected a combination of green, yellow and black it had likely been two weeks since he stepped into the tub.

The front doors of the small houses would open and the men would march towards the big gates of the foundry where they'd be greeted by the smell of smoke and oil. Minutes later as the banging of hammers and the sputtering noise of train engines coalesced, mothers would retreat to the bedrooms of their children where they lifted up the bed-sheets and threw cold water on the warm half-naked bodies to ready them for school. Dressed in tattered clothes, boys and girls would enter the street and head to school and for the time being avoid the lane that led to the foundry.

Shortly thereafter, on clotheslines in back yards, bed-sheets were hung out to dry while prayers were said to encourage the absent sun to show up. With men at work and children at school some housewives, wearing dresses that were as clean as their husbands' overalls were dirty, would begin to polish their front-door brass knobs. The women would call back and forth to each other, exchanging gossip and rumour. Often the talk was about who owed who a cup of sugar or a bottle of milk. Or whose son or daughter wouldn't get up to go to school or Mass. More often than not the chattering was about which young girl was "up the pole" and whose son was responsible for it. At the same time the street vendor Biddy Sonics, who'd got her odd surname from a marriage to some kind of East European, would be calling out the price of bad apples and wilted cabbage. Biddy's raspy voice was almost as loud as the foundry horn as she sold her damaged fruit and vegetables from her horse and cart. To keep the nag content Biddy would sprinkle its oats with whiskey from a flask she carried in her apron pocket.

Biddy's throaty voice was also the alarm for Mrs. Mack. Mrs. Mack spent her entire day if not her entire life looking out of her upraised window. The woman couldn't travel or go anywhere because she had only one leg. It was rumoured she kept her severed leg in the back yard and that was the reason for the peculiar smell on the street. On Saturday mornings when the priest came to hear Mrs. Mack's confession he had to listen and bless her through the front window because of the whiff. He often told neighbours on his way back to the church that his time as a missionary in Africa was an easier task than having to stand outside Mrs. Mack's window while she confessed to nothing. After about two or three years of being Mrs. Mack's spiritual adviser he requested a transfer to the Australian outback.

Friday evening, the end of the work week . . .

Men with their wages in their pockets would rush from the foundry like a stampede of cows fleeing the slaughterhouse and hasten to the nearby pub. Once inside, the ritual of drinking and singing would begin. Sons covered with engine oil joined fathers at the bar and displayed their youthful and inherited prowess for the consumption of Guinness. When the pub closed the men would stagger out, drunk and incoherent. Some got up on their bicycles and began the risky wobble home. A few would tumble and end up on the street, feeling their sore arses. At the same time women would hurry in the direction of the pub only to find their men sprawled on the street. The women would frantically search their husbands' pockets, hoping their men hadn't spent every penny on the drink. With the shock of finding empty pockets the women would unleash a painful lament, their screams greeted with rambling and incoherent apologies from the men.

* * *

My mother looked through the curtains, saw who was at the door and without looking back at me said "Hide!"

I was sitting in front of the fireplace counting the sparks that were floating up the chimney. As the front door was opened, I ran and hid under the small table.

The priest entered the house and my mother greeted him with a reverential bow.

With a voice that was known to knock cups off their saucers Father Joe Devine bellowed out, "Mornin', Missus!" With hat in hand he stepped into the middle of the room and viewed all the holy pictures and statues my mother had accumulated over the years. He probably thought it was as good a place as any for a miracle to occur.

Father Joe Devine was referred to by my father as 'Holy Divine' and by us thereafter as 'Father Divine'. He was also known as 'Sheep Dog' because of his habit of roaming about on his bicycle rounding up errant parishioners and herding them with due violence into the church for 'retreats' and other 'devotions'.

Rumour in the neighbourhood had it that in his earlier years he had been thrown out of a cloistered order in County Waterford because of his unnatural fixation on the Virgin Mary. Instead of money, he carried around in his pockets small mini-statues of the religious figure. It was believed that when he went to bed at night he placed a life-size statue of the Virgin next to the foot of his bed. The religious order required Joe 'Divine' to take a vow of silence but he couldn't stop talking about the Blessed Virgin and he was asked to leave the monastery. The irrational relationship Joe had with the Virgin Mary tarnished the image of the holy order. A hundred or so reclusive men who were pledged to a vow of silence in a hidden-away monastery didn't appreciate Joe Devine's very vocal obsession. Also, when Joe left the cloistered monastery, his fellow monks made sure he took his collection of plaster statues with him.

Now the Oblates Parish of Mary Immaculate in Inchicore was blessed with Father Joe, a man with deep roots in County Waterford who preferred to speak Gaelic rather than English and had little sympathy for Dublin people. He was a replacement for a priest who was exiled to Donegal by the Bishop of Dublin after he was accused by several of his parishioners of unpriestly activities. The nature of his unpriestly conduct was never made public and no one who attended Mass or received Communion in the parish ever asked why. Some parishioners were heard to say that he had plans to "Christianise Ireland properly". The parish in North Donegal was at the edge of the Atlantic Ocean and, because of the fierce cold weather there, it was said that it was only accessible during the summer months. So whatever his crimes or misdemeanours, the errant priest was well out of the way of the Bishop of Dublin.

"Mornin', Father," my mother finally and humbly said to the man who stood in front of her, dressed from head to toe in black.

Father Joe stood in the centre of the room, spoke about the Virgin Mary and looked like he was about to burst and drown the whole country in holy water.

"The blessed Mother of God stands alone and crownless watching over all of us who pray to go to Heaven. The Mother of God has withstood storms and bitter cold winters, facing and comforting all who come by Her feet to pray."

The big old statue he was referring to was there since the local church was built and nobody paid much attention to it before Father Divine arrived.

From under the old wooden table I could hear the priest's notorious voice and I trembled with fear. When he stepped close to the table I noticed his black shiny shoes. They had thick soles on them as if they had been repaired twice.

"The Virgin Mary is the closest to God that any imaginable person or thing could be. Anything she says, you can be sure God pays attention to." Father Joe then knocked on the table with his knuckles. "Mrs.Walsh, I'm here on a duty to honour Our Lady. How many times, and I needn't ask you this, but how many times have you knelt down before the Mother of God and asked her for guidance and blessings?"

My mother's voice rang out, "Many times, Father!"

"I know you have, Mrs. Walsh, and I also know that the Mother of God hasn't forgotten. She keeps a long and remembered record of your prayers."

My mother, feeling blessed, stepped closer to the man in black. "Wasn't I only there meself this mornin' after Mass offerin' up me prayers, Father. That's as true as Christ is in Heaven!"

Our Lady's statue outside the church was standing on a high pedestal surmounting the gate that led into the church-yard. She had a big rosary beads over her arm but she didn't have a crown or a halo over her head. What she did have was a man who was resolved to do something about it.

"Have you anything to offer, honour and beautify the statue of Our Holy Mother?" he asked my mother.

My mother's response was typical of her. "The few ha'pence I've left over wouldn't be enough to buy a bottle of holy water, Father."

Father Divine wasn't satisfied with my mother's answer so he walked about the room inspecting everything in the place. From where I was sitting under the table, I could smell the polish on his shiny shoes. He continued to walk about looking at everything – the pictures on the wall and every bit of furniture my mother had collected since she was married. He even lifted up the kettles and pots in the fireplace.

Finally convinced that my mother had nothing of value in the house to offer the Virgin, he walked to the door and, turning, reached out as if to shake her hand. But he took her left hand, not her right hand.

On the fourth finger of her left hand was her wedding ring. The ring that bonded my parents in marriage and perhaps more than anything else the object that kept them in the holy miserable state of matrimony. Maybe the only happy memory my parents ever experienced together. Perhaps the one thing of value in my mother's life, the thing that empowered her to endure pain and discomfort. The wedding ring on her finger was more than a bond to her: it was a sacrament. Whatever the pain, anger, and confusion, the ring held my parents together like no other force. It might even have been the only worthy thing she admired about my father. My mother's life was reflected in its shine. The band of gold had endured countless floor-scrubbings and thousands of laundry-washes. It had been there when arses were wiped and piss-pots emptied. It had been there when potatoes were peeled and when pigs' cheeks were cooked. It had touched shop stalls and meat counters when she reached out for bargains or charity. It felt my mother's breath when she prayed a thousand prayers with her hands joined. Every saint and statue in Dublin had had their image reflected in my mother's wedding ring when she prayed to them at one time or another.

Father Joe held onto my mother's hand as if he was proposing marriage to her. When he spoke his voice had changed dramatically.

"The Holy Mother of God would be eternally grateful if you could donate this ring to her crown, Mrs. Walsh. I know she'd look down on you and anoint you. If you do, it would be placed in her crown with other gold rings from other women and wives in the parish."

"Ah, Paddy put that on me finger," my mother said sadly.

"Our Blessed Lady will be crowned in May – the month of Our Blessed Virgin, Mrs. Walsh."

My mother then knelt down on the scrubbed wooden floor and offered a prayer. "Jesus, Mary and Joseph, I offer you me heart and me soul!" Her thick brown stockings had holes in them and her knees were showing.

She then arose and in an obedient manner presented her hand to the priest.

As he stood by the door in his crusade to undo contentment, Father Devine separated the wedding ring from my mother's finger. He told her it would be forever a star in the new crown of the Virgin Mary. God would look with special affection on her for giving such a gift to his Mother and she could have a front-row seat when the time came for the consecration of the Virgin's crown.

After a quick blessing and the Sign of the Cross Father Divine made a hasty exit.

My mother, who couldn't afford a pint of milk, felt she had achieved something close to sainthood.

Within a few minutes of Father Divine's departure my father came hurrying in the door. He looked pale and exhausted. He had encountered the man from Waterford who had told him about the wedding ring sacrificed so the Virgin Mary could have her crown. When my father entered the house he walked to the table I was still sitting under. He then called to my mother who was cleaning out the fireplace.

"I want to talk to ya! I want to talk to ya now!"

"About what?" my mother responded with a tone of guilt that you could cut with a knife.

My father raised his voice louder than I had ever heard in my entire life. "Isn't there somethin' missing from your finger?"

"What?" my mother answered.

It was the first direct confrontation I had witnessed in a long time.

"You had a ring on there, didn't ya?"

"I had."

"Where's it?"

"Me weddin' ring?"

"Yes. You only had one bloody ring!" my father yelled. "Where's the bloody ring I bought ya?"

Molly began to peel a potato as if to avoid his wrath. After a second or two Paddy took the potato from her hand and threw it across the room. It landed in the fireplace.

My father was then hit with what he hated to hear most.

"What good are you? You're just a labourer! You've no trade! Nobody has any need for ex-soldiers. And if they served in the English army they have even less use for them. All of Ireland knows that!"

Paddy retreated like a soldier who had run out of ammunition or one who'd got fed up with firing at the same target.

"Where's the ring I bought ya? Where's the wedding ring I spent me savin's on? Where is it?"

He then began to cry.

I wanted to crawl out from under the table but I was afraid to.

My mother, with a sense of sacrament in her voice, continued: "The Holy Mother of God will be wearing the ring in her crown."

My father fired off one last shot. "Why the hell didn't you give her the wedding dress as well?" Holding on to his suspenders he retreated like a wounded soldier to the bedroom. It was the only place he could hide.

* * *

Murphy's barbershop was located not too far from the foundry. At the time it was Inchicore's only beauty salon. I was sitting on the curb outside the shop with Danny Murphy, a boy about the age of seven, the same age as myself and the son of the owner.

"Come in here, Danny, and mind the shop." Mr. Murphy's hands were shaking and his tongue was sticking out of his mouth. "I need to go get a pint before I drop dead on the floor. I'm goin' across the street for a drop of porter. Keep the lock on the door and let nobody in. I'll be back in a bit. Y'hear me, son?"

"Yis," Danny said.

Mr. Murphy took off his apron, shook the hairs off it, put his overcoat on, reached for his hat, covered his bald head and walked out the door.

Danny looked at me. "Give me a hand with the hair," he said, imitating his father's demanding voice.

"What d'ya want me t'do?" I asked.

"Put the dirty hair in the barrel in the back room."

I grabbed as much hair off the floor as my hands could hold, walked to the back room and pushed the stack of greasy hair into a big cardboard barrel. Half of the hair stuck to me. My face, ears and nose were covered with it. I walked back to the front room and saw Danny wearing his father's apron and holding the hair-snippers in his hand.

"When I grow up I'm goin' to be the barber here. And if you're me pal you'll help me get a start."

For a second or two I wasn't sure what Danny was talking about.

"Let me do it," he said.

"Do what?" I asked.

"Let me give you a haircut."

I crawled into the chair in front of the big mirror. Danny tied a striped apron around my neck and within seconds he was snipping away at my head. Twice he snipped my ears and made me bleed. I had hair and blood-spots all over me. I looked like Magua, in *The Last of the Mohicans*. I started to cry.

As Danny tried to reassure me about my bleeding ears, a knock came to the door. "Me dad is back," he mumbled.

Mr. Murphy's voice yelled out, "Open the damn door, Danny!"

Danny sat down on the floor and began to cry. "I'll be kill't! I'll be kill't!" he moaned painfully. He was so frightened he couldn't shake the scissors out of his hand and stabbed me with it again and again as he tried. He looked like he was lock-jawed and dead at the same time.

Mr. Murphy's voice bellowed even louder than before. "Open the fuckin' door!"

Danny started to cry and pray at the same time. "Holy Mary, full of something, and Jesus, say something to me father!"

I became so frightened I began to pray also. "*Oh my God, I'm heartily sorry for having offended Thee!*"

Danny stuck his hand to my mouth. "Don't pray so loud! He'll hear you!"

I was now very worried and choking at the same time. For what seemed to be forever, I couldn't talk. Danny shifted his hand a bit and now I couldn't breathe either but I could hear Mr. Murphy yelling.

"Open the damn door or I'll whip the shite out of ya! I swear to Christ you won't sit on your arse for a month!"

Danny then pissed in his trousers. Mr. Murphy kicked on the door again. In panic I leaped from the chair, ran to the back room and jumped into the big barrel of hair. I had hair in my ears, my nose, my eyes, my mouth, my pockets, my shoes and down the back of my neck. I closed my eyes and hoped I could just fall asleep and forget everything.

"Open the door! Open the blasted door! Y'hear me? Open the bloody door, Danny!" Mr. Murphy yelled again.

Danny rushed into the back room and looked down at me hiding under a mountain of hair.

"Me father's drunk and I'll be kill't if he finds out what I did to ya."

I wasn't able to help him. I was imprisoned in a barrel of dirty hair that up until a few hours earlier belonged to half the men of Inchicore.

Mr. Murphy was going crazy. "*Open the bloody door before I kick the thing in! Y'hear me? D'y'hear me? Open the door!*"

Danny ran back to the front room. I heard the sound of the front door opening and said a few prayers to myself – "*Glory be to the Father and to the Son and the Holy Ghost!*" and "*Hail Mary, full of grace, the Lord is with Thee, blessed art Thou amongst women and blessed is the fruit of Thy womb, Jesus!*"

From the front room I heard a loud noise. It sounded as if Mr. Murphy had thrown the wooden bench at Danny.

Danny let out a scream. "*Don't hit me! Don't hit me!*"

There was a loud grunt from Mr. Murphy as if he had missed hitting Danny with the wooden bench. "What in the name of Christ are ya up to? Why didn't ya open up for me? Why? You're a right git, ya scruffy little bollocks! Get home with yourself!"

The door slammed. All was quiet again. They were both gone.

I was terrified of what my mother would say about my hair when I got home. I planned on telling her that I'd been praying all evening and had said more prayers in one hour than I had in a week. I wanted to tell her I said the Act of Contrition and the Our Father so many times I could sing them backwards.

After about fifteen minutes I climbed out of the container and walked into the front room. I tried to open the front door but it was locked. I then went into the back room, climbed to the small ventilator window, crawled out sideways and fell into the back alley.

* * *

"Sacred Heart of Jesus, what happened to you?"

My ears had two red streaks of blood dripping down the sides of my neck and face. My head looked even worse. My mother's face appeared to turn purple when she saw me. She quickly grabbed my hand, led me to the big mirror that was hanging over the picture of the Sacred Heart of Jesus. I stared at the plaster statue and for a moment wondered if it had real blood dripping from its heart. For a very short time I was dreaming that Danny Murphy hadn't really operated on my head and the greasy snippets of hair that were pasted to every part of my body weren't really there at all.

My dream was cut short when I felt my mother's hand on the back of my neck.

"Jesus, Mary and Joseph, you're unrecognisable!" She was having convulsions and hit me again and again on the back of my head.

A big bang went off in my left ear. Her hand felt like a shovel.

"You bloody git! You'll make a holy show of me if you show up for school looking like that! You'll be thrown out!"

She walloped my left ear with her other hand and I heard a bell ring. Its gong seemed to last forever but then all went silent.

A week or so later my ear was still paining me. My mother then took me to Saint Vincent's hospital and had a doctor look at it. After putting a small light beam into my ear he told my mother I should cut down on salt and stop eating eggs altogether. It was easy to give up the eggs because I only had one every second Sunday.

* * *

On Friday mornings the Sisters of Mercy from nearby Goldenbridge Convent went around the neighbourhood in a horse and cart with a big barrel of hot mashed potatoes and parts from a slaughtered pig. Where they got the pig carcasses from I never knew and I didn't want to know either. The smell of hot potatoes from the barrel on the horse-drawn wagon signalled to families like mine that it was time to eat. I approached the nuns' wagon with my can which had a smiling cow's face on the outside label. Fresh milk was expensive and rationed at the time. Condensed milk was donated by the Saint Vincent de Paul Society. With my family, the condensed milk lasted for about two days. After that the can was discarded, but the remnants of the condensed milk inside the can remained and tasted like sweet glue. I stood in line with other children but by the time the wagon got close to my house the barrel of mashed potatoes was almost depleted. Exercising her last charitable impulse of the day the nun scraped the bottom of the barrel and filled my can with crusty burnt mashed potatoes. It was just the way I liked them.

The Saint Vincent de Paul Society periodically dropped off a voucher for a pair of new shoes or sandals to every family on Nash Street. Children who went to school barefoot were singled out for the benefit. My mother decided that it was my turn to take advantage of the shoe voucher because the toes on my feet were withering away with chilblains from walking to school every day barefoot. Molly went with the voucher to Cleary's on O'Connell Street for a pair of sandals for me and brought them home in a box but even with the coldest toes in Ireland she wouldn't let me wear them right away. She insisted I wait till Sunday and wear the sandals to Mass. After that she said I could do what I liked with them. For the rest of the week I went to school in my bare feet, thinking about my new sandals that were in a box under my mother's bed. Saturday night came and I washed my feet and went to bed with such great anticipation of wearing a new pair of sandals I couldn't fall asleep. The next morning my mother handed me my new sandals. I was so sleepy I could hardly see them. Instead of shoes or boots with laces, my sandals had buckles, silver buckles that took only a second to fasten. The sandals were the first new thing I had ever owned and were a perfect fit. When I put them on my feet I thought I had died, gone to heaven and sprouted wings. In a hurry to feel the sandals on my feet I ran out the door and headed for Mass. On my way to the church I kept looking down at my feet. It felt so good I thought I was in a bus or riding a bicycle. Inside the church I kept gazing downwards at my feet. While I was doing that a person behind me slapped me on the head and told me to look up at the altar and pay attention. As soon as Mass ended I was determined to form a relationship with the leather items that covered my feet. I ran up towards the canal to test the sandals. I wanted to show them off to anybody I'd meet. I felt so free I could have jumped over the moon. When I got to the canal I decided to cross over to the other side. As I stepped on the footbridge that allowed one to cross over the canal, my right foot got caught in the chain that secured the wooden crossing. To free myself I yanked my foot and was quickly separated from the sandal that covered it. It fell into the water where it went under and drowned. I never saw it again.

When I came home with one sandal my mother threw me out of the house and I sat on the sidewalk and cried till sunset. Monday morning I was back in school in my bare feet.

* * *

I woke up in the middle of the night and my jaw was so swollen I looked like I had a doorknob in my mouth. The next morning, after a night of me screaming in agony, my mother dragged me by the scruff of the neck to the community dentist.

After we'd sat in a crowded waiting room for about two hours, a man in a white coat with the spots of blood on it came out and looked around. Behind him was a nun praying silently. The man in the white coat pointed his finger at me, then called to my mother: "He's next!" He then turned to the nun and whispered something into her ear. The nun began to pray out loud.

The nun came over to me and asked me if I had made my First Holy Communion. My mother answered for me and said I hadn't but I would soon. The nun asked my mother if I was baptised. My mother said I was. The nun then led me and my mother into a room where the man in the white coat told me to step into the dentist's chair. He looked in my mouth.

"Half of them have to come out," he said.

"Only take the bad ones out, sir," my mother pleaded.

"Sure most of them are bad," the dentist said.

The nun blessed herself as if on cue.

The dentist then took another look at my decaying teeth. "I assume he's been baptised?" He smiled and squinted towards the nun who nodded while kissing the rosary beads she was holding. "I'm afraid I'll have to put him to sleep," he added.

"Ah Jesus, can't you help him without puttin' the gas-bag on him, sir?" my mother begged.

"I'll give it a try, missus," the dentist replied.

He then put a pair of pliers into my mouth, got a grip on one of the teeth in the back that had a big black hole in it and began to pull. The dentist continued to pull and pull. I was spitting blood like a loose water tap and crying even louder. I screamed so loud I almost swallowed the pliers and the hand of the dentist as well. The tooth would not come out.

The dentist then looked again at my mother and the nun. "I was afraid of this," he said. He then reached for a rubber bag that was on the shelf behind him. The bag looked like a recently extracted cow's liver and smelled as bad. "Take a deep breath," the man with the bloodstains on his white coat said to me. Before I could inhale anything he slammed the slippery-looking cow's liver flat on my face as if he was slamming an insect with the heel of his shoe. I could hear the nun praying louder as I screamed, pushed and attempted to resist being knocked out by the rubbery bag that was smothering me. In seconds I was gone, way gone. Where I sailed to I don't know. When I came to the nun was still praying and I had fewer teeth in my mouth than ever before.

* * *

Receiving your First Communion showed everybody in the church that you were in a State of Grace and if you died a second after you received Communion you'd go directly up to Heaven because your soul was clean and white. At the age of seven, receiving Holy Communion gave you the right to walk to the altar and receive the sacrament with grown-ups. Many families walked up to the altar and received Communion together. First, of course, you had to make your First Confession and confess all your sins to the priest.

The Communion wafer that the priest stuck in your mouth was made at the biscuit factory. It was a small round light papery wafer that you had to swallow the second the priest placed it on your tongue. It was a sin to let it touch your teeth because if you did it meant you took a bite out of God. The Sacrament of Communion was like a passport to

Heaven. Receiving it meant you had no sins or black marks on your soul. You had a white soul and that was the only kind of soul that got you by the guards at Heaven's gate.

After you received your First Communion you were allowed to walk around the neighbourhood, knock on doors and show people that you were saved from punishment for your sins. When friends, relatives and neighbours saw you dressed up in your new suit with the white ribbon on your lapel, they gave whatever they could afford and congratulated you on avoiding the fires of Hell or Purgatory.

My First Holy Communion got off to an odd start. At Goldenbridge Convent which I was attending, Sister Charlotte approached me in the middle of class one day with a big happy smile on her face.

"Did you get your Communion suit?" she asked me.

I didn't know what to answer. I knew my mother had gone to the Iveagh Market looking for a suit for me but she hadn't told me if she'd found one or not.

"After class I want you to stay in your seat. Will you do that?" the nun asked me.

I could never say no to Sister Charlotte. Had she told me to walk backwards on my head, I would have. I would do anything for her but I was afraid to tell her that.

She was so beautiful I couldn't stop thinking about her even when school was over. I didn't know why my body was reacting the way it was. All of Sister Charlotte's prayers and promises were like Christmas presents. She made me believe that all things and all people were good. Even if I had no shoes on my feet Sister Charlotte convinced me that I didn't really need them. "Ah, you've such a good pair of feet, Gabriel! It would be a shame to cover them up with shoes or sandals," she'd say to me. I felt so happy and comfortable in Sister Charlotte's presence I forgot about everything else in my life. Sister Charlotte was my Guardian Angel. Guardian Angels were to remind you not to commit a sin when you were tempted. I asked myself every day in school: What would Sister Charlotte say if she knew I wanted to kiss her?

When the bell rang for the end of school that day, I remained in my seat. After the class had emptied out, a woman who used to cook in the convent kitchen came into the classroom with a big brown-paper bag.

"It's all here, Sister. Clean and pressed. Like new," she said and handed the bag to Sister Charlotte.

"Come up, Gabriel."

I timidly got up from my seat and walked to the head of the class.

"Congratulations, Gabriel, on making your First Holy Communion this week," she said.

The woman who'd brought the brown-paper bag in blessed herself and moved her lips as if she was saying a prayer.

Sister Charlotte then took a grey jacket and trousers out of the bag. "I think this will fit you, Gabriel."

The woman stepped forward. "Stretch out your arms," she said to me.

I stretched my arms out like the man on the cross. The woman placed my arms into the sleeves. "The jacket fits him," she said, turning back to Sister Charlotte.

Sister Charlotte smiled. "This suit used to belong to one of my young brothers, Gabriel. He's a lot older than you and he's living in England. It's been hanging in my room for years. I've kept it in mothballs."

"That's where I keep me husband," the woman said.

Sister Charlotte laughed out loud.

The woman measured the trousers to my knees. They too seemed to fit.

Sister Charlotte stepped back and took a look at me.

"I have a confession to make, Gabriel."

I thought she was going to say she loved me. My blood boiled and my face turned red.

"I've tried to fit this suit on boys for the last three years and it didn't fit any of them. When you first came into my class, you reminded me of my young brother. I prayed that the day would come when you could wear his suit, and now you're going to. Your poor mother will be happy about that, won't she?"

"She will and thanks very much," I said.

Sister Charlotte then put a white ribbon on the lapel of the jacket. "Wear this on your lapel when you receive your Communion on Friday, Gabriel."

The ribbon was snow white and brand new. It was to be my badge of honour when I received my First Communion from the priest.

The sister also gave me a new prayer book with a picture of Jesus on the front of it.

"You can say your prayers with this book, Gabriel. Whenever you're having trouble with everything that goes on around you, open this and read it. Making your First Communion gives you rights and responsibilities. Your Holy Communion Day is one of the most important days of your life."

As I stood in front of my Guardian Angel she reached back to her desk and handed me a small box. "Open it," she said with a glowing light in her eyes.

I fumbled with the box but managed to open it without much trouble. Inside the box was a pair of new brown shoes. I almost passed out from the smell of the new leather.

"Wear them with your suit when you make your Communion," the nun said. "Tie the laces tight so they won't fall off your feet."

I was so fixated on Sister Charlotte I wasn't able to concentrate on what she was saying to me. I felt trapped in a cage of pure love. My skin was boiling and I felt as if my hair was on fire. I could hardly breathe. I was convinced I was committing sin.

A week after I made my Communion I went to Confession and told the priest that I wanted Sister Charlotte to be my mother. The priest told me I had a mother and I shouldn't be thinking of having another one. I told the priest that I was always wishing I could see Sister Charlotte in a dress instead of the black habit she wore. And I wondered if she painted her legs brown like my oldest sister Mary did before she left home and got married. I told the priest that I had a dream when I imagined Sister Charlotte wearing almost no clothes at all. For the act of committing sin by "thought" the priest told me to say the rosary every day for two weeks as well as six Acts of Contrition.

Sister Charlotte was the nicest person I ever met. The more I got to know her the more I believed she was a real saint who should have been living up in heaven. She told me she prayed for me and hoped that I would find everything I ever wanted out of life. She said she prayed that I would even find my lost sandal. "Gabriel, you will find your sandal. You will have new sandals with silver buckles on them as well."

I had fantasies of kissing her but I knew that was a serious sin. Nuns didn't kiss or be kissed. But I think I was the only boy in her class that she held hands with. Every day she'd look into my eyes and smile and say nice things to me. In the back of my mind I kept telling her I loved her and that I wanted to see her every day for the rest of my life.

Sister Charlotte was talking about how a star in the sky guided the Three Wise Men to Bethlehem when another nun came rushing into the class and whispered in her ear. The two nuns then walked to the classroom door and opened it wide.

"Everybody go home and quickly!" they said.

The room emptied in a hurry. I didn't know what was going on and most of us in the class started to cry. One boy who wasn't crying said the Devil had escaped from hell and he was being chased all around Dublin by Catholic angels. That bit of information made us feel better. We knew no devil could beat up God's angels and when the Devil was caught he would be sent back down to hell and Dublin would again be safe for us to sit in school or do anything we wanted. Then in a fit of panic Sister Charlotte started to herd us out of the convent. When we got to the school gate another nun yelled out, "Infestation!" The boy who said the Devil had escaped from hell said "infestation" meant mortal sin. There was no escape from that unless you went to Confession and confessed all your sins and really meant it. I was trying to think of how many mortal sins I had committed when another nun called out to the Mother Superior of the convent: "Lice! Lice!" The Mother Superior blessed herself in a hurry. Lice weren't mortal sins. They were bugs with legs growing everywhere that crawled on your head and in your hair. The dogs and cats and the birds in the trees had lice. Mice had lice. Somebody said the cause of the lice was eating the dead rabbits the dogs dropped on the street.

When I got home my sisters and brothers were sitting outside on the kerb. They had been told the same thing in their schools. My sisters and brothers and all the boys and girls on the street had lice in their hair. A man came by and left a big bottle of Lysol outside our hall door. He was from some government agency and he said there was a state of emergency in Dublin because of the lice. The government handed out fine-toothed combs and paper with drawings of the lice on them. I think they drew the picture of the lice so the mothers wouldn't confuse them with mice or rats or stray kittens or anything else that was on the loose in Dublin. All the mothers in Dublin had a big combing job every night after dinner. My mother searched our hair for lice then crushed them with her thumbnail. Crack and splatter! Poor head! Poor mothers! Poor lice! Poor Dublin!

After the lice infestation and when everybody was back in school, still smelling of Lysol, Sister Charlotte called me to the head of the class and handed me six shiny new pennies. The six pennies Sister Charlotte gave me was the most money I had ever had in my life. She also presented me with a birthday cake. It was my very first present ever and the closest I had ever been to anything that had cream on top of it. *Happy Birthday* was written on top of the cake. Sister Charlotte held me by the hand and told me to smile and be happy about everything. With great difficulty and shyness I managed to lift my chin and look in her eyes. I thought I was going to die when I made eye contact with her. Angels and Heaven and happiness were floating all about me. I didn't want to stop looking. Her face was the sun shining through on a cold rainy day. I didn't know who I was any more so I started to cry.

Sister Charlotte wiped away the tears that were falling from my eyes with her fingers. She smiled at me and told me it was not a bad thing if I cried my eyes out in front of her. When she said that I stopped crying. She then walked me back to my seat and sat me down. The other boys in the class were watching with looks of serious confusion on their faces. I sat in silence and felt numb.

Sister Charlotte came back to me with the cake in a box tied with a red ribbon. "Open this when you go home, Gabriel, and share it with your family. Your mother will be happy, I'm sure of it! And a big happy birthday to you, Gabriel!"

Sister Charlotte turned to the class and asked the other boys to sing "Happy Birthday" to me. The classroom thundered with the sound. When the school bell rang she asked me to stay in my seat. She then walked up to me and wished me a happy birthday again. As I picked up my cake and was about to walk out of the classroom, she took my hand in hers.

"Gabriel," she said and went silent for a moment or two. She looked down at my two feet as if to make sure I was wearing the shoes she gave me. She then looked in my eyes again.

I was consumed by shyness, fear and confusion. Since I first met her I believed she was my Guardian Angel with white wings growing out of her shoulders. Her magical presence made everything in my life bright and clear.

Almost at the exact moment when I felt I didn't exist at all, she whispered, "Gabriel, in a few months you'll be transferring to Saint Michael's Christian Brothers School. The brothers are fine teachers. They'll help prepare you for the day when you'll be going out in the world looking for a job."

The thought of me ever having a job was as far away as my entering Heaven. I'd have to be dead first to get there. My father and loads of other men were always looking for jobs.

"You'll soon be gone from the convent here. You know that, don't you?"

I was so shy I could only nod my head. Sister Charlotte continued to talk. What she had to say came close to erasing me from the page of life that my name was written on.

"I'm to leave the convent soon."

I stood, feeling half paralysed.

Sister Charlotte continued. "I'm going away to Africa to join my fellow sisters there. My order has encouraged me to go and I've accepted. I won't be in class when you come here next week. I wasn't going to tell you or the class and I didn't, until now." Then she leaned towards me and kissed me on the forehead.

* * *

Angelo Fusco's fish and chip shop was a place where my oldest brother Nicholas and I often got a bit of extra food when we were hungry. Nicholas was only twelve but he acted as if he was as old as my father. Because I was so small Nicholas would tell me to lie down and hide on the floor under the long wooden stalls in the fish and chip shop. Angelo would bring the fish and chips to the customers in the booth. Often the customers, a lot of them men who had been working overtime at the foundry, were so exhausted they would fall asleep before they had a chance to finish what they paid for. When they started snoring Nicholas would signal to me that Mr. Fusco was back behind the counter. It was a chance for me to reach up to the plates and swipe whatever part of the fish and chips hadn't been eaten. A portion of uneaten fish was the prize of the night. Nicholas and I would swallow what was left of the vinegar in the bottles to wash down the chips.

Sometimes Angelo Fusco would spot us in the booth and whip us with a wet cloth soaked in flour batter. When he connected, the wet flour ended up in our hair, our ears and our eyes. It stuck to our faces and by the time we got home the batter would have hardened and we'd have to face my mother's anger as well as her wet dishcloth.

Nicholas had courage. The way he took chances and ignored danger drew me to him. He wasn't afraid of anything or anybody and he made sure I got part of everything he had. He was a bit loose and wild. He caused my mother all kinds of problems. He skipped school and robbed apples from rich people's orchards. Not attending Mass or going to Confession was another thing. Sometimes he stayed out all night and slept in abandoned cowsheds. I loved him with all my heart. He ignored or didn't see where he lived and never complained about anything. He was always jumping on the back of horse-drawn carts and committing daredevil acts and he was always there to protect me from my brother Michael who was older than me but younger than Nicholas. As boys we ran and scrambled about the neighbourhood like young pups. I followed Nicholas and Michael everywhere. When I fell behind, Nicholas always slowed down enough for me to keep up with them. It so endeared him to me I always looked forward to the next day when we could run all over the place even though we had no place to go.

* * *

At the age of ten, with a red ribbon pinned on my lapel, I received the Holy Sacrament of Confirmation. The red ribbon meant I was officially a soldier in God's army. I was told that when I made my Confirmation I'd be strong and able to tackle the world on my own. Even though you could go straight to Heaven after you received your First Communion, Confirmation was even more important. It meant you were strong enough to be a soldier for your faith. You could go into battle and do away with anybody who wasn't a Catholic. Being 'confirmed' meant you accepted the full responsibilities of being a Catholic. If you committed sin after Confirmation you couldn't blame your mother or father or anybody else. You couldn't blame the schoolmaster or the priest or any of your neighbours. Anybody who stole anything from you or hit you with a stick or a stone couldn't be blamed either. You couldn't blame any other kind of thing either. Even if you were starving to death or dying of the cold or had an incurable disease or if everybody belonging to you died, you couldn't blame it. If everybody you knew died in a fire and if the whole town and country burned down, you couldn't blame it. If the world fell into Australia, you couldn't blame that either. It was as if you were given a full driver's licence. Confirmation was an important promotion. You were stronger to fight any battle with the Devil and you knew the difference between Hell, Limbo and Purgatory. I had to be aware of committing sin in thought, word, deed or action. I could keep my little soul white or I could make it dark. Sins meant spots on it. If you had too many spots on it and if the white part of it was black it would not be a good soul. It didn't take long for a few of the boys and girls on the street to get into arguments as to whose soul had the most black spots on it. Or whose soul was the whitest.

Around this time I felt myself getting into trouble when the discussion turned to the subject of girls. My mind began to act like an alarm clock. Every time I looked at a young girl I began to think I was committing sin and my soul was losing its whiteness. It was a good thing I was baptised before I knew I was born or alive. I think not to be baptised was worse than not having made your Communion and Confirmation put together. If you died before you were baptised you were dropped off in Limbo. Only babies who weren't baptised and people who were born mad went to Limbo. A person born mad wouldn't know if he was baptised or not so when he died he was sent directly down to Limbo. I never heard of anybody getting a second chance in Limbo. The babies that went there didn't have mothers or fathers to take care of them. The priest or the bishops or even the Pope couldn't reach that far down to save them. The only comfort the babies in Limbo got were the prayers that were offered for them when people said the rosary or went to Mass. My mother sometimes offered up the rosary for the Limbo babies. She also prayed for the souls that were suffering the flames of Purgatory, waiting to get out and go to Heaven. My mother had personal knowledge that some of her relatives were in Purgatory. Two of her uncles who went away from Ireland when she was a child never came back. She believed that they'd committed serious sins that kept them from returning. Purgatory was supposed to be as hot as Hell but you had a chance of getting out of it if enough people said enough prayers for you. If you committed a not-too-serious sin, you had to wait in Purgatory until it was forgiven or erased by God or an angel.

When I thought back to my Confirmation Day I wanted to make it all over again in case I had made a mistake the first time.

* * *

Few people in my neighbourhood really knew the difference between a 'Christian Brother' and a 'priest'. A Christian Brother was only a half-priest it was thought and they had a mission that was different from a priest's. John O Gods they were called. I didn't know what the 'John' or the 'O' meant. The priests were to save our souls. The Christian Brothers were out to save our minds. At the Christian Brothers' school, smartness was to be beaten into you and sins were to be beaten out of you. My mother often praised the Christian Brothers. "They're fine men who devote half of their time to God and the other half to teaching the youngsters." Sister Charlotte also told me the brothers at Saint Michael's were good teachers and fine men. I couldn't imagine her ever saying anything that was not true, but others who had experienced the brothers had different tales to tell. "Most of them would frighten the flies off a dead crow" and "They'll teach ya if they have to kill ya."

For me leaving Goldenbridge Convent and going to the Christian Brothers in Inchicore was as close to being dropped into the fires of Purgatory as I could imagine. When I was transferred I was still seeing Sister Charlotte in my dreams and thought about her almost every day. I had images of her swinging through the trees in Africa with Tarzan. And I knew if Tarzan ever met Sister Charlotte he'd fall madly in love with her. She'd even get him a cake for his birthday and give him other presents as well. She might even encourage him to go to school at Saint Michael's.

Before I transferred to Saint Michael's, the Mother Superior at the convent told all the boys that it was time to go on a weekend religious 'Retreat'. She told us it was a time of transition. I didn't know what transition meant. The Saturday morning before enrolment at Saint Michael's about thirty of us arrived at the far end of the convent grounds. Inside the old church an altar boy was standing in front of the altar, shaking an incense silver bowl attached to two chains. The smoke and smell of the incense was making everybody cough. The smell reminded me of the foundry. Jamie Coombs, the boy kneeling next to me, said the incense was to remind everyone how Heaven smelled. Jamie Coombs was from Keogh Square and it was strange to hear him mention the word 'Heaven' because where he lived was known by most people in the area as *hell*.

Keogh Square was the place where the nuns and some priests earned their seats in Heaven. It was once a military fortification where English soldiers were billeted when England occupied Ireland. There were six barracks surrounding a large parade ground where for centuries the Union Jack flew and military parades and drills were held on the grassy field. When the English left Ireland the barracks were turned into a public housing project. Originally its fortress walls kept out the enemies of Britannia. Now, word had it that the walls were used to keep the residents in. The poorest of the poorest in Dublin were housed there. Bus drivers sometimes broke the speed limit just to get by the place. Pedestrians walking by often got hit with stones, bottles and empty food cans and other objects thrown over the wall. Nuns and priests competed to sacrifice their time on earth by going there and administering to the poor inhabitants. Large families of ten, eleven and twelve children lived in single rooms without electricity or running water. The long barrack corridors had community baths and lavatories. Where infantry soldiers once revelled and bathed, tenement-dwellers – men, women and children – shared the amenities without the luxury of soap or hot water. Thirty years or so after independence, stray horses and abandoned dogs as well as a few homeless men lived among broken bottles and tin cans. The residents lived mostly off food and clothing dockets supplied by Catholic charities. The hallways and stairways were so dangerous at night that when the men from the Saint Vincent de Paul's Society came they had to be escorted by other men who kept an eye out for danger. Families constantly fought and beat each other up. Then sometimes they married each other. One half of the place was related to the other half. Residents of Keogh Square, it is safe to say, saw as much combat as did any of the English soldiers who were once stationed in the place.

Two boys kneeling behind me were arguing about what it took to get into Heaven. I sat at the back of the chapel waiting for the priest to arrive and serve Communion. The boy next to me was hoping he'd die just after the priest put the wafer in his mouth.

Two nuns were walking up and down the aisle and tapping some of the boys on the head to keep them awake. Then the church organ gave out a loud blast. The door of the church swung open and the priest entered. A hush fell over the church. Two nuns instantly blessed themselves as the priest passed them on his way to the altar. In seconds he was standing in front of the assembly and smiling at everyone. The church organ blasted out again and the nuns in the aisle encouraged us all to join in singing the hymn.

"*O salutaris hostia, quae caeli pandis ostium!*" I sang as loud as I could.

The organ stopped and everyone fell silent.

The priest blessed himself. "*In the Name of the Father and of the Son and of the Holy Ghost, Amen.*" He then took a deep breath and announced, "There will be no Communion because the Communion wafers are still at the factory."

A sigh of relief reverberated throughout the chapel.

With a much louder voice the priest called out: "Boys, I want you all to pay special attention. I want you to listen and heed what I'm about to say. What I want to talk about is the time you'll be feeling urges of the flesh. The images of young girls will be there to tempt you. When these urges come to you and you know what part of the body makes you aware, turn your mind to the Holy Word of the Church. And if your mind gets stuck with the devil in your trousers, touch nothing. Find your rosary beads and get a firm grip on them. Any thoughts of fondling anything or any part of you should give way to saying a quick decade of the rosary. I remind you that only with Our Lord can you find the strength to turn away from such temptations. Boys, we'll have the Devotions and Benediction after dinner."

He stepped from the altar and walked down the aisle towards the door. The nuns signalled for us to march in an orderly fashion out of the church.

As we walked along the path that led to the dining hall, I walked in another direction and departed from the grounds and the Retreat.

* * *

My brother Nicholas had some kind of problem with his throat that made him cough all the time. One night while we were all in bed my mother took him to the hospital. Sitting in semi-darkness downstairs two of my older sisters, Rita and Carmel, kept mumbling prayers and blessing themselves. The rest of us who were younger listened and waited for my mother to come home. While waiting one of my sisters mentioned the word "tuberculosis". Tuberculosis was what everybody dreaded in Dublin. My mother often prayed for people in the neighbourhood who had it. She also prayed for them when they died of it. My father, knowing his oldest son was in hospital, got out of bed, walked downstairs, sat by the fire and said nothing. It wasn't long till my mother came in the front door crying. She told my father that Nicholas had to stay in the hospital.

"God has punished the whole family!" she cried. "God is not happy with the life we're living. We don't say the rosary enough and half the sacraments are not bothered with. Our

Heavenly Father is not happy with what goes on in this house. Look at me daughters! Look at them!"

She felt that God had paid her back because of her daughters. They wanted to wear lipstick and powder their faces. They painted their legs with make-up to substitute for nylons and, before they went out, my mother would lash at their legs with a wet dishcloth hoping to wipe away some of the paint. Also the way they dressed invited sin, according to Molly. Her own sense of glamour was based on how the nuns dressed. Going to dances at the local nightspots, The Crystal and The Four Courts, was also not condoned. When the girls came home late they often found the front door closed. My mother believed they were out committing sin and deserved to be shut out to teach them a lesson. My father was obliged to get out of bed and open the hall door. My sisters were still met with a barrage of doomsday warnings from my mother who'd be standing at the top of the stairs in her nightgown.

‹O›

For my first day in class the Christian Brother talked about Oliver Cromwell as if the man was still alive and living next door to him. He said he was the Devil himself who murdered thousands of women and children in Drogheda and drove all the true Irish out of their homes and westwards to Connaught, behind the Shannon River, shouting "To Hell or to Connaught!"

To me the Brother was like bad weather, cold, damp and the flu all rolled into one. He was a young man who looked old. Like a fish monster that had been thrown up out of the ocean. His face was easier to bear when he spoke, because his eyes didn't stay in the same place. Sometimes he put his hand up to his face and covered his mouth. When he was talking he even looked more like a fish.

He'd call out: "*Thógáil amach do leabhair Ghaeilge anois.*" Take out your Irish books now.

I hated Irish. Irish frightened me.

"Breathnach!" He called me by the Irish name for Walsh. "Breathnach! Tell me about the Gaelic Renaissance!"

I knew nothing about Gaelic or the Renaissance or whatever the word was or meant. The Christian Brother was obsessed with the Irish language. He spoke as much as he could in Irish and wrote everything on the blackboard in Irish. Few of us knew anything about Irish. The government wanted everybody in Ireland to learn it because de Valera, the Taoiseach, said we shouldn't use anything English. "Burn everything English except its coal," he said, except it was someone else who said that first in the old days, not Dev. De Valera wanted every Irish person to know Irish. It made people less English, he said. Hardly anybody in Dublin spoke it. For half the school day the Christian Brother would read to us in Irish even though we didn't understand a word of it. At the end of the week we got tested in Irish and almost everyone failed. The Brother then called out the names of those who had failed and had us line up in a row to await his punishment. One by one he lashed out at us with his cane as if he was defending Drogheda from Oliver Cromwell. He prayed in Irish at the same time. All of us would have preferred Hell or Connaught to the unleashed temper of Brother Fish Mouth. He whipped us on the palm of our hands and on our bottoms. It was six slaps with the cane and if his temper reached the boiling point he'd add three more slaps with the leather strap. The more we cried, the harder the leather strap came down. When the palms of our hands bled we wiped the blood off on the sides of our trousers.

After I retreated to my seat with swollen and bleeding hands I heard my name being called out again.

"Breathnach! You didn't hand in any home exercise work. You did nothing since you were here yesterday. Where's your homework? Did you do any?"

"No, sir," I responded.

"And why not, Breathnach?"

"My mother had her rheumatic pains last night and the whole house was kept up half of the night. I couldn't read anything with my mother screamin' and cryin' with her pain. Her legs and arms and the back of her neck were driving her mad. She made me and my sisters say the rosary loads of times but the pain didn't go away. My father boiled water and even put a hot cloth on her neck."

"What pains?" the Brother queried me again.

"Rheumatic pains! That's why I couldn't do my homework."

"Your mother has been suffering for three weeks now with those pains. When is she going to get better?"

"I think she's better now. She said she was going to Communion at the early Mass this morning, and when she does that I know she's better. She offered her prayers up to the Infant of Prague. She said the rosary again this morning."

"How many times did you say it?"

"Me?"

"Yes, you."

"I didn't say it this morning."

"Why not?"

"My mother was screamin' and prayin'. I couldn't join in on it. Neither could my brothers and sisters."

"So you didn't say it this morning?"

"No."

"No?"

He didn't believe my story about the rheumatic pains. He made his way up to my bench and saw "*FUCK EVERY-THING GAELIC*" carved into the bench. His eyes began to roll and I thought he was going to faint. The carvings had been there since I first sat there and probably had been there since nineteen-sixteen.

"Who did that?" he asked.

"It was done a long time ago. It was here before I came to Saint Michael's," I said in defence of myself.

The Brother wasn't in the mood to believe anything I had to say even if it was the truth.

"Hold out your hand."

Out I held my hand and down fell the weight and force of the hot leather again. The class fell into its usual silence. *Smack! Slap! Smack! Slap!* When it reached the sixth slap he stopped. My hand was more swollen than before. He yelled at me again. This time I thought he was really losing his mind. He seemed not to be able to control himself.

"You'll learn to study at night before I'm through with you!"

"I'll do my exercises tonight!" My hands were bleeding even more and I believed that I had slipped or fallen into Hell.

* * *

A week later while I was lying in bed I heard my sister Rita coming into the house. She had been to the hospital to visit Nicholas.

She was crying and calling out. "Nicholas is dead! Oh God help me! Nicholas, poor Nicholas!"

My mother rushed in from the kitchen and let out a scream. "Sacred Heart of Jesus, be good to his soul! Sacred Heart of Jesus, keep him at your side in Heaven!" Her overwhelming pain was now challenging her overwhelming belief.

Nicholas was dead. My brother was dead. I lay back in bed and was afraid to get up and face what I had just heard. I knew now that I was really alone. I was always calling after Nicholas and telling him my brother Michael was beating me up. Nicholas would defend me and protect me from the bullies on the street. What would I do without him? If he was really dead I'd be lost and have no one to go to when I was frightened. Nicholas was the person I loved the most in my entire life. I wanted to burst out crying but some part of me wouldn't accept that he was dead and the tears wouldn't come out of my eyes. I kept telling myself that he wasn't dead and that he'd be coming out of the hospital and we'd go running around again, playing games and having fun.

After a few minutes I heard more voices coming from downstairs. Neighbours began to come into the house to offer their sympathies. My mother was crying and blaming his death on the family's way of living. The house became very dark that morning. More neighbours came in, talked and had tea. Black dresses were brought up from some charitable society. The flowers and lace curtains were taken from the windows. The priest came up. He told my mother Nicholas was on his way to Heaven. While everybody downstairs was crying I stayed in bed.

A few days later I stood with the rest of my family at Nicholas's gravesite in Glasnevin Cemetery and kept telling myself that my brother was not in the coffin that was being lowered into the grave. Later on the gossip on the street and in my house was that the doctors in Dublin at the time didn't know what they were doing and experimented with some new form of chemical. My mother said it was radium and they blasted Nicholas's young body with an overdose of it.

* * *

Almost every moment I spent in school with Brother Fish Mouth I shook with fear. Added to that was the fact that my parents didn't have money to purchase textbooks. Without the textbooks I'd nothing to look at and I couldn't ever do any homework. It was a sad time altogether. I couldn't read. The Brother blamed my parents for not taking advantage of the Free Book scheme that the government and the Saint Vincent de Paul society were involved in. I was afraid to tell him that the books were gone by the time my mother went to get some.

The man in black put a deep fear into me. I was afraid of his face. I was afraid of his voice. Anytime he was talking about Irish and English History he'd raise his voice as if he was about to sing a song. "The Penal Laws of 1695 were made by the English to destroy Catholicism in Ireland. England punished Ireland for supporting the Stuarts against the Protestant William of Orange. Ireland was in favour of anything France did because France was a Catholic country." Brother Fish Mouth told us about the terrible troubles that began when Catholic King James the Second was defeated on Irish soil at the Battle of the Boyne on July 1, 1690. This was after Oliver Cromwell's time and Blessed Oliver Plunkett's as well.

Every time I looked at the man in black I saw two horns grow out of his forehead and his tongue was a rope of flame. I began to think and even believe that I was going insane. Every day he was on my mind. Whatever I said, thought or did, I felt his presence. I took him everywhere I went. When I played football he was there. Even when I went to the films at the Tivoli I imagined he was there as well. When I swam in the canal I could sense his frightening presence and I felt that I might drown.

One morning when he asked me about my father the Brother almost punched a hole in the wooden desk I sat on. I proudly told him that my father had spent time in the English army and it was as if I had killed his mother or his dog or something. The look of madness in his eyes when he heard that my father was once a British army soldier frightened me more than the priest who stole my mother's wedding ring.

The Brother walked away from me and with his back turned to the rest of the class he yelled out, "I can see England rolling in the dust of Babylon! The Chinese will take Hong Kong and the Spanish, God bless their hot-blooded hearts, will take Gibraltar, which rightfully belongs to them! And Ulster will come back to Ireland!"

When he got to the front of the class he turned around, bamboo cane in hand, and stared back at me again. I thought I was finished. I trembled and regretted telling him about my father's time in the British army. As he stared at me a smile crawled over his face. He began to talk as if he was making his First Communion or his Holy Confirmation. For no reason that I could think of or imagine, he sounded calmer and more peaceful than ever before.

"I've often wondered how great England would have been if it didn't have the Irish and others to fight its wars. If you ask me, the Irish were always too good and kind to the English. Pity the buggers up there in the North not knowin' if they're English or Irish. The poor Protestants marchin' around on Irish soil with Irish rain fallin' all over 'em. If ya met an Orangeman in India or England he'd quickly tell ya he was Irish. If ya met the same fella in Ireland he'd tell ya he was English."

When he finished his political rant he turned his attention to religion.

"Boys oh boys! You may know bits and pieces about the physical body but what do you know about your soul? Or anyone's soul? Even the souls of the people you love most. Souls? What are souls? What? What? Souls that are pure and clean and spotless – that's what we strive for and seek while we live on this earth. And it's only by having a clean and pure soul that you can join our Heavenly Father in Heaven. D'ya know we were all pure, spotless and sinless souls in Ireland at one time?"

There was a silence. He started again.

"We're the ones who put up them big heavy stones in Stonehenge. Everybody's been wonderin' for centuries how anyone could lift up such heavy things like that. The doctors and educated fellas can't account for that, you know." He stared right at me again. "How did we put them up?" he asked me.

I didn't know. I didn't even know they were up or what they were. I'd never heard of Stonehenge.

"Where is it?" I asked.

"Stonehenge?"

"Yes."

"In England."

"How did they get lifted up so high?" another boy called from the back of the class.

"Y'want to know?"

I didn't know what he was talking about and he was getting very excited about what he was saying. He seemed to be enjoying it.

"How?" I asked.

"Spiritual levitation. We were connected to the magnetic forces of the Earth and the Universe. We in Ireland know how to make things rise without touching them. An' you want to know somethin' else? D'ya want to know somethin' else?" He rattled the money in his pocket and went on talking. "That's why the English came over here in the first place. They were in search of their souls."

I shrugged my shoulders and hoped he was going to stop talking. He didn't. He kept playing around with the bamboo cane in his hand.

"We were the centre of commerce and trade during the Bronze Age. And most of the gold found in Mycenae came from Ireland. The treasures in our national museum here in Dublin will bear witness to that. Go to Knocknarea in County Sligo and fascinate your imagination with your heritage. Yes, by Christ, that's what you can do. Did you know that Ireland was never incorporated into the Roman Empire?" The man then crashed the bamboo cane against his desk. "Oliver Cromwell was the vilest man who ever lived!"

The class was quiet. Most of us didn't understand the word 'vilest'.

Then Brother Fish Mouth asked, "Does anybody know who said, 'To Hell or to Connaught'?"

Half the class raised their hands and yelled out in unison, "Oliver Cromwell!" Everybody knew Oliver Cromwell said it because Brother Fish Mouth was always telling us. He was always on about Oliver Cromwell and Oliver Plunkett.

I got the Olivers mixed up one morning when I was asked about a date in Irish history and said Oliver Plunkett instead of Oliver Cromwell.

Brother Fish Mouth jumped up from behind his desk and rushed towards me with his eyes bulging. "Don't ever mix up their names. Oliver Plunkett is not Oliver Cromwell!" He slapped me on the back of the head for giving the wrong answer. "Oliver Plunkett was the brave Archbishop of Drogheda who stood up to Oliver Cromwell!" He then turned around and, with his face to the blackboard, he asked, "Who was Oliver Plunkett?"

Nobody answered.

The Brother turned around, faced all of us and yelled, "Blessed Oliver Plunkett was a Catholic! He was the Bishop of Drogheda who stood up to Oliver Cromwell. In the name of his Protestant religion Oliver Cromwell pushed the Irish off their land and killed men, women and children, all because they clung to their Catholic faith. Cromwell was a scourge to our country. He was a scourge to our religion!"

He sat down as if to take a rest from his anger. About five seconds had passed when he got up and quietly addressed the class again.

"When did the barbarian invade our country?" he asked.

He pointed his bamboo cane at Éamon Quinn, the boy sitting in front of me. I was glad I wasn't asked the question.

Éamon shook with fear. "Nineteen-sixteen," he answered.

The Brother leaned over towards Éamon and whacked him on the back of the head. "No! No! Sixteen-fifty, you dope!"

Éamon dropped his head onto the wooden desk in front of him and started crying. The brother walked up to Éamon and stood next to him. He looked around the class as if to warn us about giving the wrong answer to his questions. He then placed his hand on Éamon's head.

"Did Oliver Plunkett cry when confronted with Oliver Cromwell?" he asked out loud to the class.

"No!" we all said, knowing that was what he wanted to hear.

After a second or two of silence, a boy with a new pair of shoes on his feet put up his hand. "Why was Connaught worse than hell?" he asked.

"It *wasn't*, you bloody git! Connaught was the West of Ireland. The West of Ireland had no houses or towns or farmland. No livestock, no nothing. Cromwell wanted to herd all the Catholics who wouldn't change their religion to the West of Ireland. That way they would all starve to death and he wouldn't have to kill them off like he was doing in every other part of Ireland at the time. Oliver Cromwell hated Catholicism more than he hated the Devil himself."

The Christian Brother urged everybody in class to visit Drogheda where Blessed Oliver Plunkett's skull was in a glass case for everybody to see. He showed us photographs of the skull. It was a brownish round bonehead with no eyes or anything. A bit smaller than the sheep's head my mother often bought to make soup. We were to imagine the brave Bishop of Drogheda before his flesh wasted away. I couldn't imagine any kind of face on the skull. It had cracks and a few dents on it.

* * *

After a while I decided I was going to fight back a little bit. I couldn't bear to be beaten any more. And the next time I was in his class I was determined not to let him whack me with his cane or leather strap. He started to talk about something in Irish and I had no idea what he was saying.

"Breathnach? Did you hear me?"

"I didn't understand, sir."

"Come up. Come up now!" He called me up to the head of the class.

I went.

"Hold out your hand."

I didn't. I kept my hands behind my back.

His face and neck began to swell up. *"Hold out your hand!"* he roared like a lion.

I kept my hands behind my back.

"Give me your hand!" His eyes were bulging and his mouth was opening like a big fish about to eat a little fish.

I kept my hand away from him.

He grabbed hold of me and started to twist my arm to get at my hands. I still wouldn't let my hands go in front of me. The more he pulled at my arms to get at my hands the more I kept turning and turning away from him.

I screamed at him. "Leave me alone! I've no money for books! All the free books were gone! My mother told me to tell you that!" At the same time I kicked him on the shinbone.

He let go of my arms, grabbed me by the scruff of my shirt collar, dragged me out of the classroom and deposited me in the corridor where he slapped me on both ears.

"Don't hit me! Don't hit me!" I pleaded. I fell to on the floor, crushed with pain and fear.

As the Brother walked back to the classroom he called to me. "It's the reformatory for you, boyo! You'll be there before you know it. Daingean will suit ya."

Daingean, a reformatory school in a town of the same name in County Offaly, was run by the Oblate Fathers, the same order Father Devine came from. Reformatory schools were where the church sent those who were not adjusting to the programme and discipline of the Christian Brothers. Punishment, torture and abuse were the mainstays of the curriculum in reformatory schools. Originally Daingean was a prison for convicts. When Daingean was compared with Hell, most people chose Hell. Intimidation and brutality were the commandants of daily life in such institutions.

Reformatory schools were also a heaven of opportunity and motivation for the young men who volunteered to be priests and who majored in teaching Irish and Irish history. The small white collar around their necks gave them licence and liberty to practise and indulge in any sexual fantasy their infected minds could conjure.

Countless boys my age and younger who were considered 'difficult' and 'hard to manage' were shipped off to reformatory schools every week. Few ever returned home with any semblance of innocence or optimism. Most couldn't adjust to anything or anybody they knew prior to their incarceration and were unrecognisable.

The name and threat of Daingean sent shivers up my spine. I was hoping that the Brother wasn't serious when he threatened me with incarceration there. I picked myself up from the floor and walked out of the school. I was afraid to go home and face my mother but I made up my mind that I would never go back to that classroom again. For the next month or so, during every school day, I stayed away from school and spent most of the day walking around the city or going to the cinema. When I came home every day at four o'clock I told my mother I'd been to school and that everything was going fine with my schooling. I felt obliged to lie to her because I was terrified of facing the Christian Brother and being sent to Daingean.

Within a few weeks my mother got a notice of delinquency from the Board of Education. The notice outlined my absence record at school and my behaviour towards the Christian Brother. My parents and I were summoned to go before a school board to explain my behaviour. A panel of men would decide if I was fit to remain in the Christian Brothers' School or should be sent away to a reformatory school such as Daingean.

* * *

The day of Fish Mouth's revenge came. A rainy morning. I washed my hair and my face, and wore the cleanest clothes I had. A week earlier I'd got a pair of free boots from the Vincent de Paul. They reached up to my ankles and were made of thick leather. They were as black as the soot in the chimney. I had no socks and when I put my feet into them they scratched the top of my ankles. I took a test walk around the room and my ankles turned red. Every step I took made a sound as if I was passing wind or squashing a bunch of frogs with my toes.

My trousers had cloth patches on the back that were hanging off. My mother noticed my partly exposed rear end and let out a holy scream. "Ah, for God's sake, look at ya! You'll be sent away for sure if you walk around like that!"

"The stitches came out yesterday," I said.

"Take them off right now!"

I climbed out of the second-hand trousers and stood half-naked on the floor. My mother threw a dishcloth at me and went looking for a needle and thread. I wrapped the dishcloth around the lower part of my body and spent the next ten minutes trying to identify the odour that was coming from it.

After finding a needle and thread, my mother sat down. "Christ almighty, what's to become of us?" she kept repeating as she tried to thread the needle. "Here, do this for me, will ya?" She passed the needle and thread to me. I quickly threaded the needle and handed it back to her.

The patches on my trousers were sewn back on again and within minutes my mother and I were on our way to Dublin Castle where my future might depend on how the patches on my second-hand trousers held up.

My mother and I walked into the big grey building where hundreds of years of Irish history had been played out and joined up with others who were in the same sad situation as

I was. The corridor we walked along seemed too imposing a place for the crime of talking back to a schoolteacher. In this same building in years past people were ordered to be hanged, executed, flogged and deported for disobeying English law in Ireland. With Ireland now in charge of its own affairs it was, at least on some scale, duplicating what England had done to it years earlier.

As my mother and I got closer to the room where my case was to be heard, I could hear mothers crying. Some were screaming. Their sons had been ordered to report to the police office at the far end of the hall and be sent to a reformatory school. Fear engulfed me again. I was frightened and began to shake and cry.

"Ah, Ma, help me. Don't let me go. Don't let me go, Ma. Help me. Save me, Ma. I'm afraid." I held onto my mother's hand so tightly I almost broke her fingers.

"I'm your mother and I'll stand by you, son," she said as we walked the last few yards toward the hearing room.

We entered a cold room with long wooden benches in front of a table that was on a raised platform. Three men were sitting at the table.

Before we could sit down my name was called out. "Gabriel Walsh?"

My mother remained standing. "We're here, sir," she said.

"Is he with you?" she was asked by one of the men as if he couldn't see me.

"Me son is here, sir," my mother responded.

"Step up, boy," the man said.

I was holding my mother's hand so tight I couldn't let go of it.

"Go up, son," she said while she tried to detach herself from me.

I walked to the table and looked up at the three men. My mouth opened and my eyes closed and my heart raced.

"You're a problem at school. Are you?"

"I don't know."

"You don't know, *sir*!" the man bellowed back at me. "The Brother states you don't learn and you don't care. And you don't attend. Is that true?"

I was so frightened standing in front of the three men I didn't know that I was alive. I was a heartbeat away from fainting on the floor in front of them.

"I'm afraid," I said. It was the only thing I could say. I kept repeating it. "I'm afraid. I'm afraid. I'm afraid." I kept saying it until I was interrupted.

"Afraid of what?" one of the men asked me.

I looked up at the man but I couldn't answer him.

My mother then came up to me and held my hand. "Tell the nice man what you're afraid of, son," she said.

I was happy my mother was holding my hand but I still couldn't answer the man's question.

"What are you afraid of?" the man asked me again.

"He's afraid to admit he kicked the Christian Brother if you ask me," one of the three men said.

"Isn't that some kind of carryin' on?" the man sitting in the centre said to my mother.

"He meant no harm, sir," my mother responded.

The pain of thinking about Daingean forced my mouth open but prevented me from opening my eyes. My future was looking as bleak as my present. I wished a silent suicide upon myself but I didn't know how to die. Outside in the corridor the cries of mothers who were separated from their children could still be heard. Then, as if to detract from the sad and painful wails, the senior-looking man looked directly at me and raised his voice.

"This fella is not learnin' a ha'purt in school. He's giving the Brother a lot of back talk and isn't in any way disciplined. Daingean will be the proper place for him."

When the man mentioned "Daingean" my mother's face went white. I exchanged a fearful look with her and went so numb I didn't know if I fainted or not. My mother then walked up to the man behind the bench and looked directly at him. She began to talk with the conviction of a saint or a martyr.

"Me son will change. I promise and pray that to you. He's a good boy but his father has been no help to him. His father hasn't been able to earn a penny in years and he's been back and forth to England searchin' for a bit of labourin' work. Gabriel couldn't do his school lessons 'cos the free books were gone so he had no books to look at and we couldn't afford him a pen or pencil. No boy can be expected to learn with that kind of drawback. I've prayed and I've done me best and I ask you not to send him to Daingean." She then leaned forward and raised her right hand, with her rosary beads clutched in it. "Look! Look how worn out me rosary beads are from constant prayin'!" She placed the small wooden crucifix over her heart and pleaded with the panel not to send me away. "It won't be long till he can get himself a job and earn a few shillin's. After that he'll be a great help to all of us at home. Give him another chance, I beg ya!"

'Daingean' was written all over their faces.

As I watched my mother plead for me I remained choked with fear.

The men behind the bench looked at each other and then back at me and my mother. Dublin, of course, had many oddball characters and some who might have even defied reason but my mother's performance had to be up there with the best and oddest of them.

A member of the board looked directly at my mother. "He'd be as well off in a reformatory. By our Divine Saviour, he'd learn there. This lad is bold, very bold. In my opinion, if he's not checked now it will be too late in a year or two. If he's let loose he won't know how to read or write. I've seen it all before. You'll be proud of him when he's released in a couple years."

My mother put her crucifix to her lips and made the Sign of the Cross with it. She then raised her eyes to Heaven and took off as if she was transported. She called upon all the souls of every saint in Heaven – foreign or otherwise – as if she knew them personally. Molly knew many prayers and she knew how to pray as if she wrote the words to them. She recited acts of contrition and spat out an encyclopaedia of hymns that dealt with every dimension of forgiveness. I'm sure the school board members had never experienced anything like what they saw that day. Two members of the panel simultaneously blessed themselves. They appeared to be rethinking their rubber-stamped decision.

A miracle happened. My mother saved me from the persecution and agony of the reformatory school. Her sorrowful presence and her ability to call upon saints and angels as well as deceased bishops and popes convinced the inconvincible. Dressed in her old clothes and with stockings hanging around her ankles, Molly won the day. I was saved. All the thoughts and feelings of embarrassment I had previously felt for and about my mother vanished rapidly. She was now my saviour and, with the sense and avalanche of joy of not being sent and condemned to Daingean, I felt so light I could fly.

After a moment or two a board member told my mother to have me leave the Christian Brothers' School and go to the Model School, a non-religious-order school, closer to home.

* * *

A week later I was enrolled in a school where the teachers didn't wear black. It was a Catholic school run by teachers who wore regular clothes and who went home to their families when the school day ended. Compared to the Christian Brothers' school the Model School was like a holiday home.

Nevertheless every Friday at about eleven in the morning we'd leave the classroom and assemble outside on the street to be marched to a chapel that was not too far away. It was about a ten-minute walk. For the first two years I was an obedient pupil and marched with my schoolmates to the church so that the local priest could hear our confessions. We marched in unison and in a straight line – a parade of boys marching to take our souls to the laundry. For most of us it was a celebration.

One morning close to my last few months in the school, I decided I didn't need to confess to nothing all over again. The morning started with the usual ritual. A whistle blew and the march began. As we marched towards the church to confess our sins we passed a big public house. The stench of Guinness and whiskey coming from the place cut through the air like a dirty bed-sheet drying on a clothesline. This wonderful sunny morning I was feeling freer than I had felt in a very long time. As I marched by the pub I noticed that the door of the place was wide open. Without giving it too much thought I slipped from the confessional line and walked into the pub as if I was a regular customer. Inside the pub a few men were sitting at the bar. They were talking out loud but I couldn't tell if they were talking to each other or to the big pints of Guinness that were in front of them.

When the long confessional line had passed, I stepped out of the pub and walked home very slowly. Before I got to my house I decided I'd better visit the Oblates Church to get as holy as I could before I went home. I didn't want my mother to know I had skipped the confessional line. If she knew I had, she'd believe I was afraid to confess to some sin I had committed. Any kind of sin on my white soul would be a one-way ticket to hell with the Devil as my landlord for eternity. If I came home looking holy after a visit to the statue of the Virgin who had her wedding ring in her crown, my mother might not ask any questions.

There were several statues of Our Lady outside the church but I knew the one Father Divine was in love with was the one that overlooked the churchyard, the one that now had a massive gold crown on her head and a great big halo. She was there up on her big high pedestal over the gate, day and night, in all kinds of weather, with her eyes cast up to Heaven as if she had no interest in the rest of us moving around down below. She didn't move or blink or fart or want to go to the bathroom or anything like that.

I wanted to tell the statue that my mother's wedding ring was on her head. As I looked up at it, Father Divine's voice was ringing in my ears. *"The Holy Mother of God would be eternally grateful if you could donate this ring to her crown, Mrs. Walsh. I know she'd look down on you and anoint you. If you do, it would be placed in her crown with other gold rings from other women and wives in the parish."* I tried to spot my mother's wedding ring but I wasn't able to. I couldn't see any rings on the crown, only big stars all around it. Maybe the rings the women gave were on top of it? I thought about climbing up on the statue and getting the ring back to give to my father so he could give it to my mother all over again and she would forget that he hadn't had a job in years and years. Our Lady knew where God was all day long and knew if he was busy or not. He would listen to her at any time and if she heard me praying to her she could put in a good word for me. I wanted her to know that my father was sad and lonely and needed a few shillings. I made up a prayer: "Mother of God! Mother of everybody's mother! Daughter of God! Sister of God! Sister-in-Law of God! Child of God! Virgin of Heaven and Earth! Help my mother and father to be nice to each other."

When I got to my house my mother was kneeling on the floor and leaning over a chair, with a pair of rosary beads wrapped around her fingers. Her eyes were closed. She looked more peaceful than I had seen her in a long time. I wondered if it was because my father was out of the house. Normally she would name every saint that was ever tortured or burned by the time she finished saying the rosary. A candle was burning near the statue of the Sacred Heart that was strategically placed on the cabinet that held the Sunday plates and dishes. She had just finished scrubbing the floor. A bucket of soapy water was at her right side. Her apron was soaking wet. She had pulled up her skirt a bit to scrub the floor and I could see she was wearing a big pair of thick woollen knickers that reached to her knees and several holes in the knickers had been sewn up with different-coloured thread. Her toes were sticking out of her stockings and the sleeves of her blouse were rolled up to her elbows which were red and sore-looking.

The place looked so clean the entire population of Heaven would have been content to live in it. I sat down by the fire and waited for her to finish. I wondered why my mother and father seemed to be happier people when they were not around each other. The smell of soap was everywhere. The floorboards had been scrubbed and the windows were clean.

At last my mother got to her feet and went to sit on a chair facing out onto the back yard. She didn't turn around when I walked up to her.

"Why are you home now? Didn't you go to Confession?" she asked while still gazing out the window.

I could tell my early return didn't make her happy. I decided to tell her the truth and tell her I didn't go to Confession because I had nothing to confess, that I hadn't committed any sins and I didn't want to be telling the priest in the confessional box a lie. I hesitated and when my mother looked at me I knew what she was thinking.

"I wasn't feelin' well, Ma," I answered and poured myself a cup of tea from the nearby teapot.

"You was supposed to be confessin' your sins, wasn't you?"

I didn't know how to answer. I wanted to tell her I didn't have any sins to confess.

"You ran away, didn't ya? You ran away from the holy place. I know you did. That's what you did." My mother then stood up and reached for the broom that was leaning against the wall.

I told her I went to the church to see if her wedding ring was still in the crown of the Virgin Mary and that I had prayed and prayed. "I said more than twenty prayers, Ma. I talked to the nuns, the priests. I prayed to the statue. I didn't go to Confession, Ma. I'm sorry. I wasn't feeling good, Ma. I had a stomach ache." I told her I was sorry for anything I had done wrong.

Molly turned from me as if all her prayers had fallen out of Heaven and onto her head. She seemed smothered with anger. She looked at me and lowered her voice but it seemed louder than ever. For a moment she seemed disconnected to it.

"*Ya won't do what's good for ya!*" she yelled. In a fit of anger she made a swipe at me with the broom.

The handle hit me across the arm. When I put up my hands to prevent another swipe from hitting me, my mother smacked me even harder with the broom-handle. I wanted to cry for my father but he wasn't home.

"You're just like your father. There's no changin' you either. Not a bit!"

When my mother moved closer to me I closed my eyes, hoping she wouldn't strike me again but she continued to pursue me around the room, laying into me with the broom. At first I hid under the table but I was still hit by the broom handle.

"Ma, ma, don't hit me! Don't. You're hurtin' me. Don't, Ma! Don't!"

My mother was silent and that frightened me even more. She kept striking me until I began to faint and not know where I was.

Out of nowhere I heard our neighbour Mrs. Fortune yelling from outside our door. "Mrs. Walsh, leave him alone! Stop! Stop it!"

My mother immediately stopped and sat down on a nearby chair. She looked down at me and started to cry.

"I'm sorry, son. Forgive me. Forgive me."

Mrs. Fortune then came into our house. "What in the name of God are you doing, Missus?" she yelled at my mother. She reached down to me and saw that my hands and arms were bleeding. She turned back and stared at my mother but said nothing. My mother sat there in silence.

After a minute or two I heard a knock on the hall door. Another neighbour, Mrs. Waters from across the street, wanted to know what was going on as well. Mrs. Fortune put her finger to her lips and Mrs. Waters left.

"I'm goin' to take that boy down to the hospital," Mrs. Fortune said to my mother.

"I don't know what's come over me, Missus," my mother said. "I'm not feelin' well lately. I don't know what's come over me. I don't know how I'm going to put a few crumbs on the table. There's nothin' in the house. I've pawned everythin'."

As Mrs. Fortune took me by the hand and led me towards the door, my mother stood up and put on her coat. "I'll take me boy to the hospital."

Mrs. Fortune slowly walked back out the door. After I washed the blood from my arms and head, my mother took me to Stephen's Hospital where I had my wrists stitched in two places. When the doctor asked my mother what happened, she told him I fell down the stairs.

* * *

The next day the parish priest, Father Brady, came into the classroom. His face was red and he seemed to be in a hurry. He walked around the classroom with a small bamboo cane in his hand that he kept tapping against his knee. His eyes met mine but I turned away and pretended I didn't see him. He walked up to the front and whispered something into the teacher's ear. The teacher then looked back at me and I knew I was in trouble. I'd been spotted. Somebody had seen me skip the confessional line.

"Gabriel Walsh?"

"Yes. Father."

"Come up here."

I took the walk up the aisle and stood at the head of the class. The teacher turned his head away from me. That meant something. The priest looked down on me. Then, he turned his face to the class and pursed his lips and, without saying a word to me, he landed his right hand on my face with the force of a boxer. I fell sideways. I was too hurt to cry and too afraid to say anything.

75

"That will teach you to cheat on God!" he said as the teacher, seemingly sympathetic, turned me back toward my seat.

My mind was buzzing and spinning and I didn't know where I was. The entire class fell silent. In my frightened state I silently cried as the pain raced through my face. When I reached my seat I could hear the voice of the priest calling after me. "Say an Act of Contrition!"

I couldn't answer. His voice became louder and louder but I still couldn't talk. I couldn't move my jaw.

"Do you hear?"

I murmured back, "Yes, Father."

"Say it while the sin is still in your mind."

"Yes, Father."

The other boys looked at each other and nervously shuffled their feet under the desks.

"*Our Father who art in Heaven, hallowed be Thy name,*" I began.

When I uttered my first word of the prayer the feet-shuffling stopped.

"That's not an Act of Contrition, that's the Lord's Prayer!" Father Brady roared.

He rushed towards me, raised his hand again and hit me in the jaw. My teeth and brains began to shake and rattle and the light outside went on and off. I couldn't remember the prayer but I knew it was for saying sorry for committing sin. I felt sorry for everything. I felt sorry for everybody and I felt sorry for myself.

"Do you know what is meant by an Act of Contrition?" the priest demanded.

I didn't answer. My jaw was hurting me and I thought I was swallowing my teeth. I looked up at Father Brady and hoped he'd see my fear and pain. I was hoping that the fear in my eyes would convince him I was more than sorry for my sin.

He looked down at me and spoke in the slowest voice I had ever heard coming from a human mouth. "You're sorry. You are sorry for what you did. You admit to God that you are sorry for the sin you committed and you promise not to sin again. You beg and beseech God for forgiveness for committing sin. That's paramount in God's mind. He must know that you are truly repentant. He must know that you are truly and sincerely sorry and that you have no intention of ever committing sin again for as long as you live your life on this earth. Go on now, say it. Say an Act of Contrition." He began to say the prayer himself: "*Oh my God, I am heartily sorry for having offended Thee . . .*"

I repeated the words: "*Oh my God, I am heartily sorry for having offended Thee.*" I stopped and was more frightened and confused and more awkward than before. I didn't know what I was saying. I was hoping I would remember the words to the prayer. I prayed to myself as Father Brady stood over me: Dear God, little Jesus in the crib with the ox and the animals breathing on you, help me remember the Act of Contrition! I then began to mumble, "*O my God, I am heartily sorry for having offended Thee and I detest my sins above every other evil . . .*"

As I continued with the prayer Father Brady turned away from me and walked to the head of the class. He looked over the entire class and slowly walked out.

◄○►

At thirteen I was considered fit and able to seek gainful employment but finding work of any kind that would bring a few shillings into the house wasn't simple or easy. It was almost impossible. In order not to be thrown out of the house I'd make a few pennies by boiling water and making tea for the plasterers on building sites who were plastering the interiors of new houses in what used to be considered 'countryside'. This means of survival didn't last long. Most of the plasterers were from Scotland and when they finished their work they went back to Scotland. When that happened I was unemployed and sat around the house for weeks and months on end. This didn't please my mother or other members of my family who were working and making money. Three of my older sisters were in factories and my brother Michael was training as a house painter. Every day he'd come home covered with paint and smelling of paint-thinner. Wherever he walked or sat in the house it smelled like he had just painted the place. When I complained about the smell, my mother said, "Shut up and get a job! If you don't get a decent job soon you'll end up like Black Bart Joe Deegan!"

Joe Deegan who lived down the street was supposedly allergic to soap and water. He let the dirt pile up on his skin until he looked like the cowboy named Black Bart in the movies. Black Bart had a black hat, a black suit, a black pair of boots and rode a black horse. Nobody ever saw his face because he wore a black mask. When my mother compared me to Joe Deegan I was convinced she didn't like me all over again. Joe was not only idle and dirty but he was considered mad as well. He ran up and down the street with a wooden rifle, shooting at anybody who passed him. I used to pretend to shoot back at him with an imaginary revolver. He would fall down on the street moaning and groaning and stay there until someone came along and offered him assistance. Joe would lie on the street rolling about in pain for an hour sometimes. His acting at dying was close to the real thing.

After being compared to Joe I was determined to find employment. Danny Dorgan's shoe shop was across the street from the pub where the men from the foundry drank.

Danny was often a customer in the pub and he was very well known. I had heard that his last messenger-boy quit and went to England to work in a bicycle factory. Half the boys who were sixteen or older had left Inchicore and gone to England to work. I was told that Danny needed a messenger boy so I went into Dorgan's and asked for a job.

"Ya need anybody?"

"For what?" Danny Dorgan said without looking up at me. He was cutting the shape of a heel from a big swathe of cow leather. The place smelled but I liked it.

"For work."

"Who sent you here?"

"Nobody."

"How'd you know there was a job goin'?"

"Is there?"

"Can you ride a bike?"

"Yis."

"D'ya have one?"

"I can get a loan of one from my sister."

"What's she goin' to do?"

"She gettin' married soon."

"Yeah?"

"She's going to live in the city."

"You think you want to be a cobbler?"

"I like the smell of the place."

"Good. That's what you need first. You have to like the smell of glue and leather."

* * *

"Need any boots or shoes mended, ma'am? Soles and heels mended cheap. Delivered free with a new pair of laces thrown in!"

I rode a bicycle around Inchicore and knocked at doors to see if anybody needed boots or shoes repaired. When they did, I took their footwear to Dorgan's and he repaired them. During the week I collected boots and shoes and sandals. On weekends I returned them repaired. I was delivering and collecting anything made of leather. Mostly boots and shoes but sometimes ladies' handbags and straps and belts.

I met a girl one day after I knocked on the door asking if they had any shoes that needed repairing. She laughed at me and made me fall in love with her. She had red hair and an inviting smile. She appeared to be happy. I couldn't understand why she seemed to be so happy but she was. I wanted to be around her all day long even though I was only thirteen. She could make me happy if I was with her long enough. I thought about her all day and all night long. Her name was Maureen Quinn. I prayed that her shoes would wear out so I could collect them from her. I wanted to kiss her every time I saw her. I cycled up and down her street hoping I'd see her. Many times I pretended to be collecting shoes just to see her sitting outside her door. I used to get off the bike and pretend it needed a patch for the tire. Every day I came to work I was hoping that Maureen would come by with her shoes.

Three weeks passed and I hadn't seen Maureen. I was beginning to miss her so much I was forgetting pick-ups, deliveries and tagging. I'd be thinking of Maureen so much I'd put brown polish on black shoes and after a while it began to drive Danny Dorgan mad.

"What in the name of Christ did ya do here?"

I pretended I didn't hear him. "What?"

"What, me arse! Take a look at this!"

"What?"

"This shoe is brown and you've put black polish on the blasted thing!"

"I'm sorry."

"Fuck bein' sorry. Pay attention. What's the matter with ya?"

"Nuthin'."

"You must be sniffin' too much glue here."

"I'm not. I hate the smell of glue."

"Are ya all right?"

"Am I mad, you mean? Is that what you're askin' me?"

"Somethin's gone wrong with ya."

I don't know why he didn't fire me.

Danny had been repairing shoes and boots for so long he forgot his mouth had purposes other than holding nails. When I talked or asked him something he would shake his head and point to his mouth with his hand. The first thing he did when he opened the shop in the morning was to put a handful of nails in his mouth.

I didn't tell him I was thinking of Maureen Quinn all day long. One day I asked him if I could go and look for customers. Danny nodded yes.

The first house I went to was Maureen's. I knocked on her door asking for shoes. Maureen's mother opened the door.

"Who are you?"

"I work for Danny Dorgan."

"Danny Dorgan? Who's he?"

"Didn't you get your shoes mended this year?"

"What?"

"You got any shoes to be mended?"

"No."

"You don't?"

"I said no."

"What about Maureen?"

"Maureen? Me daughter?"

"Yis."

"Maureen's gone to Australia for God's sake! What's the matter with you?"

"Australia?"

"That's what I said."

"She's gone?"

"Gone."

"Australia?"

"Yeah. You know where that is?"

"It's far."

"Very far!"

"How far?"

"Farther than America."

"Jesus!"

"What did you say?"

"I said I hope Jesus doesn't go there."

"To Australia? Jesus *is* in Australia. Don't you know that?"

"When's he comin' back?"

"Who?"

"Jesus! I mean, Maureen."

"Who are you workin' for again?"

"Danny Dorgan."

"What d'ya want to know about me daughter for?"

"She wanted somethin' mended."

"She did?"

"Yes."

"What?"

"She told me she had a pair of . . ." I didn't know how to finish the conversation.

I walked away in pain. I felt depressed and abandoned. I had so many fantasies of sitting with Maureen Quinn and telling her everything about my feelings for her. I felt I loved her so much she would have no choice but to love me back. I planned in my mind to marry her when I was eighteen.

Now it was too late. I never got a chance to tell her anything. She didn't know that she was the last person I thought about before I went to sleep at night. She didn't know that I walked up and down the street hoping I'd see her. She didn't know I was hoping her shoes would wear out fast.

Maureen never came back from Australia. Later on, a year or so maybe, somebody said she got married to a fella she met at work there.

After my painting brown shoes with black dye and black shoes with brown dye and doin' everything else backwards Danny Dorgan decided to let me go. I didn't blame him.

A few months later I was cycling by his shop and it was closed. He had swallowed a mouthful of nails and was taken to the hospital.

* * *

Mrs. Nolan was a frail little woman with wire glasses leaning on her strange flat nose. Someone said her husband came home one night and gave it to her when he couldn't wake her up from having one too many shots of whiskey. She was known in the street as 'Whiskey Breath'. Mrs. Nolan said it was prescribed medicine that people smelled when they stopped to talk to her. She kept a flask in the pocket of her apron and never took her hand off it. Whenever she had a sip too many Mrs. Nolan was always generous with handing out a few pennies. She provided me with a bit of employment every Monday and Friday.

"You're up early, boy."

"Yes, ma'am."

"How's your poor mother? I see her pass every morning. On her way to Mass, I suppose. God love her. I'm sure He does too."

I could smell the whiskey.

83

"Son," she muttered again, "I want you to go to the pawnshop on James's Street." She stuck her tongue out as if to air it. Then her eyes came back to me. "Can you go?"

"Yes," I said.

"Bless you. My husband's suit is there and I want you to go and release it before he gets up."

She moved back into the front room to look for the ticket. I stepped inside and watched her.

"My son's shoes are there too, but I can't get them yet," she said to herself, lifting everything that had a lid on it as she searched for the pawn ticket. She found a batch of dockets and pulled one from the top of the bundle. "Here it is." She handed it to me. Her hands were shaking and she looked nervously back into the house as she took some money out of her apron pocket and told me to give it to the pawnbroker. She'd give me a few pence for myself when I came back safely with the suit.

Mr. Nolan was upstairs asleep in bed. It was Saturday and he would be sleeping late. He snored like my father. If he woke up and came down and wanted to put on his suit there'd be hell to pay. The man had no idea his suit was resting peacefully in the pawnshop on James's Street. After a week's hard work at the foundry most of the men in the neighbourhood slept till noon. On Saturdays the wives did their shopping and bought everything for the week. That included a bottle of whiskey that Mrs. Nolan hid away for herself. At the end of the Saturday shopping spree there'd be no money left for anything. The families then coasted until the next payday, Friday. To get extra cash during the week the wives pawned everything and anything of value. For most, the only valuable items they had were clothes or sometimes a clock or an iron or something brass. Anything of value was consigned to the pawnshop Monday morning after the men entered the factory gates. Mrs. Nolan's husband had a new suit, which he won in a church raffle and Mrs. Nolan made sure it remained new for as long as possible. He was only allowed to wear it to Mass on Sunday and for his dinner after. After Sunday dinner Mrs. Nolan (and most other wives) stripped her husband of his suit. She covered it with brown paper and hung it up in the wardrobe behind some other items. Mr. Nolan wouldn't see it again until the following Sunday. He never knew his suit spent the week in the pawnshop. The pawnshop gave a loan on the suit and Mrs. Nolan was able to replenish the small bottle of whiskey.

* * *

The pawnbroker stood up on the counter and held up the items.

"Murphy! Brass clock?"

"Here I am, sir. I want to redeem that before me oul' fella passes away. We got it as a wedding present over twenty years ago." A woman stretched her hand out with her pawn ticket. The man handed down the clock and she passed along some money with the ticket. The man reached back on to the shelf and began taking down every conceivable item you could think of. Brass buckets, stags' heads, holy pictures, statues, cups and saucers. The women milled about, pushing each other aside. They all wanted to have the ornament at home for the weekend. Monday to Friday didn't matter just as long as they had something nice to put up for the weekend when the country relatives came to visit after Mass.

When the pawnbroker moved to the clothing department a wild rush followed him. The people in this bunch seemed more eager than the ornament seekers. He pulled out overcoats, trousers, blazers, suits, and shirts. There was something about the smell of the packed clothing that made everybody rub their noses. When the man called out the name "Nolan" I let out a yell. The women next to me looked to see where the voice had come from. I was lost between thirty fat women. When I raised my hand showing the ticket, the women pushed me up to the counter and a few of them hoisted me up on it.

"Here it is! Your first pair of long pants!" the man said as he threw the suit over my head.

I gave him the ticket with the money. I couldn't find room enough to get back onto the floor so I just stood there on the counter with Mr. Nolan's suit. "Here y'are, son, let me give ya a hand!" With that I was carried all the way across the women waiting for their familiar threads to appear.

I got out of the pawnshop as fast as I could. When I got back on the bus I was happy that my mother didn't have any suits at home that were worth pawning.

* * *

By the time I turned fourteen half of the neighbourhood had emigrated to England, young women as well as young men. Money was as scarce as sun in Dublin. With nothing to do, a pal of mine and I found a new world for ourselves.

Billy Whelan was considered by the neighbours to be in the same league as Biddy Sonics. Some even said he was as odd as Mrs. Mack. He might have been as odd as both of them put together but to me Billy was a hero. He lived every minute of the day believing and behaving like he was somebody else. Had anybody in Inchicore taken Billy seriously they would have called him Mandrake the Magician.

Billy was also the first to see every new film that opened in Dublin. Watching films was Billy's idea of Heaven. He wouldn't want to go to Heaven if it didn't have a cinema. If I didn't have the money to go Billy would sit down and tell me the whole story from beginning to end. He acted out each part. I spent a lot of time with Billy. We saw nearly every movie that played in Dublin. In the morning we'd start off at the Lyric on James's Street, then we'd go to the Tivo (the Tivoli) on Francis Street. In the afternoon we'd walk across town and go to the Mero (on Mary Street). Late at night we'd cross the Liffey Bridge and go to the last show at the Phoeno (the Phoenix). The next morning we'd be up early and be first in line to get into the Cameo on Grafton Street to see foreign films. The cinemas of Dublin in the forties and fifties were as culturally important to the minds of the poor as the churches were to their souls. I saw so many films and serials at the Tivo and the Mero I was in danger of losing touch with reality. Laurel and Hardy, the Three Stooges, the Marx Brothers and Bud Abbot and Lou Costello made me laugh and each laugh was like a new beginning. The American films of the fifties turned our damp days in Dublin into a world of Technicolor.

The Tivo was also one of Dublin's dating arenas, a place where boys and girls met each other. The older boys would come in and look around for a girl who was sitting alone. When they spotted the girl they'd do everything they could to sit in the seat next to her. When a girl came to the Tivo alone it was accepted she was looking for a fella. It was never questioned. The ritual of sitting next to a stranger was part of the excitement of going to the Tivo. When the lights went down sex went up in the dark. Boys and girls felt each other up without taking their eyes off the screen. A girl and boy sitting next to each other would touch and feel everything they had between their legs and not even see each other's face. Both parties let their hands roam without missing a moment of the film. When the film ended one or the other of them would just get up and leave. They would have sat through two films and felt every bodily part of each other without ever looking in each other's eyes. Billy and I did our fair share of feeling-up.

Although Keogh Square was famous for its roughness and danger it was also well known as the best place in Dublin to swap comic books. Visiting Keogh Square took more guts than living in it. Billy Whelan had a different take on Keogh Square. He was able to put out of his mind any sense of danger in regard to the place. Billy was more than mad about comic books. He was a fanatic. Every penny he ever had he spent on going to a film or buying a comic book. He had collected stacks and stacks: *Batman*, *Captain Marvel*, *Wonder Woman*, *The Blackhawk*, *Mercury* (the man of speed with wings on his tin helmet), *The Green Hornet*, *Plastic Man*, *Super Boy*, *Batman meets Superman*. Fantasy was to Billy Whelan's blood as drink was to others. Billy Whelan was the comic-broker. He peddled and exchanged paper fantasies. I also had a passion for films and comic books but not nearly as intense. If Billy didn't have the latest edition he'd walk around Dublin looking for somebody who had. Hail, rain or snow Billy would be searching anywhere and everywhere for the latest comic book. When he found an individual who had the comic book he wanted he'd barter and bargain and swap two old editions for the latest. I traipsed around Dublin at night with Billy. He knew who had what comic book through a whole network of other boys. He knew not only where they lived but also at what hour they'd be in at night. Having comic books to swap was the same as having a passport and safe passage in or out of Keogh Square. The boys in Keogh Square welcomed anybody in who came with comic books. And they admired the courage it took to go there.

The Tivo had more to offer than the fantasy on the screen. Getting the pennies for admission to the cinema was not always easy. When it couldn't be had, we'd sneak in through the back toilet windows. There was always a crowd waiting to climb in the window. We waited for the film to start then we'd climb up the wall and drop through the window to the bathroom floor. When the men's toilet was crowded, myself and others ran around to the other alley where the girls' toilet was. It was even more crowded and the smell was just as bad. When the girls saw us climbing through the window they'd scream and yell and run out. The whiff of the place was enough to knock a horse down. Management had to leave the windows open to let the fresh air in. If they didn't the entire movie house would be so smelly nobody would be able to watch the film. Often the toilet was so crowded some people didn't bother getting up from their cinema seats to go to it. They pissed under the seat in front of them and the urine would flow down the slanted floor towards the screen and end up in a puddle. Nobody wanted to sit in the front row. When they did they ended up with wet shoes and stinky feet. My own trousers were stiff from the piss I had to let go of because I couldn't get into the toilet and my mother would always know where I had been hiding all day.

Billy favoured certain movie stars. He loved Jeff Chandler but he also especially liked Tyrone Power, Cornel Wilde and Robert Taylor. Something about their black hair slicked back appealed to him. He'd argue with me over who was the best-looking and who made the best films. Billy said Errol Flynn was the best Robin Hood. I said John Derek was. The fight between John Wayne and Randolph Scott in the film *The Spoilers* was the best fight ever because John Wayne hated Randolph Scott in real life, according to Billy. How he knew that I don't know. To Billy, Jeff Chandler was a real American Indian because of the way he played Cochise in the film *Broken Arrow*. He said Jeff Chandler's grey hair was grey because he put white shoe polish in it to make it look grey. Apparently he did this because there were too many movie stars with black hair and moustaches. Another thing about Billy: he didn't like wearing shirts or jackets and definitely not together. If he wore a jacket he wouldn't wear a shirt. When he had to go to Mass or go outdoors he slung an old tweed jacket over his shoulder and stuck his chest out no matter what the weather was. This was probably something to do with Jeff Chandler's bare-chested role as Cochise.

Singers didn't escape Billy's obsessive nature either. He spent a lot of his time listening to his neighbours' wireless by sitting outside their door. On different days, Billy would comb his hair and make himself look like the singer he heard last. Each day of the week he was a different personality. On Mondays he was likely to be looking and sounding like Johnny Ray. By Sunday he'd be Frankie Laine. Billy walked around the streets of Inchicore imitating Mario Lanza, Billy Daniels and Al Jolson. Billy knew as much about the singers and the hit songs as he did about film stars.

One day after seeing a film at the Tivo Billy decided he didn't like his nose. It was slightly fatter or broader than those of most other boys in the neighbourhood. For Billy, it was an unwanted reminder of a reality that he didn't want to know or live in. His nose wasn't a thing to smell with. It was something that made him look like he was poor and unattractive. No matter what way he combed his hair or what colour shirt he wore, his nose wouldn't let him be fully free. It was the herald that reminded him of his perceived imperfection. Billy was always comparing his nose to that of some movie star. When he thought he looked like a certain actor he'd point to his nose and say that was the only part of him that was different to the leading man on the screen. Whenever I went to the pictures with him he wouldn't stop pointing to the screen and describing the features of the film star and at the same time pointing to his nose. He'd continually ask me to tell him who he looked like. Every film I saw with him I had to tell him he was just like the movie star on the screen. If I saw four different films with him he was all of the actors. One day he was Rock Hudson, the next his favourite Jeff Chandler, another day he was Tony Curtis and John Derek. Because of his lifelong attendance at the movies, Billy could contort his face and manage to make himself look like all the movie stars he was mad about. The only thing he couldn't twist was his nose. It was as if his nose was a trap he couldn't escape from. It bothered him that there was no independent way of moving or reshaping his nose. He often resorted to using one of his hands to demonstrate how he wanted it to look. "If me nose wasn't like this I'd be as good-lookin' as Jeff Chandler, wouldn't I?" Billy would press his fingers against his nose and made it flat; he'd then squeeze it with his two fingers and make it look thin. When he squeezed his nose I'd tell him he looked like Jeff Chandler. He'd pull his nose out a bit with his two fingers. "Who now? Who am I like?" I wouldn't know who he looked like or what to say. When I'd hesitate Billy would let go of his nose. "I'm like Tony Curtis, amn't I?" I'd quickly catch on and tell him what he wanted to hear. "Yeh, you're as good-lookin' as him." After I agreed with Billy's idea of himself he'd look very happy. He'd then begin to sing. Billy not only wanted to look like his favourite film star, he also wanted to sound like his favourite singer. Of all the singers Billy imitated, his true obsession and real idol was Frankie Laine. He knew every song Frankie Laine sang backwards. He was furious that Tex Ritter sang "Do Not Forsake Me Oh My Darlin'" from *High Noon*. Billy fervently believed Frankie Laine's rendition was the better one. When Billy passed a shop window he'd stop when he saw his reflection and break into a Frankie Laine number. "I Believe" was of course a favourite. Billy rarely talked to anyone; he sang to them. Billy was trapped between thinking he looked like Jeff Chandler and sounded like Frankie Laine.

One week Frankie Laine was at the Royal Theatre in Dublin and Billy asked me to go with him. When I agreed he burst out into one song after another. Along with about a hundred other Frankie Laine fans, we stood outside the Theatre Royal for four hours to get a glimpse of the singer. After we spent about half a day calling up to a small window on a side street, Frankie Laine stuck his head out and began to sing "Danny Boy". With all the cheers and calls from the crowd, and with Frankie having no microphone, we could hardly hear him. That night both of us walked back home singing and pretending we were Frankie Laine. When I tried to imitate Frankie, Billy drowned me out. I think he sensed that he would lose his audience of one if I persisted.

When Billy concentrated on being Jeff Chandler he'd walk about bare-chested with a white scarf around his neck. The look in his eyes caused by his twitching head made him look like an Apache Indian. When he sensed he was Tony Curtis he'd pour a bottle of hair oil on his head and his hair would become black and shiny.

One day I met Billy on the corner and he wasn't singing and he wasn't even happy-looking. I'd never seen him so sad.

"What's wrong?" I asked.

He squeezed his nose with two fingers then let go. Then he pressed his nose with his thumb. He told me he needed my help. I said I'd help him. He made me swear on it and I did.

He then stuck his face directly in front of me.

"What d'ya see?" he asked impatiently and earnestly.

I didn't know what he meant.

He kept staring at me. "What d'ya see?"

"I see Jeff Chandler," I said quickly.

He yelled back at me, "No!"

I instantly said what I thought he wanted to hear. "I see Tony Curtis."

"No! Take another look!"

"Frankie Laine? No? Billy Daniels? Johnny Ray? No? John Wayne? No?"

Billy was looking more and more outraged.

I then screamed at him. "Who am I lookin' at, Billy?"

"You're lookin' at *me*!" He took his fingers away from his nose. He was almost in tears.

I was lost. I didn't know what to say. I began to think that he had gone mad all the way. And that the fuckin' foundry noise had finally got to him.

"Didn't you see me two weeks ago?" he asked me.

I'd seen Billy every week for years. I spent every second day around him. He was always on the corner or at the pictures.

"You swore you'd help me out, didn't ya?"

"I'll do me best for you, Billy. What are ya askin' me for?"

"I want ya t'come with me."

"Where?"

"I'm goin' to the hospital."

"For what?"

"I'm goin' to have an operation and I need your help."

"You're goin' to have an operation and you want me to help ya? You're nuts altogether, Billy. How can I do anythin' about that? What kind of help could I be? What kind of operation are you thinkin' of havin'?"

"On me nose."

"Your nose?"

"Yeah."

"What's wrong with it?"

"It's not shaped right. It's growin' wrong."

"I don't see anythin' wrong with it, Billy."

"You're not lookin'. Take another look!"

I looked closer at his nose and couldn't tell anything. It looked the same to me as it always did. "You're imaginin' things, Billy."

"Are ya me friend or not? Am I not your best pal?"

"You are."

"Look at me nose again."

"I'm lookin' and I don't see anythin' that's different."

"You're the one who sees me every day and you'd be able to tell the doctor what you saw."

"What I saw? I didn't see anything."

"You saw me nose, didn't ya?"

"I see your nose all the fuckin' time, Billy! What can I do about that?"

"Can't you tell the doctor it was smaller two weeks ago?"

"Your nose hasn't got bigger."

"It fuckin' has! Take a closer look at it." Billy stuck his nose in front of my face. He then turned to show his profile. He pinched it with his two fingers. "I know it's bigger than it should be and I'm goin' to the hospital to get a job done on it."

"It hasn't grown, Billy. I'm not coddin' you. I don't see any change. It's the same nose you always had. It isn't any bigger, Billy. I swear to you."

"Can't ya tell the doctor you noticed it gettin' bigger? If I don't have a witness he'll think I'm out of the madhouse."

I was beginning to think I was goin' nuts myself. Billy begged and I finally agreed. We took the bus to College Green then went up Grafton Street and walked in the doors of Dublin Hospital near the College of Surgeons. A doctor came out and called Billy into the examining room.

After about ten minutes the doctor stuck his head out the door and called me in. Billy was sitting quietly in a chair. He was wearing his jacket but no shirt and his chest was sticking out like a rooster at sunrise.

"How long have you known Billy?" the doctor asked me.

"More than ten years," I said. I wasn't sure how long.

"Billy said his nose had grown considerably. Have you noticed that?"

I'd sworn I'd tell the doctor that it had grown in the past few weeks. "His nose is a bit bigger than it was."

"A bit longer? A bit fatter?" the doctor asked me.

I looked at Billy. I didn't know whether he wanted me to say it was longer or fatter or both. I hesitated with my answer. The doctor then looked at Billy and then at me.

"Why don't you wait a month or two, Billy, and we'll take another look at it?" he said.

Billy got up from the chair and walked out the door. When I got outside the hospital Billy was gone. He didn't wait for me. I had to walk home on my own and I felt that I had let Billy down.

For the next week or so Billy stayed home. When I knocked on his door looking for him, his mother answered.

She said he couldn't come out because he had stepped on a nail and his foot was infected. The next day I came by and looked through the window of his house. Billy was sitting on the stairs inside and looking out through the curtains. He looked very sad. I asked him to come out and go to the films or to Keogh Square to exchange comic books but he didn't move. He wouldn't talk to me. I told him I would go back and tell the doctor his nose had grown but Billy wasn't interested. Having to accept his own nose had crushed part of Billy's fantasy. After that I had to get used to walking around the city on my own.

* * *

A few weeks later, while walking past Jury's Hotel in the city centre, I came across a group of American tourists getting off a tour bus and going into the hotel. They were talking out loud and sounded like some of the actors I had seen in the films. Their clothes and hats were as colourful as any I had seen in a Technicolor movie. The group looked like a little bit of sunshine. The men in the group had big hats and blue suits and wore black cowboy boots. I was tempted to ask them where they had all come from and maybe even ask for an autograph. I was sure I saw John Wayne walk right into Jury's Hotel right in front of me.

This was one day that my wanderings about this part of Dublin paid off. If Billy was with me he would have forgotten about his nose. I stood and watched the Americans go into the hotel, then I followed them into the lobby.

Within an instant I heard a loud voice. I thought it was one of the American tourists. It wasn't. The hotel hall porter was calling me. When I turned in his direction he looked at me as if I was a worm on the floor.

"What are you doin' there?" he asked me.

At first I didn't know what to say to him. I then quickly told him I was looking for work. He nearly fell over.

An American man in the group then handed me a dollar bill. I was about to faint when the hall porter grabbed my hand.

"Give that back!" he said.

I held on to the dollar with a clenched fist.

The American with the cowboy boots and cowboy hat laughed and said, "Leave him be!"

When I heard that I knew I had always done the right thing by going to the American films.

The hall porter was flustered and embarrassed. He turned his head around a half dozen times to see if anyone was watching. He then stuck his nose so close to my face I thought he was going to spit all over me. "How'd you get in here?"

"I followed them people who got off the bus."

"Where do you live?"

"Up in Inchicore."

"Inchicore is not up," he said.

"It's not?"

"No! Are you daft?"

"Inchicore is not up?"

"Don't you know that?"

"It's up past Kilmainham Gaol. Where all the fellas from 1916 were shot."

"Who told ya that?"

"Somebody said it was."

"Who?"

"I think it was my brother."

"How much do you know?"

"About what?"

"Stop askin' me fuckin' questions when I'm askin' you them!"

"I didn't know what you meant."

"I meant to find out if you're any good at payin' attention to orders and instructions."

"I'm very good at that."

"Can you read and write?"

"Course I can."

"How old are ya?"

"Fourteen. My birthday was last week."

"Why don't you work in the C.I.E. foundry?"

"I couldn't get a job there."

"Why?"

"I can't tell you."

"I know the answer to that."

"You do?"

"Because your father isn't workin' there. Am I right?"

"Yeah."

"Are you sure you don't live in Keogh Square?"

"I don't."

"I heard that before. You look like you might."

"I don't mind Keogh Square."

"You go there?"

"Sometimes."

"For what?"

"To swap comic books."

"Can you read?"

"I told you. Course I can."

"You don't live in Keogh Square?"

"I live in Nash Street. Past it."

"How much do you know about hotel work?"

"I don't know much."

"How are you goin' to talk to people if they ask you somethin'?"

"Why would they ask me anythin'?"

"People, hotel guests might ask you somethin' and how are you goin' to answer back?"

"Ask me about what?"

"About where you live. A lot of people who come here want to know if you know anything at all about your own bloody country."

"How am I supposed to know anythin' about my country?"

"Did you go to school?"

"Course I did!"

"What did they teach ya?"

"Who?"

"The fella who stood up front with the leather strap in his hand?"

"The Christian Brother?"

"Did ya go to the Brothers?"

"At first I did. Bastards if you ask me."

"You learned nothin'? Is that what you're saying?"

"I heard that Oliver Cromwell was the worst man ever made in the history of God. He was the man who said, 'To Hell or to Connaught'. Oliver Plunkett was against Oliver Cromwell. Did you know that? Blessed Oliver Plunkett. The man whose skull is in a glass case in Drogheda. Did you know that?"

"How do ya think I got this job here?"

"You must'a went to the same school I went ta."

"Jaysus, everybody knows who Blessed Oliver Plunkett was!"

"I was always gettin' the two Olivers mixed up. The Christian Brother put bruises on the back of my head for sayin' Oliver Plunkett was the man who said 'To Hell or to Connaught'. I've never been as happy as the day I got out of that school."

"Are you sure you're not a half-arsed knacker?"

"No, I'm not. I got the Primary Certificate from the Model School. I used to go to Saint Michael's up in Inchicore as well."

"Did you make your Communion and Confirmation?"

"Course I did. You're the only person in all of Ireland who would ask that question to a fella lookin' for a job."

"What's the name of your priest?"

"There's more than one."

"I'm referrin' to the one who looks after you and your family the most."

"There's Canon Doyle from St. Michael's and then there's the fella called Sheep Dog."

"Jesus, that's no way to talk about a holy man."

"Well, some people call him that."

"What's his real name?"

"Father Devine from the Oblate Fathers."

"Who goes to your house in time of need?"

"They all do," I answered.

"I'm happy to hear that. I don't want no sinner boy workin' here. This hotel is too respectful. I might go up and ask Father Devine about you."

"Father Devine came up to my house once in time of need. It was only in time of his need though. I could tell you a thing or two about Father Devine. You know that statue of Our Lady up at the Oblate Church, the one with the big crown?"

"Of course I know it. I'm no pagan. I've been to Mass there a few times when I went up to visit a cousin of mine who's buried in the Bluebell cemetery."

"Well, Father Devine took the wedding ring from my mother's finger for that crown. I wouldn't confess to Father Devine if you gave me this hotel."

"I don't want any riff raff. That's why I asked about you gettin' and havin' the sacraments. I'm happy to hear you're confirmed."

For about five minutes I'd been involved in a conversation with the hall porter at Jury's Hotel and I didn't know what I was talking about. I think the man enjoyed asking me questions. He wasn't finished yet. He inquired about my father and what county my mother came from. He wanted to know how long I'd lived in Inchicore. After asking me if I had hair oil to put in my hair, he said he'd hire me. He told me to go up to Callahan's on Dame Street and have myself measured for a uniform.

I was over the moon with excitement.

The first thing I did was run to Billy's house. I knocked on his door and his mother answered.

"Is Billy in?" I asked.

"No, he's not. And when he comes in he's stayin' in."

"When he comes in will you tell him I got a job in Jury's Hotel where American film stars stay."

As soon as I said that Billy stuck his head over his mother's shoulder.

"Will ya get John Wayne's autograph when he comes in?" he asked with a recurrence of his old enthusiasm.

"Course I will, Billy."

Billy retreated into his house. His mother quietly closed the door. I went home hoping John Wayne would show up at Jury's.

◄◆►

John Wayne didn't show up.

At work I operated the hotel lift, polished brass door-knobs, radiators, buckles, handles, bottle-tops and desk bells. Anything in the hotel made of brass, I polished. I called taxis and fetched newspapers. I became a walking loudspeaker when someone was wanted on the phone.

"Paging Dudley Hornsby! Paging Major Winbeck! Lady Thompson!"

Running through the halls and hearing husky and squeaky voices.

"Oh, boy, this fire in the lounge is going out – do you think you could do something about it?"

"Yes, ma'am."

"Good lad."

Down to the dark dirty smoky airless cellar for a bucket of coal. Back up to the lounge with the heavy black lumps.

"Now, ma'am, the fire is full blaze again."

"Make sure you come back with more coal in thirty minutes."

"Yes, ma'am."

Going out the door I'd mumbled under my breath, "You old bitch!"

"Would you close the door tight?"

The door banged behind me. Back to the coalhole where I left the dirty black bucket. Back again to the lift.

A man from Kerry or Cork, a big farmer type with a tweed jacket and cap and big brown shoes, approached me. He'd been there yesterday and didn't give me a penny.

"Here's a shilling, boy. You do a good job on this lift. Take me to Room 252."

Into the lift he stumbled as I closed the gate on his toe.

"Ouch!"

"Sorry, sir."

"That's all right."

"It's this modern electric stuff they put into the motor."

"That's hardly modern," he replied.

"Well, it is for this hotel, sir. A few years ago the porters used to carry the guests up on their backs."

"Quite a sense of humour you have, boy."

"Thank you, sir! What floor did you say again?"

"Second floor!"

"Yes, sir!"

As I was putting my hand to the starter the hall porter, whose name was Larry, beckoned to me from his desk in the hall. He had spotted one of his regular customers and wanted to show off his authority. I saw him approach the customer and hold his hand out to offer assistance and to let the customer know that it was time for his monthly gratuity.

"This way, Mr. Taylor," he said.

I put the lock on the gate.

"Page, page, wait a moment for Mr. Taylor!"

I turned my head to the man in the lift and pretended not to hear the hall porter. "Up, sir?" As I pressed the starter the lift began to rise upwards and as I looked down I saw the porter with his hands going through the gates, calling, "Page, page, page!"

When I came back down the porter was still waiting for me. His face was red and he was dying to say something to me but with Mr. Taylor beside him he held back. I could see his fists clenched.

I took Mr. Taylor up in the lift and came back down again.

The hall porter was still waiting for me, fuming.

"Did you polish the radiators?" he said.

"Yes, sir."

"Well, polish them again. Someone has spit on them since."

"I'll do it in a minute, sir."

"Do it now and shake your arse!" His lips continued to move but he didn't say any more.

"I'm waiting for Mr. Thompson to come down. He said he'd ring in a minute."

"Never mind, I'll wait for him. Go move your skinny rump for Christ's sake!"

Back down to the dirty cellar looking for a can of Brasso. More black dust on my face and hands and uniform. I hated polishing the dirty things. They were all green with dried spits burnt into them. My hands became smelly and sweaty. Why the hell didn't the hotel get new radiators? But the brassy things had to be polished. I cleaned them and they shone until you could see your face gleaming. Back to the lift to continue with the ups and downs.

Tea break at three o'clock. Back again for the slack period of sleeping inside the lift until the customers showed up around mealtime.

"Wake up, boy, and take me to the fourth floor."

The lift shook and shuddered as I jumped from the chair. I closed the gates and pressed the handle for down so fast the man fell on his arse with shock and surprise. And so did the hall porter. The man grabbed me by the neck and pulled me to him.

"What are you up to?"

"Sorry, sir, I pressed the wrong way. Dozing around this time of day does that to my senses."

I pulled the handle forward and the lift flew upwards with a speed I never thought it had. As we went dashing by the main floor I almost took the hall porter's fingers off as he was standing there gripping the gates, watching to find out what was wrong.

"Fourth floor!"

The man sneered at me as he stepped out.

"Move, you Protestant bastard!" I called after him.

"What was that?"

"Nothing, sir!"

Down again to the main floor. The hall porter had gone back to his desk. The phone was ringing off the wall. He picked it up. Then looked over at me. I thought I had done something wrong. He started to wave his hand in the air.

I didn't know what he wanted or what he was doing. I thought he was telling me to sit down or go away or come over. I walked towards him. He began to shake his hand even faster. He still had the phone to his ear. He yelled at me, "Page! Page!"

"What?"

"Go back to the lift! Stay at the lift!"

He put the phone down and ran out the front door. In a split second he was back in and running towards me. I thought he had seen an accident outside or something.

"What's up?" I asked.

His face was red and he was breaking out in a sweat. "Go back in the lift," he said again.

I stepped into the lift. He ran back to the front door, stood at attention and opened it. Three men then entered the hotel. One of them was a short chubby fellow who was dressed in a pinstripe suit. He had a black silk hat in his hand and a white scarf around his neck. The hall porter led him to the lift. One of the others got in with him.

The hall porter stood outside. "Lower floor, page," he said.

The third man walked down the stairs to the lower lounge. I closed the gates and pressed the lever for the lower floor. I turned and looked at the small man. I thought he was going to a dance or something fancy.

"Working late, young fella?" he asked me.

"Ah, I'm almost off now, sir. I go home at seven."

"What time do you come in?"

"Six, sir," I answered.

The other man said, "Long day!"

Within a second or two the lift arrived on the lower floor. I opened the gates and the third man who had gone down the stairs was already standing in front of the lift. The short man dressed in the fancy suit got out and walked with the other fella to the lounge bar.

I took the lift back to the ground floor where Larry the porter was waiting for me. He looked me over like he was about to buy me.

"Do you know who that man is?" he asked me.

I guessed he was asking me about the small one because of the suit he was wearing.

"I don't. Who is he?"

"That's Seán T. O'Kelly."

"Seán T. O'Kelly?"

"He's the President of Ireland in case you didn't know or learn that in Inchicore!" Larry walked back to his little desk area at the front door.

I sat back down on my small chair in the lift. I was reminded again that Larry didn't like Inchicore even though he'd never been to it. The clock on the wall was turning to the number seven: the hour of my release.

* * *

Thursday again. Back at Jury's Hotel. My brass buttons were shining. I'd enough hair oil in my hair to drown a crocodile.

Larry the hall porter was walking about the lobby with his hands in his pockets. It wasn't his favourite day of the week or the month for that matter.

It was the day after the horse sales at Punchestown or Fairyhouse or some other place where they buy and sell horses.

"Page, did you polish the doorknobs?"

"Yes."

"Is there coal in the fireplace on the second floor?"

"Yes. I just filled it up."

"Did you wash your hands?"

"Yes."

The hotel was full of farmers from all over the country. Up from Cork! Across from Clare! Down from Monaghan! Men wearing big warm coats and looking very comfortable. Some wearing leather boots that reached to the knees. Others were wearing heavy clogs with steel studs on the soles of them. The smell of whiskey was everywhere. I had the duty on the lift. The big fat-faced whiskey-nosed farmers thundered into the lift and ordered a ride as if they were kicking the shit off a cow's arse.

"Up, boy!"

"Yes, sir."

They all sat around the fireplace in the lounge talking about the dealing and buying of animals. I never knew the size of a cow's tit or the length of a bull's bollocks until I heard the farmers talking that day. Some of them drank until the whiskey came out of their nostrils and when they sneezed the whole lounge was showered with whiskey raindrops.

"Come on, boy, take me down to the lounge in a hurry!"

"You're only one flight up, sir."

"Never mind that, me bucko! If I put you on the farm it would take the potatoes out of your ears!"

I hardly had to press the down-button with the weight of him.

Another farmer, wanting to go up to the first floor.

"Sir, would you like me to get you some cigarettes?" Trying to sift a tip from the bastard.

"I've got all the cigarettes I want."

Arriving on the first floor.

"First floor, sir. Watch your step, please."

The lift didn't come in line with the landing. He hit his boot off the edge and about four pounds of horseshit fell off his sole into the lift.

"Thank ya, boy."

"You're very welcome, sir." And a muttering under my breath, "And thank you for the horseshit you forgot to leave at the fair. I hope to Christ you fall off your wallet, you miserable country mug!"

Down to the ground floor again. Gates open.

The two other pages looked into the lift and saw the cow shit. "Are you shitting in the lift again?"

I didn't answer.

"The porter won't like that. He'll put you to cleanin' the spits off the brass radiators."

"Some vein-popping-faced mug was too damn lazy to lift his farm boots. How about giving me a hand with cleanin' this dung?"

"Clean it yourself, you got the tip."

I was as mad as the country maids that cleaned the lavatories. "Them lousy horse-traders wouldn't give you the steam off their piss."

Out I go and get the shovel and broom to clean the lift. Seven o'clock.

Time to go off duty.

* * *

Billy Whelan was waiting outside my door when I came home from a long day at work.

"Any sign of John Wayne?" he asked me.

"No." I got off my bicycle and put it against the window-sill.

"Any movie stars come in?"

"I didn't see any."

I could see my mother inside the window behind the curtains. She was cleaning the small statue of the Infant of Prague. There was something special about the statue. I think it was because it had a crown on its head and because of the robes it was wearing. It looked like a little rich person, maybe a prince or a princess.

Billy's voice called to me again. "You know what I think?"

The sight of my mother in the window with the statue had made me forget what Billy was talking about. "What?"

"I think they went to the other hotel."

"Who?"

"The American film stars."

"What other hotel?"

"The Gresham."

"How do you know that?"

"I was standin' outside it today and I saw somebody go in."

"Who?"

"I think she was an actress."

"Who?"

"Dorothy Lamour. In *The Hurricane* with Jon Hall?"

"Are you sure?"

"I think I'm sure. Looked just like her."

"Did she have black hair?"

"No. Blondie."

"Blondie? Dorothy Lamour has black hair. She's half-French and half something else."

"So it wasn't her? I think you're right."

My mother then pulled the curtains across and stuck her face next to the pane of glass. She called out and tapped on the window at the same time.

"Come in out'a that, will ya? Your dinner's on the table!"

I waved back, indicating I was on my way in.

Billy had a film magazine in his hand and he pointed to a photograph in it. "Look at this!"

"What?"

"Robert Taylor is comin' here to make a film."

"What's it called?"

"*Knights of the Round Table.*"

"I read in the paper it was *Quo Vadis.*"

"What kind of a fuckin' name is that?"

"It's Latin. Listen to the priest and you'll find out."

Billy then added, "Elizabeth Taylor is in it as well."

"Where did you get that magazine?"

"Shamie Finnerty gave it to me."

"Shamie from Keogh Square?"

"Right."

"Where'd he get it?"

"He stole it."

"Can I borrow it?"

"Yeah." Billy gave me the magazine.

I walked into the house.

Billy called after me, "Don't forget to ask John Wayne for his autograph if he comes in!"

"Okay!" I called back as my mother slammed the door behind me.

I wasn't in the house but a minute when I heard a knocking on the door. I went to open it and Billy was still standing there.

"I want me magazine back," he said.

I walked back to the kitchen table and got it for him.

"Shamie will go bleedin' nuts if I lose this. I'll let you have it tomorrow," he said and walked away.

* * *

Blister Dempsey was about two years older than I was. For most of the day we stood next to the lift and waited to be called by the hall porter. When either one of us wasn't operating the lift we'd run messages or polish anything that needed polishing in the lobby. Blister didn't like the fact that I was assigned the responsibility of operating the lift. He knew the customers who took the lift were the best tippers. Everybody knew that. Whoever operated the lift made the most money. The hall porter didn't want Blister on the lift because he had a very pimply face. His face was filled with pimples and half the time they were boiling over and the yellow stuff would drip down his jaw. Nobody ever said that was the reason Blister wasn't assigned the lift but it was obvious.

Blister and I often talked about leaving the hotel and going away to England or even some other more exotic place. It might have been because we had very little to do sometimes. On a slow day we would talk for hours. Blister had a great head of hair but it was so caked with oil the back of his neck looked like a wheel axle. Blister sometimes took over the lift when I went to lunch and supper. His mother worked in the hotel kitchen mopping up the gravy and soup that fell out of the large boiling pots. He wasn't happy having charge of the lift part-time. He wanted to operate it all day. He was very hungry for the tips. When rich-looking customers entered the hallway he rushed to operate the lift, but I always beat him to it. I managed to get my hand on the handle that controlled it. He also knew the hall porter wanted me to do the operating.

One day he told me about a plan he had. He was going to go away on a ship. He said he had found out all the information from a friend of his. A shipping company in England, the Orient Line, was hiring waiters for service on board their ships that sailed all over the world. Blister said he had made arrangements to go to Tilbury in England to be hired as a waiter on one of the luxury liners. The ship was to sail to Trinidad and places like that. He told me I could go with him. At first I didn't believe him, but then he told me to go down to the kitchen and check with his mother. If his mother knew about it I would believe him. I turned over the lift to him and went downstairs to the hot kitchen to see his mother.

I was very excited about the idea of leaving on a ship. Mrs. Dempsey was scrubbing the concrete kitchen floor when I got there. The smell of chicken soup was all over her. Somebody had knocked over one of the large cooking pots and spilled the soup. Mrs. Dempsey was mopping, and the sweat was flowing from her forehead. I walked up to her, avoiding stepping in the spilled soup.

"What d'ya want?"

"Can I ask you a question, Mrs. Dempsey?"

"What?"

"Can I ask you a question?"

"*What?*"

"Is Blister going away on a ship?" I asked her.

She looked up at me and began to drink the beads of sweat that poured from her forehead into her mouth. "A ship?" she said, suspicious of my question. She squeezed the rag she was wiping the floor with into the bucket. "Blister said that?"

"Yes."

"A ship?" she said again.

"Yes, he just told me he filled out the papers with the Orient Line, in Tilbury, England."

"England?"

"Tilbury. It's the docks near London."

"Blister said them things?"

"That's what he told me."

"When did he say them things?"

"A few minutes ago. Is he goin' away to work on the Orient Line?"

"He is. He's goin'. Isn't that what he told you?"

I nodded my head, turned away and let her continue with her work. Back up in the front hall I told Blister I believed him. We then talked and made plans. We were both to go to the hall porter and tell him we were finished with working. We decided to go together.

Blister stopped me as we were halfway across the floor.

"Look, why don't we do it one at a time?" he said to me.

"Okay."

"You go tell him first, I'll follow you."

He was bigger and older than I was and I wondered why I should be first. When I told him to go first, he reminded me that he was the one with the plan and papers. I finally got up my nerves and held them tight. I walked over to the head porter.

"I want to hand in my notice."

Larry the hall porter looked down at me.

"Your what?"

"My notice. I'm not goin' to be working here any longer."

"Where you goin'?"

"I'm goin' to England."

"For what?"

"To work."

"Where?"

"I'm gettin' a job on the Orient Line."

"Doin' what?"

"A waiter. A steward. Servin'."

"You've no experience."

"Well, how's it goin' to matter? I'm able to do it."

"Who told you all this?"

"Blister."

"Blister?"

"Yes. He's got all papers and info."

"Blister?"

"Yes."

"Does your mother know about this?"

"No."

"You're too young."

"No, I'm not."

"You have to be eighteen. Does your father know?"

"My father doesn't talk to me."

"You better tell him."

"He won't care."

"Who knows about this?"

"Nobody knows about it. I'm going away. I'm leavin' Dublin."

The hall porter turned away as if to ignore me. Hoping that I'd leave him alone and go back to the lift.

I just stood there.

"What?" he asked me impatiently.

"I'm givin' in me notice. I'm goin' away."

"You're talkin' through your arse, Walsh. Go back to the lift."

"I'm leavin'. It's the truth."

"You the same fella who didn't know if Inchicore is up or down? You don't have a trade and your father doesn't have a trade."

"Leave my father out of it!"

"I'm sayin' if your father doesn't have a trade the likelihood is that you'll be down on the balls of your feet walkin' around Dublin lookin' for a job."

"I'm gettin' a job on the Orient Line in England. I don't want to be standin' up against the wall over there all my life."

"Listen to me, will ya? As long as your arsehole faces the ground you won't do better than what you've got here. I'm tellin' you."

"I'm leavin'. And this is my week's notice," I said back.

"Well, get outta me sight. Go away with yourself. Go down to the office and tell the pay clerk."

"So it's official?" I asked.

"Yes, it's very official. And if you ask me you're a bit of a nut case. I think you left your brains in the skull of Oliver Plunkett when you went up there to Drogheda."

"I never went up to Drogheda!"

"Well, you shoulda. All I can say is, I hope your poor mother knows what you're up to."

I turned from the hall porter's area and went back to Blister.

"I've done it, I'm outta here! Go on over! He's in a good mood."

Blister was silent. He looked at me, then turned his face the other way. I kept telling him about the good mood the hall porter was in but Blister wasn't listening. It dawned on me after a minute that Blister had played a trick on me. His mother had played a trick. I had left my job and now Blister wasn't going to leave with me. I asked him about the ship and travel plans and he admitted it was all a joke, just to get me out of the lift. He said his mother needed all the pennies he could get his hands on. He wasn't making enough tips standing in the hall running for papers and taxis. For a few seconds I thought about going back to the hall porter and telling him it was a joke but, as I stood there without the sense of having to stay, I kept thinking. I looked at Blister with all the greasy pimples on his face. He was half-crying.

I didn't know what to do. I was afraid to back down and tell the hall porter I didn't know what I was doing. For a minute I wanted to hit Blister in the face but I held back. I had just pulled the world down on myself and I was getting more frightened by the second.

I was out of the job I loved. I decided that I would leave anyway. I would stick with my plans to go and work on the Orient Line and sail away to Trinidad and Fiji. The thought of travelling so far away made more and more sense to me. I was feeling freer, even though I knew it would only last till I spent my wages. I turned away from the lift and Blister walked into it. He sat down on my chair. His face was red. The oil he had in his hair was dripping down on his forehead just like the sweat from his mother's head.

I passed through the hotel, telling everybody I had finished with my job. Most of them didn't believe me. I was off to work on the Orient Line. When I passed everybody and faced the gate of the hotel I realised I was walking out for the last time. I would never be able to get John Wayne's autograph for Billy Whelan. I felt bad and sorry for myself and was feeling lonely again. I was already missing my friends and unhappy with what I'd done, but I just wasn't able to turn back and tell the hall porter I'd made a mistake. Tears came to my eyes. I began to cry out loud.

I walked out the gate of Jury's, stepping over sacks of onions, carrots and potatoes. It was raining outside. My brass buttons were gone. No more coal buckets, no more farmers' horseshit. No more spits on brass radiators. I could see Blister sitting in my chair in the lift. I had allowed my fantasies to take me away from the world I was happy in. I had never thought Blister Dempsey was smart but he out-smarted me because he knew I would want to sail away to a distant place. I wished I hadn't been such a fool. I started to walk away and didn't know what direction I was going in and I didn't care. I walked towards O'Connell Street and nearly got run over by a car and a hundred bicycles. I wandered about for hours wondering what my mother and father would say when they found out about me.

I wandered over to the outdoor stalls on Moore Street. The stalls were laden down with every imaginable kind of meat, fruit, and fish, including fly-covered tripe, cows' tongues and pigs' cheeks. Every once in a while a dog or a cat managed to get hold of the cow's tongue or the nose of the pig and run away towards Henry Street. If the anxious animal was lucky it escaped with the food. Usually it was grabbed by the tail and its head ended up with the fish-heads under the stall. Anyone walking on Moore Street got called and coddled into purchasing something. Even if they didn't want what they were talked into buying. Often passers-by found a head of cabbage or half a pig's cheek in their hands when they walked by a stall. The chesty vendors with charm and determination convinced reluctant customers to buy the food and only asked for whatever they could cadge out of the person who didn't like cabbage and who couldn't stand the sight of half a pig's head in their hands. The vendors' voices on Moore Street could be heard streets away. A 'secret' on Moore Street would be as rare as an undamaged apple.

"I've got to use me bladder."

"Widdle by the lamppost."

"Merciful God!"

"Ah, the rain will wash it away before the day's done."

Anything going off was sold for almost nothing. The character of Moore Street was more Dublin than anywhere. It might be the only street in the Western World where people could talk and listen at the same time.

As I walked past a stall a big red-faced woman handed me a pig's cheek and a cabbage. "Don't forget to eat this before Frida', son! I don't think it'll last." She sniffed at the bag. "Ah, it's still with us but not for long." The woman seemed to recognise me from one of my many visits to Moore Street with my mother when she was looking for bargains. "Your poor mother is a saint. Holier than anyone I ever met in me life."

* * *

My father was sitting by the fireplace when I came in. I was going to show him the pig's cheek but he didn't move his head. I went out into the back yard and put the meat in a pot and left it on the windowsill for my mother. It was cold outside and it wouldn't go off too quickly. Back inside I felt the teapot on the table. It was warm. I poured myself a cup of tea. Two big logs were burning and making a noise as if they were talking or complaining. I sat down at the wooden table facing the back yard. I could see my father's reflection in the window. I was too sad to turn and face him. I sipped on my tea and continued to look out at the back yard.

Most of my life I wanted my father to sit down and have a conversation with me. I wanted to hear him talk about his time in the army and what he saw of the war and maybe even talk about what it was about him that was like me. Everybody in the family said I was "the spittin' image of Paddy". My oldest sister Mary said I was "shell-shocked" like him as well. In the past I was happy to hear that I was so much like my father.

Yet today for the first time in my life I was hoping he wouldn't talk. The pimply face of Blister Dempsey was still in front of my eyes. I edged over to the fireplace, pretending I was too preoccupied to talk and I was concentrating on something. I knew if I didn't talk to my father he wouldn't ask or question me much but I also knew when he was around his presence kept my mother's temper from boiling over.

My mother entered the house and was surprised to see me. "Why are you home so early?"

From the side I could see my father getting up from his chair and walking slowly about the room. He was looking for something. My mother turned around but didn't say anything to him. After a moment he found his hat, put it on his head and walked out the door. My mother, noticeably annoyed, walked over to the door and closed it as if to say, 'Don't come back'.

Then she sat down and poured herself a cup of tea.

I mumbled in as soft a voice as I could, "Ma, I've no work now, I'm not at Jury's any more. I lost my job. It's gone.

"What are ya talkin' about 'gone'?" She couldn't believe it.

"The job's gone. I'm outta work. I don't work at Jury's any more, Ma."

"What's that you said, son?"

"I'm outta work, Ma. I don't have my job at Jury's. I lost it. I'm sorry. I'm sorry, Ma. I made a mistake."

Her face turned redder than a beetroot. She bit her bottom lip with her false teeth and I felt she wanted to slap me across the face. She threw her handbag down on the table.

"Ya can't hold onto anything! You'll rue this day!" she yelled at me.

I was sick and sorry for what I'd done to myself. In her mind I was definitely on the path of my father.

When I finally managed to tell her what happened she showed little sympathy. I became so frightened I began to think of going back to the hotel and begging the hall porter to take me back. I would admit to him that I made a mistake. I would hit Blister Dempsey with a punch in the mouth. I would pour cold water over his mother's dirty hair. I'd get into the lift and be smiling and happy again.

My father returned from outside. He took off his hat and placed it on the mantelpiece. I was never so happy to see him. He not only surprised me, he shocked me. Had he come back to save me from my mother's anger? I wanted to believe he did.

"Go back and tell the hall porter you're sorry," my mother commanded.

The more I thought about going back to the hall porter, the more I felt I couldn't. I had made too big a show of myself and I had bragged too much about where I was sailing off to. I had made it too clear that I was able to tackle the world on my own. I was now licking the tears off my own face.

My mother walked up to me, "Go back there and tell them you're sorry. Tell them you're sorry!"

My voice trembled with fear. "Ah, he's finished with me, Ma. He's finished with me. I know he is. I let him down."

My father got up from the table and walked towards the window. "Maybe it's a strain in the MacDonalds," he said.

My mother jumped up. "You're not just a drop-out, you're a left-out! A man hardly wanted in his own country!"

All of a sudden everything became very silent. Even the hens in the back yard seemed to go quiet.

My mother turned her eyes from me and looked out to the small garden at the back of the house. "I could sow a few potatoes and a bit of rhubarb out there, couldn't I?"

"You could, Ma," I answered.

"I had a bit of cabbage last year. Do you remember?"

"I don't, Ma," I said.

"You ate it, didn't ya?"

"I suppose I did."

"What about Mick's hens? I wish he'd let me cook one of them," she said, continuing to look at the two birds in the back yard. "There's a bit of bacon in the oven – will you bring it to me?"

I went to the kitchen, opened the oven door and took out a plate that had a thick slice of bacon on it. My mother took out her false teeth and put them into her cup of tea. She bit into the bacon with her gums but she couldn't get a grip on it. The bacon slipped from her mouth. She picked it up again and held it with her fingers. She struggled with the piece of bacon like a dog chewing and snapping when it's been fed too big a piece of meat. Paddy then walked upstairs to cover his head with the bed-sheet.

My mother walked over to the small colourful statue of the Infant of Prague. Its little painted blue eyes seemed to be glaring at me, telling me that everything was fine and not to worry.

After a moment Molly began to mumble. "Child of Prague,

open your holy eyes to show me son the way. This son of mine doesn't know any better. He'd just as soon hang around with loafers and sit on the street corner listening to the Devil talk, with all them no-good whelps who don't want to pray, work or find a job. Child of Prague, guide his way to finding the light of our beloved Jesus the Son of God Almighty. Wouldn't he be better off in that nice little job than idling about on the street? Child of Prague, help this son of mine find his way!" Molly then turned away from the statue and faced me. "You must have done something wrong. You got cheeky with the hall porter, didn't you?"

I turned around from the fireplace and looked at my mother. "I'm sorry, Ma. I am sorry for what's happened. I made a mistake."

As I was attempting to defend myself my father came downstairs again, reached out to me and shook my hand.

"Welcome to the Land of Unemployment," he said.

I held on to his hand for as long as I could and then let it go.

"Don't be bothered, son. You have the rest of your life to find another job."

My mother took her hat and walked towards the front door. She stopped, turned around and called out to me, "I'm goin' to say a few prayers!"

I could see the deep look of disappointment in her eyes.

After a few moments of silence my father retreated upstairs to the bedroom. I remained alone staring into the fireplace.

—◦—

In 1953 my brother Michael, who had turned sixteen, decided he'd had enough of Dublin. The place was "too bleedin' small" for him, he said repeatedly. Several of Michael's friends had gone to England and had jobs in factories and were earning money. When they were in Dublin they hung around street corners and gambled the few pennies they got from the Dole by playing cards or 'pitch and toss'. The Dole was public assistance and enough to keep you from dying. When Michael's friends came back from England for a visit they had suede shoes and silk shirts with colourful ties and talked about the money that could be made working in the factories in Manchester and Birmingham. Billy Breen and Seán Doyle came back and said it was like having landed on the Moon or someplace in Hollywood. Seán told Michael how easy the women were and that the Catholic Church wasn't on every corner keeping an eye on you. The stories convinced my brother to give up his job as a house painter and set out for England.

Michael had only one problem – he didn't want to go alone – so he convinced me to accompany him. I didn't tell my parents.

"What time is the boat?" I called from the kitchen.

"The boat leaves at seven," he called from the toilet. "We have to be there half an hour early."

I turned on the tap to drink some water. Michael came in, fastening up his trousers.

"Are ya ready yet?"

"I'm ready," I said.

Down at the North Wall dock a herd of cows were led onto the boat. As they ran across the gangplank the frightened animals began to scutter. The smell of the cow shite was everywhere.

My brother and I stood back a bit from the crowd and watched. I put my brown suitcase with an old necktie of my father's tied around it near my feet. A man was talking to a young girl and I heard him saying, "Did ya bring yourself any toothpaste?" Why would anyone who could afford toothpaste be going to England on the cattle boat? The dockside was full of fathers and mothers and wailing girls all kissing goodbye and hugging each other. Most of them were in tears. Where did they find the love they had for each other and what was it that caused them to have it? My brother and I didn't have anyone to hug and cry and say goodbye to. We hardly even talked to each other. I began to imagine what my mother and father would say when they saw that my little bed was empty. In the back of my mind I hoped my mother wouldn't throw away my old blanket. It had covered me for the last ten years. I was so used to it I could hardly fall asleep without it being next to me.

Somebody across the street was singing 'The Girl from Donegal' to an accordion, about the girl's heart being broken when her boyfriend sailed away to foreign lands. It was an odd song to be singing to people who were going off to England. The moans and the noise from the confused cows and horses blocked out the accordion player on the dock. After all the animals were in place the ship's horn blasted the signal for everybody to board. We picked up our luggage and joined the queue.

The boat pulled away and Dublin became dimmer and dimmer and dimmer. Very soon I was sailing across the Irish Sea to England. The place my father had gone to join the army many years earlier. Looking around me I knew things couldn't have changed too much since his time. A man came around selling tickets for bunks to sleep in for two-and-sixpence extra. Some of the passengers rushed to buy a bunk. I was glad because it left the deck with a bit more space to sit down on. Most of the people were standing up to save money till they landed. Later the smell of tea came from the cabin and everyone rushed down to buy a cup. We went down and bought a cup of tea for a tanner and a biscuit.

The room was crowded with people sitting on the floor, babies running up and down everybody's legs. Some of the passengers were Travellers. That's what they called themselves but my mother and father and everybody else who lived in my neighbourhood and on my street called them gypsies because they lived in caravans and wandered from town to town all over Ireland without having any one place to live or stay. They were also known as tinkers or knackers. They wouldn't stay long in any one place. Their address was always the next town. They had wild-looking horses that roamed into gardens and ate the grass, and dogs that were scraggly and starving half the time. Because they begged from poor people they were considered stupid as well. Whenever they came wandering in our neighbourhood, me and everybody I knew hid away. They knocked on doors and asked for money or food. The men in the caravans used to mend pots and pans. If they got enough old pots and pans to repair they'd start a big fire and melt down tin to repair them – that's why they were called tinkers. Sometimes the fires got out of control and the fire brigade had to be called to put out the flames. What would they be going to? Who would be waiting on the other end of the journey?

They sat on the floor, drank as much porter as they could, sang songs and begged for money. After they finished singing the mothers sent their rag-wrapped and shoeless children around the crowd of other passengers to see if they could cadge or shake any money out of them. A few tried to pick pockets but were caught and sent away with a slap on the face or a kick in the arse.

Most of the passengers didn't have a penny to spare. Practically everybody on board was making the journey to England to find employment. Half of them had to borrow the fare. Few even had luggage or suitcases. Brown-paper bags and sacks held all their worldly goods. The possessions generally consisted of a pair of hobnailed boots and a shirt as well as heavy tweed trousers. Some who had made the journey before talked about England and what it was like there. The younger fellas who had been to England wore fancy clothes. Thick-soled suede shoes and stovepipe trousers, blue jackets with black velvet collars. Everybody called them 'Teddy Boys'. The Teddy Boys liked to dress up. They were more interested in looking fancy than anything else. The first thing they bought when they got money in England was a shiny blue suit with a black velvet collar. Having a Teddy Boy suit was a mark of success. The fancier the clothes and shoes the more it reflected success in England. If they had a white silk shirt it meant they earned more money. Every so often I'd see older boys from my neighbourhood back from England and they'd all be wearing the Teddy Boy suit and crepe-soled shoes. Once you saw them you knew they'd been to Birmingham or Manchester or Liverpool. My brother Michael wanted to be a Teddy Boy. He talked a lot about getting a blue suit with a velvet collar and a black shirt with a white tie.

Michael also loved to sing but he wouldn't sing in front of anybody. If you weren't looking at him he'd break out into song and would continue singing until you turned to look at him. As soon as he saw you looking at him or even asking him the name of the song he'd stop instantly. It was as if he was caught stealing. My brother was different from me in a way that was almost like my mother and father were different from each other. I believed my father and I were always looking for something fairer and brighter in our lives but felt we could never attain it. Michael and my mother had a tighter grip on their reality and didn't seem to question it much. This evening on the cattle boat bound for England Michael was much more certain about his ambitions. He said when he got to England he'd look for Billy Breen or Seán Doyle.

"Are they in Liverpool?" I asked him.

"I think they are."

I got the feeling he didn't want to tell me where Billy and Seán were. They were pals of his who went to England a year or so earlier. They came home one Christmas wearing their Teddy Boy suits and crepe-soled shoes and acted like returning millionaires. The girls stuck to them like flies to flypaper. Michael wanted to be part of that.

"What kind of jobs have they got?" I asked.

"Who?"

"Billy and Seán."

"They're workin' in a factory some place."

"Where?"

"How do I know?"

"How're you goin' to meet them if you don't know where they are?"

Michael walked away from me. I got the feeling he didn't want to tell me anything. I even got the feeling that he didn't want me with him.

"I want to go with you," I said, frightened and on the verge of tears.

"Go where?"

"When you meet Billy and Seán. I know them too a bit, you know."

"They're older than you. What are you goin' to do? Hang around cryin'?"

"I won't be cryin.'"

"That's what you say now."

"Can I go with you?"

"I'm not goin' anywhere!"

Michael turned and went down the stairs where most of the passengers were singing, smoking and drinking tea. I stood on the deck and began to feel sea sick. After a few minutes of trying not to cry, I burst out in tears.

An elderly man came up to me. "Are ya sea-sick, boy?" he asked.

I was too afraid to answer him and I went down the stairs after my brother.

Many passengers who sat in the hot steamy tearoom had girlfriends and relatives in different parts of England. Some talked about Manchester. Others knew Birmingham well.

I asked my brother what the tinkers were doing going over to England. He told me they travelled all the time. It was their way of life. Some of them sitting on the floor had dogs tied with twine that were barking at everybody who passed them on the deck. Women wearing colourful woollen blankets around their shoulders with holes and food stains on them sat on the floor and leaned against the wall. They had big broad faces that resembled what I thought the wind would look like if I could ever see it. Wrapped inside the blankets, babies sucked on their mothers' nipples. The cries of the children mingled with the sound of someone playing a mouth organ. I wanted to talk to the tinkers but I was afraid. Something about the way they didn't care about anything or anybody made me want to be with them. I couldn't understand my feelings at the time but I knew there was some connection in my wishes. I'd often heard it said that the Travellers were the original Irish who were thrown off their land when the

English invaded Ireland years and years ago. They might have been the bearers of Cromwell's curse and cruelty. The look on their faces and the way they walked and talked reminded me of Ireland itself. The wilderness, the forests and mountains of Ireland. They were fierce, windy. Wild, wet and warm all at once. Rain and sun mingled. Rainbows and mist and green hills and steep cliffs all crushed together by memories of a time gone by. It was as if they were walking talking trees. Wanting and aching and wishing and hoping. Abused and victimised and still resilient. Ghosts and shadows of another time who were left with the look of fear on their faces as well as a great strength and handsomeness. They had got used to owning nothing but the clothes on their backs and the caravans they roamed the country in. The life of detachment from anything official. From anybody in uniform. From stamps and lines and waiting rooms. From alarms and warnings. From threats of weather to obligations of holidays. From any need to be anywhere at a certain time. Had they discovered something since the days of their evictions? Had they stumbled upon some simple secret to life that most everyone else couldn't see? Had detachment and homeless-ness forged in their hearts and minds the true way to live? I wondered if they knew how free they were. How unaffected they appeared to be by everybody else who looked at them and ran away in fear. Maybe it was the freedom they seemed to have in their life that made others afraid of them. I never was told why they were so bad. Everybody I knew looked down on them but some shadowy part of me longed to be with them. But I was shy and afraid to ever mention it to anyone.

The boat's engines roared. The cows in the lower deck began moaning as if to protest against the journey to Liverpool.

A few men sitting on one of the large wooden benches were pale and sad-looking. Across from them on the opposite bench others were singing and celebrating their departure from Dublin.

The journey was now real. The tinker children ran up and down the stairs, pulling at each other and fighting like scraggly dogs just let out of a kennel.

"Sit down for the love of God Almighty, will yis? Sit down!"

The women shook their shawls out and bits and pieces of bread fell to the floor. The children ran and picked up the morsels and ate them in a hurry. Their parents drank what remained in the small bottles of whiskey. Some of the men, by now half-drunk, fell over others already asleep, provoking yells and curses louder than the ship's bellowing horns or the cows mooing below.

Michael found himself a chair and sat down with a cup of tea and a scone. I sat next to him and watched him drink his tea in silence. He didn't appear to be worried about anything. I thought he was very brave.

I got a cup of tea and went up on deck again and saw seagulls flying low and landing on the railing. It was then I knew that we were very far out.

"Goodbye, Dublin – goodbye, Dublin!" I said.

Half-afraid, I sat down on a bench and sipped the warm tea I held between my hands. Wave after wave was bringing me closer to England.

Later, in the dark night, I thought of God again and began to talk to him: Somewhere throughout this pushing night you must be watching and smiling on this boat full of cows, horses and people. Whatever you do, don't let this boat sink. I can't swim that far back to Ireland. Whisper in my mother's ear that we're all right.

The silence on the boat didn't last long. Those who were asleep were now awake. Voices got louder and began to sing. Cows mooed as if to complain. A child ran around the deck and a mother ran after him. Somebody said "How long does it take?" About fifty opinions followed. The sun was coming up and the deck was spread with tired bodies of people snuggling against each other.

"Birkenhead! Birkenhead!" a loud call woke me up.

Everybody jumped up.

"It's England, it's England!"

The land was there for everybody to see. Boats and ships and buildings could be seen from the deck. Seeing it was like discovering a missing piece to a massive jigsaw puzzle. England was a real place with real people. In about an hour we would be in Liverpool. We began to pass the shipyards and everything looked so big along the shore. We turned into a big dockside shed. It was a place for the cattle to get off. After that we were let off.

* * *

At Customs a screaming English voice attacked my ears. "Bags up 'ere! Anything to declare, lad?"

I just looked at him with gawking open eyes.

"Wot's in the case, boy?"

"Everything," I said.

"Give it 'ere then. Where's the key to it?"

I had forgotten that the old suitcase ever had a key.

"Get to it, laddio!"

I could see he was getting very impatient. "It's open, sir," I said.

He pulled at my father's tie and searched my suitcase with his hand till he came to my bar of used soap. He pushed it out of his way and I had to rearrange my alarm clock and two fried-bread sandwiches.

When we'd both passed through the line, Michael asked me if I understood how these Englishmen spoke English. I'd heard enough English voices at the hotel and I wasn't bothered at all.

My brother and I got lost trying to find Lime Street. Lime Street Station was as large as Liverpool itself but still we wandered from street to street looking for it. We asked everybody we saw. As we walked around in a circle I noticed the old taxis driving by. The damn things had no doors on them. At last we came upon a man who was sitting on a bench eating out of a brown-paper bag. Before my brother asked him anything he asked us for a light. We didn't have any matches.

"Where's Lime Street Station?" my brother asked.

"You're on the bloody thing and behind the bloody thing!"

"We're on our way to Birmingham," I said as we moved away.

"Why don't you Irish bastards stay the hell out of this country? Stay where you belong. The bloody place is full of you, goddamn it!"

I thought he was drunk or had made a mistake. We had just met and he already wanted a fight. Michael and I continued walking. I wondered if he knew anything about the Irish over in Ireland saying the same thing about the English.

It wasn't long till we pushed into the swinging doors and heard the loudspeakers announcing arrivals and departures. The first thing my brother did was to leave me guarding the luggage while he went to the men's room to take a piss. Lime Street Station was huge. I could only think that all of Dublin would fit into it. Then my brother came out of the men's room and bought a newspaper. He couldn't wait to read the papers that were banned in Dublin. He came rushing over to me with a copy of the *News of the World*. His eyes were wide open as he scanned the paper to read or find words that are never printed in the Dublin papers. In Dublin, after Mass on Sunday, the boys gathered behind the church to talk and discuss the *News of the World* that someone had smuggled in from England that weekend. Michael found what he was looking for: a photo of a girl with no clothes on.

We got the tickets to take us to Birmingham. It was to be a three-hour ride. I was turning my head in every direction. Boys were calling out and selling papers just as in Dublin. In a few minutes we were on a train heading towards Michael's friends Billy Breen, Jimmy Doyle, Harry Combs. They had jobs in factories.

The conductor came into the compartment for the tickets and as I handed him mine he spat the tobacco he was chewing on the floor. The train pulled out and I began to feel faint. I saw row after row of small houses, clothes hanging on lines and house-windows broken, cats sitting on walls and dogs running everywhere, people smoking cigarettes and women with their hair-curlers.

I didn't know why I was in England at all. It looked just like Dublin. I got depressed. What was I doing in England before my fifteenth birthday? Why did I get fooled by Blister Dempsey? I could be sitting in the lift and getting ready for dinner at Jury's. I could be shaking my pockets with all the tips. I could still be wearing my uniform with the brass buttons. As the train neared Birmingham I asked my brother what I was going to do for a job. He had nothing to say about that.

When we got off the train in Birmingham we walked out to the main street. When I tried to walk alongside him he complained and said I was too slow. I told him it was the heavy suitcase.

He stopped walking and turned to me. "Look, I'm going on me own. You go wherever you want."

I felt I had just been crucified. My brother walked away from me. I called after him but he didn't turn around or say anything. I began to cry. I sat on my suitcase, wondering why my brother didn't even shake hands.

After a few minutes I tried to forget about how afraid I was and I walked around Birmingham looking for the biggest hotel. I saw a big hotel across the street and I walked up to it. When I got to the main entrance I was told I was too small and too young to be out looking for work. After that I roamed up and down the streets not knowing where I was going or what I would do. The thought of finding a church entered my mind. The church would protect me because of all the prayers I had said during my lifetime. After looking for hours I couldn't find a church that was Catholic. I then realised how different Birmingham was from Dublin. God's houses in Birmingham weren't Catholic.

Later that night I walked into a crowd who had gathered around a group of people carrying a sign reading: *Join The Communist Party*. They were waving the signs in front of everybody who passed. I began to remember what the word 'Communist' meant in Dublin. It was compared with Hell and the Devil. What was happening to me? Fire-everlasting was fleeting through my mind. I thought of Purgatory. Now I wanted to love God. I thought I was being punished for not liking him during the Retreat at the convent. Why did I run out of the convent that weekend when the priest was only trying to tell me about the bad things in the world? I should have listened more to him. I should have prayed more. Why did my brother leave me alone? I wanted to be back in Dublin with my mother and sisters and my snug home. I was cursing and hating Blister Dempsey and his mother.

Coloured people began to march around carrying the signs and I thought they were soldiers of the Devil. I had never seen coloured people before. Every face I saw seemed to bring me close to the image of Hell I had in my mind. I was beginning to believe that everything I was told was true and I hadn't paid any attention. I had not concentrated when the priest and the Christian Brothers told me to behave and pray with meaning and sincerity. I was a sinner who was now paying the price. I had made a mistake and my life was now falling away from me.

"Dublin, where are you?" I cried. "Dublin, one of your sons is going to die in this foreign land! Help me!"

The crowd got bigger and bigger. Men were screaming at each other. A fight broke out when somebody jumped up and knocked over the microphone. Everybody was shoving about. The white people were fighting with the black people. Women were screaming. A couple of black fellas ran by me and knocked me off my suitcase. It was beginning to drizzle when policemen came along to break up the crowd. I walked away.

How I longed to hear someone say, "It's time for Mass."

I found my way back to the Birmingham railroad station and had a cup of tea. Over the loudspeaker I heard a voice calling out for passengers to go to Liverpool. That's nearer Dublin, I thought. I went to the ticket office and was told that there would be another train for Liverpool in two hours.

I remember falling asleep and waking up to get on the train for Liverpool. I don't remember the journey but I do remember waking up in the Lime Street Police Station. They told me that I was found loitering around the railway station.

"Why were yea sleeping in the waiting room, laddie?" a voice with a Scottish accent was saying down to me.

"I'm from Dublin!"

He licked the rest of his breakfast from his teeth and replied, "Oh now, that's a fine place to be from."

"I want to go back to my mother. I don't like this country. I want to go back to Dublin for as long as I live."

"Well, what brings yea over here by your wee lonesome self?"

"My big brother brought me over here and left me without anything in my pockets. I want to get out of this country and go back to Dublin."

A Scottish smile spread on his face and I knew he was going to help me. He had another policeman escort me to the dockside. The policeman left me sitting on a barrel while he went over and talked to somebody in uniform on the ship, probably the ship's captain. The man looked over at me as he shook the policeman's hand. After a minute or two the policeman came back and told me to go on board.

I walked onto the boat as I had walked off it. I hardly knew where I'd been but I was anxious and happy to be on my way home again. To the sound of cows and screeching ropes I sat in a lounge identical to the one I came over on. Similar faces with the same kind of expressions were speaking with an Irish accent. After a minute or two somebody gave me a cup of tea. Shortly thereafter a horn blew. The ship departed the dock. I sat on my suitcase once more and felt safe and secure again.

* * *

Nine hours later the boat pulled into Dublin. Half of the passengers were standing on the deck cheering and singing. I stood among the crowd as the boat anchored. In the distance I could see the mouth of the River Liffey and O'Connell's Bridge. It was early morning and I wondered if everybody in my house was still in bed asleep. And if either of my two younger brothers Larry or Gerard had slept in my bed while I was gone. As I walked along the dockside with my old suitcase, I realised I didn't even have a chance to open it – except going through Customs. I only used it to sit on.

When I turned the corner at Nash Street Billy Whelan and Noel Ward were walking to the North Wall.

"Where you goin'?" I asked them.

"Liverpool," Noel said happily.

"We're gettin' on the B & I boat," Billy added.

"I was on that boat," I told them, feeling I was some kind of authority on the subject.

Billy and Noel looked at me as if I was telling them about a film they hadn't yet seen.

"When?" Billy asked.

"Last night!"

"Jeez, I never knew that!" said Billy.

"I went to England with Mick. I was up in Birmingham as well."

"Workin'?" Noel asked.

"No. I was only there for two days."

"Where's Mick?" Noel asked.

"He left me in Liverpool. I went up to Birmingham on my own."

"Y'didn't get a job?" Billy wanted to know.

"They told me over there I was too young. England is different."

"What's different about it?" Noel inquired.

"Don't ask him. He was only there for two days!" Billy

shouted and started to move on. When he got a little bit further away from me he turned and called back. "Did you get John Wayne's autograph?"

"No. He didn't show up at the hotel!"

"If ya ever see him tell him I saw all his pictures!" Billy yelled back at me and vanished as he and Noel turned the corner.

* * *

When I got home my mother was in the kitchen peeling potatoes. She turned and looked at me but didn't say anything. I put my suitcase next to the staircase and sat on it. I couldn't tell if my mother was angry or happy to see me back. I'd been hoping she'd be happy. I'd been hoping she'd give me a hug and welcome me back home and tell me she missed me and had been praying for me. I waited for her to inquire about my whereabouts for the last few days but she continued to peel the potatoes and was silent.

As I sat on my suitcase I tried to imagine what the house had been like without me being in it. Was everything the same when I wasn't here? Did anybody ask about or worry about me? What did my father say about me when he found out I was gone? Did either of my younger brothers sleep in my bed? Who did they miss the most, me or Michael? I couldn't understand why my mother was so silent. As I sat on my suitcase I thought she might have been thinking and worried about Michael. I wondered why she didn't ask about him.

I was walking up to the bedroom with my suitcase when my brother Michael passed me on the stairs.

"Hey, what are ya doin' here, Michael?" I called to him, hoping he was happy to see I made it home on my own.

He didn't say a word and just passed me by.

He'd come back to Dublin on the same boat the same day we arrived in Liverpool.

In the bedroom I solemnly pushed my old suitcase under the bed as if I was putting away my dreams and whatever I thought of the future.

--<O>--

The next morning I lingered in bed because I couldn't stop smelling my old bed blanket. It was an experience I was glad to be having again. For years it had been the only thing that had reminded me of myself. Holding it close to my nose was like hugging and kissing a friend. My mother was at the seven o'clock Mass and I knew I had a bit of time to think about the journey I had taken. Minutes later I could hear the church bells ringing for the eight o'clock Mass. The sound of the bells would signal the arrival of John Joe One-Ball, an old man who fancied himself a singer in the mode of Bing Crosby. He always showed up in the middle of the street. He appeared to be singing ballads he didn't know the words to. The man was a regular on Saturdays. He wore two different kinds of shoes on his feet and a rag of an overcoat on his back. When he bent down to pick up the few coins that were thrown to him, the holes in the seat of his trousers exposed a dirty crusty bottom. People called him John Joe One-Ball because he had only one testicle. I don't know how they knew that about him, but that's the name he had. A neighbour said it was because he attempted to sing high notes too often. When he reached for a high note he put his hand between his legs and held himself until the high note passed. When John Joe's voice faded I knew he had gone on to the next street.

After a minute of silence I jumped out of bed and got dressed as quickly as I could. I didn't want my mother to find me in the house when she came home. Grabbing a crusty bread slice that was left on the kitchen table I exited the house as quickly and as quietly as I could. I made my way towards the church in case I bumped into my mother. If she saw me heading in that direction she'd think I was going to Mass.

As I got to the church two elderly sisters who lived down the street from me overtook me and passed me by in a hurry. They looked like they were running for their lives. They had a reputation of being the first to enter the church to attend Mass. They walked past me waving their hands in unison as if they were greeting everybody who passed them. The two sisters were rarely seen. They stayed home most of the time with their widowed father who was a foreman at the foundry. Mass seemed to be the women's only form of recreation. The parish priest, before he was exiled to Donegal, said the girls were suffering from 'Saint Vitus Dance'. In hindsight I came to realise that the stories I heard about Saint Vitus were probably made up to compensate for the lack of sunshine in Dublin or were told in a mocking way to entertain those of us who didn't have a radio in the house. One telling of the story that stayed in my mind for a very long time was that when St. Vitus was a young man in the Middle Ages he swallowed poison rather than deny that God was a first cousin of his. After he swallowed the poison he started twitching so much it looked like he was dancing. His twitches were considered dance steps and because he danced so much he was made into a saint.

Whenever I saw the two sisters I was afraid to say hello in case they'd start dancing.

* * *

Two weeks after my ill-fated trip to England I was sitting on the edge of the local football pitch. The area was a small square where grass used to grow about a hundred years ago. The patch of land was between a row of houses and the foundry. When the men who worked at the foundry went to work in the morning they crossed the dusty football pitch; when they came out of the foundry at five in the evening they walked across it again. After kicking the ball around for about half an hour I sat down behind the goal posts (two old shirts with stones on them to keep the wind from blowing them away).

Seán Kelly, a neighbour about my own age, had just returned from England. Seán had attended Goldenbridge Convent with me years earlier. The last I heard of him was that he was put away in a reformatory school for stealing from luxury shops in the centre of Dublin. I hadn't seen him around the neighbourhood in years. Seán was wearing a Teddy Boy suit: a jacket with a velvet collar and stovepipe trousers. His hair was dyed black and he wore a pair of bright yellow socks with heavy thick-soled shoes.

Before I could ask him where he'd been all that time he started talking to me as if he was somebody else altogether.

"Have you been to London, Walsh?"

"I was in Liverpool once."

"Liverpool? That's just over the water. Did y'go any place else?"

"Birmingham for about four hours."

"Four hours?"

"I was lookin' for work but I was too young."

"Did y'get your gee over there in England Walsh?"

"Gee?"

"Yeah. Your gee."

"No. I was only there for a few days."

"You shoulda gotten your gee when you were there, Walsh. Them English girls are mad for a good ride."

"Did you ride any of them?"

A smile the size of the football pitch grew across his face. He obviously couldn't wait to tell me about his exploits.

"They don't have to go to Mass or Confession. The English girls can do it all the time and not to have to worry about tellin' the priest about it. Gettin' a ride is not a sin over there. Not like here. If you could get a ride and not have to commit a sin, wouldn't you be mad for it?"

Seán Kelly kept the big grin on his face. This was the first time I'd seen him with his mouth closed. He looked at me and his head shook as if he couldn't wait for me to answer him. What he said to me made sense. I was beginning to think I should have stayed longer in England. I could have met gangs of girls who wouldn't have worried about committing sin if we did it. The whole idea of getting a ride and not committing sin at the same time was very exciting. No wonder so many Irish went over to England. Maybe that's why my own father went over there in the first place. Maybe that's why all the boys from Keogh Square and Inchicore went there. It wasn't just to work in the factories or foundries. The English boys and girls could do it and not have to go tell a priest. It must have been a great feeling for them.

I wasn't sure what it was that kept me from committing more sins and having more pleasure. Somehow before this moment I wasn't able to put the two concepts together. I was suspect of pleasure and aware that any time I felt good about anything or anybody I was on the verge of committing sin. It was like I was carrying a big black umbrella around in my head that I had to open up whenever I felt a shower of pleasure coming on. The umbrella would keep the good feeling away from me and I would remain in a state of holy dry grace.

Seán took a toothbrush out of his pocket and began to brush his teeth. Most of his teeth were missing and the two or three that were still in his mouth had holes in them. After brushing his teeth Seán put the toothbrush back in his pocket. He licked his teeth with his tongue and started talking to me again.

"You didn't get your gee there, did you, Walsh?"

I shook my head in disappointment. "No," I answered and walked away.

"Where ya goin', Walsh?" Kelly called after me.

I didn't know where I was going. I had neither plans nor direction in mind at that moment. The sense I had of myself and where I was or where I was going just didn't seem to exist. Failure was falling on me like the rain coming out of the sky. As I turned the corner I saw the bus departing the bus stop. It was headed for the city centre. Without thinking any further or even checking to see if I had the fare I jumped on the bus and ran up to the top deck and sat in the back seat. Halfway to the city the bus conductor approached me for the fare. I told him I didn't have it. By the time he decided to throw me off the bus it was already at the James's Street bus stop and it was no bother walking the rest of the way to the city centre.

Twenty minutes later I was standing outside the Shelbourne Hotel.

I hardly had time to place my feet on the pavement when the hotel doorman, dressed in a green-and-gold military-like outfit approached me.

"What are you standin' there for?" he asked me.

By the look on his face I sensed he was wishing he had a broom to sweep me away from the hotel entrance. My attire may have prompted the man's curiosity and question. The shirt and trousers I was wearing previously belonged to my older brother and both were not only worn-out, they were at least two sizes too big for me. The effect of wearing over-sized clothes made me look younger and smaller than I really was. The trousers, made of Donegal tweed, had been purchased second-hand by my mother. In another lifetime the expensive material had more than likely belonged to a rich man. By the time I was in possession of the tough fabric it had acquired a few holes in it, mainly at the knees, and after countless years of sitting a shine on the backside.

The man in the uniform leaned towards my face and repeated: "What are ya standin' there for?"

Hardly knowing what I was saying, I blurted out, "How can I get a job in there?"

Mr. Doorman looked at me as if he had accidentally stepped into a pile of shit. He straightened his body backwards and I could see there was no trace of a welcoming smile on his face. Before I could ask him anything else, he yelled at me again.

"What d'ya want?"

The man's voice terrified me so much I couldn't close my eyes or turn away.

"Can I get a job in there?" I blurted out.

The doorman appeared to be caught off guard by my question. When my knees stopped shaking I heard his voice again. This time it was calmer and I sensed an encouraging tone in it.

"What did you say?" he asked me as if asking me to return his wallet.

"I'd like t'work here. Can I?"

"Here?" he said as if I'd spat on his polished shoe.

The man was used to greeting and being greeted by the rich and famous and the sight of me trapped in worn-out oversized clothes didn't enhance respect for his job. My shirt had missing buttons and a safety pin fastening the neck was sticking out from under the large woollen pullover I was wearing. The pin, mainly because it was used so often, had snapped open. I'd made several attempts to clasp it back but couldn't. To avoid being stabbed by the pin I kept my chin up and looked as if I was about to say something important. This might have been the reason the doorman kept staring at me. On the other hand it very well might have been the clothes I was dressed in.

He put his hand to the back of his neck, maybe to feel his pulse and to make sure he was not seeing or hearing things.

I asked again. "Can I get a job in there?"

Of the hundreds of people who crossed his path every day of the week the doorman didn't seem quite prepared for this one. He took a white handkerchief out of his back pocket and wiped his forehead with it. He pressed it against his nose and, appearing to be of two minds, pointed and without even looking at me said: "Go around the corner to the service entrance." With a great sense of relief and feeling I had survived a major confrontation I walked around the corner to where I saw a man in a long yellowish coat standing at a door.

As opposed to the man at the front entrance, the back-door man looked lonely and abandoned. I approached him with more assurance than I had previously exhibited.

"I'm lookin' for a job," I said.

"A job?" he asked.

"Yes."

"What do you do?"

"Nothin'."

"How old are ya?"

"I'm nearly sixteen."

"Who told you there was work here?"

"Nobody."

"You just showed up?"

"The man around the front told me to come here."

"Gerry?"

"He didn't tell me his name."

"Where d'you live?"

"Inchicore."

With a very sorrowful look on his face he repeated, "Inchicore?"

"Yeah. Is there any chance of me workin' here?"

The man put his hands into the two large pockets on his long yellow work coat. I thought he was feeling around for a few pennies to give and send me away. But he didn't.

"Mr. Brown's the assistant manager – does all the hirin' and firin'. Go up to his office on the first floor but don't tell him I sent ya."

I followed the direction his finger was pointing. I walked down the corridor to Mr. Brown's office. His name was painted on the door. I knocked and the door opened.

"What's up? Did you knock?"

"I'm lookin' for a job."

"Who told you to come here?"

"The man with the yellow coat at the back gate."

"Pat?"

"I don't know his name."

"Come in."

I went in.

"What kind of work are you looking for?"

"Any kind."

"Y'know anything about serving?"

"I worked in Jury's Hotel."

"Doin' what?"

"Page boy. I met a lot of waiters there."

"Why are you not there then?"

"I was tricked into leavin'."

"How?"

"Another page boy tricked me. He said he was goin' to England and asked me to go with him. I was the first to give in my notice. When I did that, he changed his mind and stayed on the job."

"He didn't leave with you?"

"No. He took over my job on the lift."

"So he tricked you into leaving?"

"Yes."

"Who told you there was work here?

"Nobody."

"You just showed up?"

"Yes."

"Do you have a black bow-tie?"

"No."

"A white shirt?"

"Just my brother's. He gave it to me after it wore out."

"Can you buy yourself a couple?"

"I've no money."

"Where d'ya live?"

"Inchicore."

"You didn't work for the C.I.E.?"

"No."

"Why not?"

"My father."

"What about him?"

"He didn't work there."

"Where's he workin'?"

"He's not."

"On the Dole?"

"Yes."

"No trade?"

"No."

"Inchicore's a bit out of the way."

"It's not that far."

"How would you get to work here?"

"I'd walk."

"You don't have a bicycle?"

"No."

"Are you out of school?"

"Yeah."

"You got your Primary Certificate?"

"Yeah."

"I don't know how you could work here without a white shirt, a bow tie and a bicycle. You'd have to be in by six in the mornin' or half six at the latest."

"This is the best hotel in Dublin, isn't it?"

"I'd say the Shelbourne is the very best in Dublin. In fact, it's the best hotel in Ireland. Everybody that's important comes here."

"Out front I saw a lot of rich people arriving."

Mr. Brown continued to brag. "This hotel has class and tradition."

"And maybe it has the best assistant manager too," I added for good measure.

Mr. Brown liked my remark. "Thanks! You got me on a good day. Can you get a bicycle?"

"I can steal one."

Mr. Brown leaned back in his chair. "Ah, don't do that!" He laughed a little to himself.

"I was only jokin'," I said.

He looked at me again, now much more seriously. Time passed. It might have been less than a minute but it felt like an hour.

"Inchicore? Isn't that up near the Naas Road?" he asked.

"Yes." I could tell he wasn't from Dublin. He was from one of the 'counties' down the country somewhere.

The men from the 'counties' represented a different style and culture from those who were Dubliners. Dubliners were less interested in tomorrow than country people. Country people were filled with ambition and seemed to hold almost all of the important jobs in Dublin. The country people played hurling and Gaelic football. Dubliners were more inclined to be involved with English football, soccer. However, when it came to accommodating the crowds who attended the Gaelic and hurling finals, only the Croke Park stadium in Dublin could accommodate them. The stadium was smack in the middle of the city. When the 'counties' clashed in sporting events their followers had not only to come to Dublin to play the games but they also had to pass through it on their way back home, particularly if the teams came from any of the counties in the south. Inchicore was a junction on the road to and from Croke Park. Every summer, Corkmen, Kerrymen, returning home from a hurling or Gaelic final at Croke Park had to pass through Inchicore. What's more they had to drive under the bridge. Everybody I knew in Inchicore believed that the country people had too much power, too much land, too many cattle and too much money. On Sundays when the countrymen were driving under the bridge in their cars with their county banners flying in the wind, they got pelted with

149

stones and sods of grass by a gang of boys who stood cheering on the bridge waving the blue and white colours of Dublin. I was never sure if any of the men from Cork or Kerry noticed.

"When I was younger and there was a big match at Croke Park, me and some other fellas used to stand on the bridge and throw sods of grass at the cars that went by."

"You did?" Mr. Brown asked with serious interest.

I tried to undo what I had confessed to and quickly added, "Not anymore. Denny Mack and me splattered muck on a car once and we got taken in."

"In where?"

"Into the police station."

"You have a police record?"

"Ah no. It was only in fun. It was a car from Cork."

"I'm from Cork," he said and he laughed at the same time. "Maybe you're the fella who threw the bricks at us when we drove by last year."

"Jeez, no! I never threw bricks. I only threw sods of grass. Grass wouldn't do much. We sometimes dipped the sods of grass in water before we threw them but we never threw bricks!"

"You must have hit me once or twice."

"Ah no! I always missed on purpose."

"You're a right bunch of whelps – all you fellas up there in Inchicore! Throwing stones at unsuspecting cars! You could have hurt somebody or caused a crash or something."

"I stopped throwing stones years ago. I swear. I haven't thrown a stone at a car from Cork since I was twelve. Others still do it but I don't. I'm tellin' you the truth."

Mr. Brown leaned back in his chair. "I might be able to do somethin' about the shirt and tie." He stood up, walked to the door, and opened it. "Follow me."

He walked down the corridor where he opened another door that led to the back stairs. I walked behind him. In a minute or two we were in the basement walking past mountains of food crates and sacks of potatoes piled up to the ceiling. Laundry carts filled with bed-sheets and towels were pushed by men and women in striped aprons. Everybody said hello as if they knew me. In a second or two I was in the waiter's dressing room where five or six fellows were either getting dressed or undressing. A few were inspecting themselves in the mirror. Mr. Brown walked to the centre of the room. Everybody turned to him.

"I've a new fellow who's goin' to be working here next week. He'll be up on the fifth floor. Early morning shift. Breakfasts."

Some of the faces turned to get a look at me. They then turned back to grooming themselves. "Can anybody loan him a white shirt and a black bow tie?"

There was a silence. I was looked at from head to toe by the waiters.

An old waiter, Mick McQuaid, called from his locker. "He can have one of mine! I'm retiring next month."

Another waiter stepped forward and put a black bow tie in my hand without saying a word. I thought it was very nice of him.

"Thanks very much," I said.

A few other young fellas were polishing their shoes and appeared to be hiding their heads away from Mr. Brown. I was feeling at home.

Mr. Brown walked up to one of the fellas. "I heard you bought a new suit this week, Sam?" Sam reached up to the top shelf on his locker, took down a brown-paper bag and handed the bag to Mr. Brown who in turn pulled a pair of black trousers out of it. He handed me the black trousers. "Make sure they fit. Be here at six o'clock in the morning next Monday."

With that he turned and walked out of the dressing room.

I stood holding a white shirt, bow tie and black trousers. I then stepped out of my own trousers and tried on the one Sam gave to me. It was a perfect fit. While I was at it I put on the white shirt and black bow tie. When I looked at myself in the mirror I almost fainted. I was so dressed-up-looking and ready for a fancy-dress ball. I didn't want to get out of the trousers so I left them on. I held my old tattered pair and felt like throwing them into the wastebasket.

The other young waiter, Dessie O'Neill, leaned down and picked up the brown-paper bag. "Put it in this."

I put my old trousers in the bag, thanked him and the other waiters and walked out of the room.

A minute after I left the waiter's dressing-room I got lost in the hotel basement and after searching for a door or a window I ended up in the kitchen. The main kitchen of the hotel was like a jungle, hot and steamy. I could hardly see in front of myself. Stoves with barrels of bubbling soup and chickens hanging downwards everywhere. Chefs were screaming at each other and everybody else in the kitchen. I stuck my finger into a cream cake but I was abruptly grabbed by a chef and pushed out the door. He yelled something in French at me but I didn't know what.

Seconds later and as lost as I had ever been in my life I found myself walking through the laundry room.

A woman folding bed-sheets noticed my confusion. "Are ya lost, son?" she called.

"I'm goin' to be workin' here!" I yelled over the steam presses.

"Grand. Grand! I need a bit of help down here."

"I'll be serving breakfast!" I called to her.

"Breakfast?"

The woman stopped what she was doing, took me by the hand and led me out. "Y'll have to be in early for that shift," she said.

She took me to the service lift. I got on it.

"When d'ya start?" she asked.

"Monda' mornin'."

"I'll do your shirts and aprons for a few pennies. Don't forget that now."

The woman pressed a button. I went upwards. The lift stopped on the first floor. I got off but I was lost again. I was standing where everything was polished and clean.

I didn't know which way to turn. I walked down the corridor where two rich-looking English types were stepping into the lift. I followed them into the lift and descended to the main floor. The doors of the lift opened. The rich-looking couple stepped out. I stayed behind for a few seconds. I sensed I had arrived in a place I wasn't supposed to be. I thought of pressing the button and going back up but decided to walk across the main floor. My brown-paper bag was under my arm and everything I was wearing, except my trousers, was worn-out. Apart from the trousers, nothing I had on me had a memory of newness.

As I walked towards the front door of the hotel I heard a loud "Hey!" I instinctively knew the "Hey" was referring to me. It was the doorman who'd sent me around to the back of the hotel to ask for a job.

He ran across the lobby and leaped at me. "What in the name of Jaysus are you doin' here?" he asked with his eyebrows stretched to the ceiling.

I couldn't answer. I must have looked like a newly electrocuted cat.

"What in the Devil's arsehole brought you through here?" he blurted out with a shower of spittle.

I'd never heard anyone mention the Devil's arse before and when he said it I was reminded of Purgatory and the sins that got burnt off the bottoms of the sinners who went there before they were allowed to enter Heaven.

The man opened his mouth so wide I could see the back of his tongue. "How'd you get here?" he yelled again. His eyebrows were now back in place and he had sucked his tongue back into his mouth.

"I'm lost," I said.

"How did you get in there?" he questioned me again, almost whispering this time.

"I went the wrong way."

"What d'ya have in that bag?"

I opened the bag and showed him the tattered trousers.

He looked baffled and I wondered if he would make the connection with the brand-new trousers I was wearing. He didn't.

"What d'ya have in your pockets?"

"I've nothin' in my pockets. My pockets are full of holes and they don't hold anything."

"Show me what ya have in your pockets this minute!"

I pulled the two hole-infested pockets of my trousers out to show him.

"I did nothin'!" I said and was about to burst out crying.

The man straightened himself up. "You bloody ragged git, slide your dirty arse out of here before I make a holy show of you!"

As I proceeded to walk across the marble floor he made a grab for me.

"Go out the back way!" he yelled.

"I don't know where it is."

"I'll show you the way. And be quick while you're at it. Don't let me see your filthy arse around here ever again."

I continued to walk towards the front door.

"You're goin' the wrong way!" he yelled at me.

But it was too late. I had reached the swinging doors and walked out onto the street with the rest of the swanks, feeling a bit different already.

◄○►

In the dressing-room after a day's work the waiters who were stiff and formal while on duty would soon descend into a mad ragtag group who talked about the customers they had just served.

"That bitch! Did ya see her? She wanted more gravy! Her prick of a husband with his sun-baked face wanted more brandy!"

"And who was the creep next to her who kept telling me to watch me elbow whenever I served him peas and carrots? I had to bend down to serve him, didn't I? If I served him standing up I'da poured the mashed potatoes on his greasy head that smelled like a whorehouse. I was almost into a fit of sneezin' by the smell of piss from his trousers. And the two who kept sending everything back because the beef was too hot or too much or they had changed their minds over and over!"

"And what about that bastard with the big fat cigar stuck to his lips? He was a fuckin' Arab or Egyptian. King Baldy Farouk. He's no Farouk. Or maybe he was French. Fuck him whoever he was. He kept askin' me for a light. I'm holdin' two hot dishes of veg and he's asking me for a light as well!

I shoulda burnt his moustache. If he had come over to light up his cigar I'da been lagged in for murderin' the bastard. He kept puffing and puffing the smoke in me eyes. I wanted to stick that stub of ash up his arse. Me feet was wore out runnin' back and forth gettin' him cigars and cigarettes. Every brand in the world he had on the table in front of him. The smell was horrible."

"And did ya see the English pisser dressed in his jodhpurs and the horse shite still on the heels of his boots? The white silk shirt with the brandy stains on it? He walked across the carpet and left a trail of dung that made the place smell like a stable. The fuckin' Frenchman almost grew hair when he saw what was on the carpet. '*Mon dieu, mon dieu, mon shite! Parlez-vous beaucoup?*' Monsieur Tripe doesn't even speak English, or he won't."

"And No Knickers Lizzie O'Rourke with her bleedin' vacuum! Buzzin' all over the place when she was told only to vacuum the spot near the door! She just came down to see who was eatin' what and how we were all doin' on the job. I think she's been screwin' too many old men up there on the fourth floor."

"What was the name of that film star that was here a coupla years ago?"

"What film star?"

"The big black-headed fella from Hollywood."

"They're all from Hollywood. Rock Gibraltar Hudson?"

"Was that him?"

"The fella who was playin' the part of Captain Lightfoot?"

"Him? That was years ago!"

"I know it was. He was a good tipper. I think he fancied you, Barney. Did you give him a bit of your Lightfoot?"

"Ah, shut up and go off with yourself!"

"And him a symbol of cockology the world over!"

"Who'd want me anyway? Me own wife only wants me money."

"I've got lounge duty today! Tea and toast! Tea and biscuits! The brandy guys who sit around all day wearin' out the newspaper with their eyes! Y'ever see them with the newspaper? They read it and they read it. Then they turn the page and then they turn it again and again. Then they bend the fuckin' thing and soon it's lookin' like a small notebook. The whole fuckin' paper vanishes right before your eyes. I think then they eat it. I swear to Jesus."

"Another brandy! Another pot of tea and more sliced tomato and cheese sandwiches, please! Lyin' around all afternoon readin' the newspaper! Are they not all duly elected officials we nominate to govern us down there in Parliament House on Kildare Street? Some are politicians. I know that. They're all politicians. This is where they talk about the destiny of our beloved little nation. My past, present and future is spelled out and bothered up there in the lounge every day at four o'clock. Can you imagine? I'd a read ten fuckin' books by the time they read the newspaper!"

"I think they're lookin' to see if their pictures are in it. When they can't find themselves they can't believe it. They just go back and forth and almost eat the bleedin' pages lookin' for a snap of themselves standing next to somebody important."

"How much did we make today?"

"It was a good day. A lot of finance!"

"We'll have a good payday Friday when it's all divvied up."

"What about these young goats from the breakfast shift? How much will they get?"

"Ah, we'll give 'em something. They've earned it. Jesus, they work fast. It's all that quick breakfast-servin' they do early in the mornin's. They've done a day's work while we're still in bed. I'm glad I don't have to ride that hard-arsed saddle on me son's bicycle. Give me the bus any time!"

"You're too old to ride a bicycle."

"Piss off with yourself! You're too old to ride your wife."

"Shut up! Keep me missus out of it. She'll be happy when I tell her Friday's pay is goin' to be good. I'm always in the mood to throw a good ride into her when the pay packet is big. I get big like me pay packet."

"Stop boastin'."

"I'm not boastin'. I'm braggin'."

"Ha!"

"Good Christ!"

"What is it?"

"Someone stole me fuckin' white collar! I left it on the top of my locker this mornin'! Anybody see a white collar? I only got me laundry back before I went on duty. Who took it? Who took it? Check everybody's hard neck! Laugh your arse off if you want but that collar was brand new. I bought the fuckin' thing in Cleary's."

"You went to the sale there on Saturday?"

"I didn't go, me sister did."

"Your sister?"

"Yes, me sister."

"I didn't know you had a sister."

"I got five sisters."

"Well, which one went to the sale for you?"

"What the fuck do you care?"

"I don't care. I'm only askin'."

"Mind your own business. Y'can't leave a damn thing

around any more. What's happenin' to this hotel? Last week it was me shoes. Now it's me white collar. It was a brand-new nylon collar."

"Why did ya' leave that collar on the top of your locker anyway? Aren't ya supposed to be lockin' it up? Isn't that why you got a fuckin' lock? Isn't it? Maybe somebody thought you threw it away."

"Who'd be that stupid?"

"Look in the wastebasket. That's where you throw your dirty stockings and shorts."

"Some of the new fellas can't afford shite."

A silence for about a minute. Talk again.

"Where in the name of Jesus does that poufter manager find these fellas?"

"He advertises in the newspaper."

"That's the parts the politicians skip when they read the papers."

"What would you do if you didn't have a penny to buy yourself a white shirt?"

"Don't be askin' me questions like that. I'm too old to be answering. I'm almost retired. I left a shirt out last week and the other day I saw one of them commis waiters from the breakfast shift wearing it."

"What did you do?"

"Nothin'! What could I do? It was my own fault. I forgot to lock it up. Anyway I couldn't really prove it was me white shirt. And by the way if you leave shoe polish out don't be surprised if it goes too. Don't forget how many people work here with black shoes. Me feet are killin' me."

"What time does the laundry open?"

"An hour before dinner. Pick up me clean laundry for me tomorrow, will ya?"

"Who?"

"You!"

"Y'takin' the day off?"

"I'm not takin' the day off – it *is* me day off. I worked last Sunda', remember?"

"What'll you do tomorrow?"

"Fuck all. I'll sleep. A few pints then I'll sleep again. I wouldn't mind takin' Fifth Floor Mary home with me. Did ya see her?"

"The one from Kerry? Is that where she's from?"

"Cork!"

"I heard she's from Kerry. Good Christ, she's some heifer. She carries more milk than a herd of cows. I'd like to be the farmer who milks her. I'd love to get a ride off her. Has anybody got any from her yet? She's up on the fifth floor. Ask one of the fellas from the breakfast shift."

"Hey, Twohig? Twohig?"

"Twohig's not here. The Welsh fella is here."

"Who?"

"Welsh!"

"Welsh?"

"Who's been clearin' away your station all day?"

"That little fella?"

"Him."

"Holy Christ, I'm sorry. I forgot to ask him his name. Hey, young fella, what's your name?"

"Walsh."

"What your first name?"

"Gabriel."

"Gabriel? That's a girl's name."

"No, it's not."

"It's a fuckin' angel's name if you ask me."

"Nobody asked you."

"No kidding. Is that your real name?"

"Yes."

"Where you from?"

"Inchicore."

"Inchicore? *'Sure there's nothin' like the Pride of Inchicore!'* Isn't that the song?"

"No."

"It goes somethin' like that. Where's Inchicore?"

"If you knew anybody who worked in the C.I.E. you'd know where bleedin' Inchicore is."

"Up by Kilmainham? Saint Pat's? They play up there, don't they? You ever see Shay Gibbons play? He played for Ireland an' I heard he always had a few pints before he walked onto the pitch. I only heard that now, mind ya. I don't know how true it is. What does your father do?"

"Nothin'."

"Unemployed?"

"Yes."

"You like this hotel?"

"I do."

"Don't mind all the blabber you hear here."

"I don't mind it. They don't talk that much when they're workin'."

"You were so good today I didn't notice you. I didn't have to tell you anything. That's a good sign. You kept the station clean and neat an' you took them dishes away in a hurry." He then turned back to the other older waiter. "I know who has your collar."

"You do?"

"Yes."

"Who?"

"Me."

"You?"

"I saw it on top of the locker and I thought it was thrown out. I'm wearin' it now. I didn't know you wanted it. Y'can have it back. I'm sorry."

"No. Never mind. It's yours – you can have it. I shouldn't have left it up there. It's yours. I mean that. Keep the damn thing. Thanks for tellin' me."

A voice called from the door. "There's a union meetin' on Tuesday! Make sure you're all there. I hear' there's strike talk."

"Who told you that?"

"I heard it."

"Is it true?"

"They want to strike at the Gresham and the Hibernian hotels but not here. If you don't speculate you won't accumulate. If you don't court you'll never marry."

The old man turned back to me. "Christ, I'm glad to be out of this stiff collar. I've a fuckin' rash around me neck from wearin' it."

"Go to the doctor?"

"Welsh? I mean Walsh?"

"What?"

"Are ya happy at your work?"

"I am."

"That's the lad. Keep it up and you'll be in the union before long. How long have you been here now?"

"A month."

"Good Christ, time goes fast, doesn't it?"

Other voices flying about the place.

"Don't leave dirty dishes lyin' about. The bleedin' things stack up and fall all over the fuckin' floor."

"Make sure the station is always clear and clean. No pots, pans or dishes. Get them on the tray and back into the kitchen in a hurry."

"All we need is that Frenchman to come over and inspect our station. Out you'd go in a flash. He wouldn't waste a sneeze in firing you."

"Who?"

"Him! Louis, the head waiter! Fuck him! Everybody who works here! Fuck 'em all!"

"What are you doin', Walsh?"

"Changing. I'm off work till tomorrow."

* * *

I loved my job. It felt as if I now at last had a family, the members of which took the time to talk to each other. What's more, we laughed and joked together. Without being fully aware of how to live a normal life of reasonable contentment, most everyone in my family, knowingly or not, did their best to make each other unhappy. My five sisters, three remaining brothers and me were soaked in my mother's perception of living when it came to accepting and liking each other, and any suggestion or impulse that led to a sense of mutual happiness was ignored as if it was some kind of ailment or illness or a threat to what lay ahead in the afterlife. With the exception of my sister Rita who had a natural kindness about her, we begrudged each other very conceivable friendly positive thing that might result in anyone being happy or comfortable for five minutes. Happiness only happened to other people who had strayed away from the teachings of the Church. In my house, for the most part, happiness meant that one was not living up to the religious standards set by my mother. Any kind of human emotion or caring for one another was likely to remind us that it was the wrong road to Heaven. The deep belief that pleasure was an enemy permeated almost everything we did and thought. It kept us from knowing and supporting each other. It excluded us from just about everything that was collectively comfortable. We all had a full-time job in disassociating ourselves from any kind of gratification, contentment and joy. Affection was a foreign concept. Even the air in the household was filled with distrust. My brothers and sisters were so alienated from each other that they lost their ability to share the personal and private pain they were suffering. Wanting and wishing for any kind of mutual affection were thoughts that led to the plucking of the feathers of the wings we all thought we had growing out of our shoulder blades. With feathered wings we could all fly away to eternal paradise when life on earth ceased. Without wings we were all condemned to Hell where we'd be roasted like chestnuts in a never-ending inferno. In a strange and almost incomprehensible way the alienation in my family gave my mother hope. She believed that her way of bringing up her children was the way God and the clergy wanted it and as such she felt she had contributed to the creation of a new sacrament.

* * *

"*Garçon, garçon! Ici! Ici!*" Louis the French maitre 'd ran out of the tea lounge.

I was about to turn the pastry dolly into the dining room when the Frenchman grabbed me by the back of the neck.

"Where you go?" he asked me.

"The dining room," I answered.

"*Allez-vous* back to the tea lounge!" He turned the dolly and pushed me towards the tea lounge.

A group of people were sitting next to the big window. A few of the men were wearing turbans and several of the women were dressed in long flowing robes. I was reminded of the film *Gunga Din*. As I stood staring at the group, Louis tapped me on the shoulder.

"Serve! Go! Show the pastries, please!"

I moved forward with the pastry trolley.

A very dignified woman remarked, "My, look at all of this! Do you bake them all here?"

"Yes, ma'am." I didn't want to tell her the bakery oven in the hotel had broken down and the pastries were shipped in from Bewley's Bakery on Grafton Street.

"Oh, I love these!" She reached forward and took one of the almond ones.

At that a man with a yellow turban on his head reached over and grabbed the remaining almond pastries.

"I'll get more," I said to the lady.

I was about to rush back to the kitchen to replenish them when the woman in question quietly took hold of my arm. "Not to bother. No need to."

I was glad she said that because I didn't want to tell her about the broken-down oven.

The man who'd swiped all the almond pastries placed one in front of the woman. "Here you are, Indira."

The woman smiled at him and smiled at me. She then placed a pound note in the palm of my hand.

When I returned to the dining room I was met by Louis.

"Everything good?" he asked.

"Yes. I got a pound from the woman with her back to the door."

"That woman is Indira Gandhi, the daughter of the Indian Prime Minister," Louis said and walked away from me.

* * *

I had barely unclasped my bow tie from around my shirt collar when a tray with a bottle of whiskey was put in my hands. I was told to rush it up to the large meeting room on the second floor. After a few leaps and a dash I knocked on the door and stuck my head into the room.

A man sitting at the head of the table, smoking a cigar, called to me. "There you are, lad! Come in."

I stepped into the room and noticed everyone had a note pad in front of them. There was a woman, quite short, sitting in front of the big window holding a young girl.

I put the whiskey bottle down on the sideboard where there already were glasses and a big jug of water.

The man turned to the woman. "What'll you have, sweetheart?" he asked.

The woman responded, "Lemonade for both of us."

The man took the cigar out of his mouth and turned to me. "You got that?"

"Yes, sir," I said.

"Good. Okay. Now along with that whiskey we're going to have two gin and tonics. Can you get me that, lad?"

"Yes, sir," I said.

"It's decided we'll film in Cork," the man with the cigar said.

For a moment I thought he was talking to me but he obviously wasn't. I was so excited to hear this man talk about making a film in Cork I rushed back down the stairs and almost fell over myself. The barman told me John Huston was the man in charge upstairs and if I hurried back up I might bump into Gregory Peck. Within minutes I was back in the big room, serving everybody around the table.

Drinks served, they raised their glasses.

"Here's to *Moby Dick*, Mr. Huston!"

166

"Gentlemen, I've a train to catch for Galway. When that script is typed up, will you send it to me as fast as you can?"

A few hours later I came back to pick up the empty glasses and bottles. There was no sign of Gregory Peck.

* * *

Montgomery Clift came into the tea lounge. A year or so earlier I had seen him in *Red River*, a cowboy film with John Wayne. And I'd recently seen him in *From Here to Eternity*. I walked up to him and introduced myself.

"Hello, sir, I'm Gabriel Walsh."

He looked at me as if wondering whether he knew me. "Oh," he said with something of a pained look on his face. He then sat down. "Can I get something to drink?"

"Course you can, sir," I responded. "What would you like, sir?"

"Bring me a brandy first, would you? Then I want . . . well, what? Get me a pot of tea and something to eat with it. Bring me an order of toast."

I rushed back to the kitchen and placed the order. After a few minutes I was rushing back with his brandy and the tea and toast. I placed his order in front of him.

"Did you play the trumpet in *From Here to Eternity*?" I asked.

He looked at me and smiled. "Somewhat. I learned to play a little so that it would look like I knew what I was doing."

I turned away from the table. By now the waiter was back from his cigarette break.

"What are you talkin' to that customer for?"

"I only asked him a question."

"Did he order?"

"Yes."

"What?"

"Tea and toast. And a brandy."

"Nothin' else?"

"No."

The waiter turned towards the kitchen.

"I got it for him."

"You served him?"

"Yes."

"Why didn't you tell me?"

"You were out smokin'."

"Why didn't you wait?"

"He couldn't wait. What did I do wrong?"

"Next time wait till I get back. I hope you didn't mess up."

"I didn't."

"Did you put a clean plate on the table and change the ashtray?"

I quickly picked up a clean plate and ashtray and darted back to the table.

"Sorry sir, just to make everythin' a bit more tidy."

Mr. Clift didn't say anything.

I walked back to the waiter, leaned against the wall and looked back over at the film actor. I was happy I asked him the question.

"That's the actor fella, isn't it?" the waiter said to me.

"He's Montgomery Clift. I saw him in the film *From Here to Eternity*. He said he only kinda played the trumpet in the film."

"You asked him that?"

"I did. Can I ask him if he wants more hot water?"

"You're the talky type, aren't ya, Walsh?"

"Me?"

"No. Yes, *you*! Who'd'ya think I'm talkin' to? Me arse?"

"Shhhh. He might hear you." I was embarrassed.

"Fuck him. He's a film star. So bleedin' what?"

"He's famous."

"Walsh, before you piss in your trousers go over and ask him if he wants anythin' else."

I jumped at the chance to go back. The film star was looking in his notebook. I think he was looking at a map or something. I stood waiting for him to take his head out of the notebook. After a moment he sensed me standing in front of him.

"Yes?" he asked calmly and quietly.

"Would you like more hot water, sir?"

"Could you get me a glass of orange juice?"

"Yes, sir." I walked away.

"What does he want?" the waiter asked.

"He wants a glass of orange juice. Can I get it for him?"

"Go ahead."

I ran to the kitchen and back with a glass of fresh orange juice for Mr. Clift. I rushed into the lounge and placed it in front of him.

"Thank you."

"A pleasure, sir."

I walked back to the wall. By now the other waiter on tea-lounge duty was back from his smoke break.

"Did I miss anythin'?" he asked the other waiter.

The other waiter pointed his finger at me. "Yeah. Walsh pissed in his trousers."

"I did not."

"You did so."

"I didn't."

"What did you piss in your trousers for?"

"I didn't."

"Go down to the dressing room and change."

"I didn't piss in my trousers. He's only jokin'."

The two waiters laughed.

Mr. Clift turned, made a gesture with his hand.

"He wants his bill. Give him the bill, Walsh."

I walked over to the table and stood at attention.

"Your bill, sir."

"Thanks."

I gave him the bill. He signed his name and left. I forgot to ask him for his autograph.

◄O►

The morning staff at the Shelbourne Hotel might have regretted that they hadn't had an extra pint or two the night before they came to work. The chitchat in the dressing-room wasn't about the smell of sausages coming from the kitchen or how long it took to cycle to work with a flat front tire. On this September morning it centred on the fact that a certain woman had checked into the hotel the night before. Word about her arrival had spread faster than butter on a hot slice of fresh toast. While they dusted off their bow ties and climbed into their serving suits, waiters and porters alike were having a field day with what they knew and didn't know about Margaret Burke Sheridan.

Miss Sheridan's presence in the hotel was enough to cause some staff members to call in sick and claim they had an early attack of the winter flu.

"The other night they were talkin' about her on the wireless," a waiter, polishing his black shoes, mumbled. "I wouldn't touch anythin' belongin' to her if you promised to canonise me." The talk and reaction to Maggie's arrival, even though expressed individually, was chorus-like and uninterruptible. Without apology or notice, one comment was layered upon another.

A waiter, apparently mimicking her voice, sang: *"I dreamt I'd a pair of marble balls with something or other beside me!"*

Another, not to be outdone, warbled: *"Eileen, I'm sure there is somebody knittin'! If you come over here I will piss on your kitten!"*

Clearly some waiters didn't want to be known only as talkers but as singers as well.

One of the older waiters, adjusting his bow tie with trembling fingers, started up, "She was in the dining room a few years ago and returned every dish she ordered. The potatoes went from boiled to mash to steamed and in the end she ended up eatin' none of it. She had little else to do if you ask me. Before she left here the last time, she caught me lookin' in her photo book. It was on top of her big trunk outside her door. That day when I thought she was takin' a walk around Stephen's Green she appeared in front of me and demanded to know if I was lookin' into her private life. Divine Jesus, I nearly lost what was left of me mind when she saw me. I didn't know what she was talkin' about. I only picked up the book and saw them photos of her when she was young."

A soon-to-be-retired old porter volunteered: "About three years ago I served dinner in her room and I was exposed to that screechy record machine she has with her all the time. Me eardrums were burstin' and poundin' with the noise comin' from it! All the loud stuff was in Italian as well to make it worse. I think she put it on to torment me."

Those who didn't speak favourably of Margaret Sheridan wished she had stayed away, not only from the hotel, but from Dublin as well. Nevertheless the news of Margaret Sheridan's arrival replaced the regular complaints of how hard and difficult it was to live and survive in the Dublin of the 1950's.

A hall porter turned from his locker and looked as if he was about to leave the dressing room but instead sat down on the bench and presented himself as if he was about to give a lecture to the mice who inhabited the place when he was away on duty.

"Do you know anythin' about Madame Sheridan?" he asked anybody who was listening.

Turning from the dressing room mirror an elderly waiter mumbled, "She's a Japanese, a singer."

"A Japanese singer?"

"Yis."

"Madame wasn't and isn't a Japanese singer."

"She's not?"

"No."

"What is she?"

"An opera singer! She sang the part of a Japanese!" the porter yelled and continued. "You wouldn't know much about opera, would ya?"

"What the fuck is that?" the newcomer from Donegal asked.

"You don't know what it is, do you?"

"No."

"How could you? You're from Donegal where the only exposure to culture is the west wind that blows up your arsehole."

"As long as *you* know!" the newcomer responded with a tinge of sarcasm in his voice.

"Yes! Down here in civilised Dublin some people have a bit of an education."

From the other side of the locker room somebody farted. The hall porter stood up and looked as if he was about to punch anyone who disagreed with him. Nobody challenged him and he presumably felt he had got his day off to a good start. With a broad grin on his face that underlined an expression of superiority he gripped his coat lapels and continued to blabber on.

"An' she's from Mayo. Just a country girl from Castlebar. Mayo!"

A voice from across the room bellowed out: "I wish to God somebody would send her back down there!"

"Castlebar is up! Not down, you eejit!" the porter called back.

A fellow wearing a kitchen apron and white hat approached. "I saw a picture of her in the *Herald* with President de Valera the last time she was here. She was never married and if you ask me that's always been her problem." He tied the apron strings around his waist. "Didn't somebody say she was half-mad about an Italian Count who shot himself dead one night when she was singin' some kind of religious song in Italy? The poor fella didn't know who he loved the most – Mayo Maggie or whatever they call wives over there in Italy."

"I've heard the stories," said the porter. "She fell in love with a married man and lost half her brain over him when he wouldn't leave his wife."

"I've heard John McCormack a few times on the wireless. He was a singer as well. The Pope made him a Count. Miss Sheridan was made into something like that in Italian."

"Something like what?"

"She was made into something like the Pope made John McCormack into! Count John McCormack, a Prince of the Church!"

"John McCormack was a great singer."

"How'd ya know all that?"

"Me?"

"You, ya gobshite!"

"I read newspapers. I've read newspapers more times than you've wiped your arse."

For the hotel staff, talking about guests was something of a hobby. But when it came to talking about Margaret Burke Sheridan it was close to being an obsession. It probably had to do with the fact that she was in many ways just like them. She was Irish and it was easier and maybe more comforting for them to criticise one of their own. When it came to discussing her they were all experts.

"The fella who invented the wireless is said to be the one who paid for all her singin' education. He heard her one day singin' in some rich person's house in London. I think it was Churchill's mother or cousin or somebody close to that family."

"I thought you said she was sent to Italy?"

"She was sent to Italy by an Italian fella who was married to a woman from Galway."

"Wasn't it the man who invented the wireless that sent her?"

"Yes! He was Italian! Or at least he had an Italian name. Marconi."

"Marconi? Who's that?"

"The man who invented the wireless! The thing you listen to with them big ears of yours every day."

"Didn't you hear the other story?"

"What's your arse talkin' about now?" the hall porter said as he moved closer to the door.

"It's not me arse that's talkin'. I'm repeatin' something me father told me."

"What did he tell ya?"

174

"When she went to the House of Commons and yelled something in Irish. Didn't you hear that story?"

"Yes, I fuckin' heard it!"

"What did she yell?"

"She yelled 'What about Roger Casement?'"

At that the hall porter called out as he left, "Go to work, you pack of bollocks!"

* * *

"That man sitting over near the winda' there sent boxes of arms and ammunition to Israel from Ireland."

"Who?"

"Him."

"The old fella with the hat?"

"Right you are."

"Mr. Briscoe?"

"You know his name?"

"Of course I do. Everybody knows his name. His picture's been in the paper enough times for God's sake. Wasn't it about the floatin' coffins or somethin'?"

"Who told ya that?"

"I had an apparition from the Virgin Mary."

"Don't get blasphemous."

"I'm too religious to be whatever it is you said."

"Blasphemous. It's a word you hear when you enter a public toilet."

"Just because you went to the University of Toilet Paper."

"I'm a historian."

"You're definitely somethin'."

"I should be more than a waiter sufferin' from varicose veins."

"Give me the skinny on your man there."

175

"Mr. Briscoe?"

"I know who he is now."

"Your arse, you do."

"I do."

"Who is he?"

"He's the Lord Mayor of Jerusalem."

"Wrong."

"He the Lord Mayor of . . . here? Isn't he?"

"I'm not goin' to tell you."

"Well, I'm askin' ya."

"You want me to tell you?"

"I wouldn't ask if I didn't."

"You want t'know about the floatin' coffins and all that stuff?"

"Go ahead. Resist tellin' me."

"When he lived in Cork he put rifles in coffins and sent them to Israel."

"You're jokin'? How did he do that?"

"He opened the top of the box like any eejit would do, you half a gobshite!"

"Lower your voice."

"I'm only whisperin'."

"He sent the boxes from Cork?"

"He sent coffins from Cork."

"With nobody dead in them?"

"That's not what I was attemptin' to get at, you dried-up ring of Clonakilty puddin'!"

"What are ya gettin' at then?"

"I don't want to continue educatin' you."

"You said he was puttin' somethin in boxes and sendin' them out a Ireland, didn't ya?"

"Ya heard me?"

"I did. You said he put arms and legs in boxes and sent them to –"

"I said he put arms and ammunition into bleedin' coffins and sent them out a this country to Israel. Y'didn't know that, did ya?"

"I think I heard it someplace."

"I didn't say a bleedin' thing about legs. Jaysus sakes! You and your arms and legs! Why don't you clean out them ears of yours? I didn't say a thing about legs, you pot of stale piss!"

"You're dyin' to show you know how to read. So go on."

"He put the guns into coffins and shipped them to Israel. That little fella over there sippin' his tea is a very important man. Robert Briscoe. Lord Mayor of this kip! He's a hero here and he's a hero in Israel."

"He put guns in coffins. Jaysus!"

"The Brits thought the coffins had dead bodies in them and let the coffins in. It goes to show ya how the Brits have more respect for the dead than the livin'. Briscoe knew that about the Brits and he sent everythin' to Israel pretendin' it was dead."

Harry Guiney, the know-all waiter, then turned to me as if he wanted to teach me a lesson in Irish and Jewish History as well.

"Is that man there Jewish, d'ya think?" he asked me.

"I don't know what he is," I said.

Mickey Quinn couldn't resist taking up the challenge. "Of course he's Jewish. He lives up on the South Circular Road."

"You have to be Jewish to live up on the South Circular Road?" said Guiney. "I'll tell you somethin' else."

"What?"

"They're not all Jews up there."

"Did I say they were?" said Quinn. "I didn't say that, did I?"

"You said somethin' like that."

"You didn't listen."

"Did ya know that all the Jews in Dublin live up on the South Circular Road?" Guiney asked.

"Doesn't everybody know that?"

"You didn't know it until I mentioned it."

"Me father mentioned it once to me."

"Your father, me arse. He didn't know where he lived himself!"

"Where do *you* live?"

"Cabra!"

"You like it there?"

"I'd like to move to tell you the truth. You know the song: '*Abracadabra, I don't want to live in Cabra – oh no, no, no!*'"

"Can I ask you somethin'?"

"Go ahead."

"Do you live near the Jews up there in Cabra?"

"Do I live near any Jews in Cabra?"

"Are you askin' me a question?"

"No! I'm askin' me dead mother the question! What the hell are you askin' me if I live near any Jews for? I don't know if I do or not. I don't know."

"I know you don't know."

"Do you?"

"You're askin' me the same question I asked you."

"What did you ask me?"

"Do you live near the Jews in Cabra?"

"Are you tryin' to tell me I'm Jewish?"

"No, I'm not. I don't know what the fuck you are."

"I go to Mass so how can I be Jewish?"

"You live in Cabra and you don't know who you live near?"

"I live near the person in the house next to me."

"Are the people you live next to Jewish?"

"What people?"

"You have neighbours, don't ya?"

"Of course."

"Are they Jewish?"

"I don't think so."

"What makes you say that?"

"Two of the girls are nuns."

"How do you know?"

"They were walkin' around with them black clothes on them. I know what a nun looks like. I go to Mass, don't I?"

"You talk like you know everythin'. If you know so much why are you only a waiter down on his heels?"

"I'm not down on me heels."

"You are so! You ought to go over and ask Mr. Briscoe to give you a helpin' hand. He's good for that, you know. That's why I asked you if you lived near any Jews up there in Cabra. If you did you'd probably have a better shirt to wear when you come to work. You need help. There's a charitable Jewish organisation up near where you live and you ought to ask for a bit of assistance."

"Go piss off with yourself!"

I was standing by, listening like an anxious schoolboy. I looked over at Mr. Briscoe, the man Guiney said was the Lord Mayor of Dublin. He looked very serious. I was afraid he had heard the chat that was going on behind him. Normally when he came into the lounge for his afternoon tea he'd bid hello or tip his hat but today he didn't. Had I known earlier the things Guiney said about him I would have paid more attention to him.

Guiney tapped me on the shoulder. "Walsh, go make sure Mr. Briscoe has enough hot water."

I went over to the table. "Is everything all right, sir?"

Mr. Briscoe took his eyes away from the newspaper and stared at me. I was expecting him to answer right away but he didn't. He continued to look at me and I began to regret my intrusion.

"Would you like another pot of hot water, sir?"

All of a sudden he looked happy. "I would, thanks. Kind of you to ask."

I rushed back into the kitchen and filled a silver teapot with boiling water and ran back out to Mr. Briscoe's table. I put the pot in front of him.

"Here you are, sir."

"Are you new here?" he asked me.

"I'm here a short while."

"Sit down," he said.

"Me?"

"Yes, you. Who else would I be talking to?"

"I'm workin', sir. If I sit down I'll be sacked."

Mr. Briscoe raised his voice a little bit. "Sit down!"

I sat down.

He looked across the room at the other waiters as if to taunt or defy them in some way. The waiters were somewhat mystified by the sight of me sitting. Mr. Briscoe folded his paper and placed his hat on top of it. He looked as if he was about to get up and leave but he didn't. I made a feeble gesture to stand up but just as I did Mr. Briscoe raised his voice.

"Them fellas standing against the wall look like a row of penguins. They pay more attention to the customers than they do to their work. Don't think I haven't been able to hear what they were mumbling about. I'll tell you something. There used to be a lot more Jews up on the South Circular Road than there are nowadays. Half of them are gone. I bet you don't know why?"

I didn't even know who lived where or what the difference was.

"Jewish girls in Dublin have to leave here and go to Scotland or England to meet fellas of their own kind. It's a pity but it's true. Lookin' at that crew standing against the wall there is reason enough for them to go. If you want you can tell them that."

I glanced over at the waiters who were now still and silent. They looked as if they were waiting for something else to happen.

"What's your name?" Mr. Briscoe asked me.

"Gabriel."

"Gabriel?" He laughed. "An odd name for an Irish fella!" His smile seemed to indicate he was enjoying holding me prisoner at the table. "Gabriel's a Hebrew name, you know. It means . . ." He stopped.

I waited for him to continue but he just poured the hot water into the teapot and quickly poured himself another cup of tea. As he retreated to his paper I quietly got up, turned away and walked back to my workmates who were standing against the wall looking and acting like nervous penguins.

Quinn turned to me. "What did he want?"

"After I gave him the hot water he said you fellas frighten Jewish girls and they have to go to Scotland when they want to get married."

Harry Guiney slapped me with his serving towel and left the room.

A few minutes later Mr. Briscoe got up from his chair and left also.

* * *

Mary the fifth-floor maid was resting and leaning against the corridor wall. A bundle of clean pressed linen was between her feet. She looked tired and exhausted. The sound of a guitar was coming from one of the nearby rooms.

"D'ya hear that? D'ya? He's been at it all bloody night," Mary said to me. "The guests next door have been complainin' about that fella in there."

"What fella?" I asked Mary.

"Yar man with the music thing!"

I stopped and listened. "It's nice."

"Nice?" Mary blabbered back with her eyes almost bursting through her reading glasses.

"Yeah. I like it. It's very good."

Mary leaned down and picked up the bed linen that was between her feet. As she walked away from me she called out: "What in the name of God would you know? You're just a Dublin jackeen!"

"And what are you? A country mug without a handle?"

"No bloody manners at all if you ask me." Mary liked calling Dubliners 'jackeens'.

The breakfast I was in the process of delivering was for the man who was making the music. When I arrived at the door I knocked. After a moment I inserted the passkey and entered the room. A man was sitting up on the bed playing a guitar. He had whitish hair and was wearing a white shirt that was probably his nightgown. His fingers kept plucking away at the guitar strings. I walked to the small table next to the bed and placed the breakfast tray on it. The man didn't appear to notice me. He just kept staring at his moving fingers. I stepped away and walked back towards the door but as I got to the door the music stopped.

I turned around and the man called to me. "I've been up all night trying to do that. It's there. It's between the cords.

The quivering string is frightened. It must be made secure. Love it. Love it and it will speak its sound. Feel! Feel it."

I wasn't sure if he was talking to me or not but he seemed happy.

"Is it tea or coffee?" he asked as he lifted the top of the pot.

I wasn't sure what was in the silver pot. I had rushed out of the pantry in such a hurry I forgot to check it.

He put his nose to the pot and smelled the aroma of coffee. "Coffee! Ah, yes! Thank you."

When I got back to the service pantry the breakfast rush had subsided. And Fifth Floor Mary was vacuuming the corridor. John Kilady, another boy on duty that morning, was sitting at the small table drinking tea and reading the newspaper. John was so intense he never opened his mouth except when he was listening to you. The more you talked to him the wider his mouth got. It was as if he was ready to swallow your head. He lived in Killeen, a posh part of Dublin and was more of a "trainee" than a regular service waiter. Everybody who worked with him knew he didn't have to work for a living. John had whiter shirt collars than any other waiter in the hotel. He also had new shoes. His ambition was to be a hotel manager or own his own hotel one day. One of his uncles owned a hotel in Kerry and John spent his holidays there.

"What's your uncle's hotel like?" I asked him one morning when both of us had a break in the room service.

"Very good. We have a beautiful view of the bay down there. I love it. I want to manage me uncle's place some day. I'll tell you that."

Being well off, John had many opportunities to travel abroad as well and he didn't hesitate to talk about it. He bragged about his visits to London and Paris and about the big hotels there.

"If you saw the size of the Savoy in London you'd spit out your Adam's apple. It's so big you could hide this hotel in its basement." Or: "If you want to know first-class silver service you have to know how they do it in Paris."

Even though I knew how he got his money to travel abroad I still enjoyed asking him questions. "How'd you go to them places?"

"Me father."

"Your father took you?"

"Don't you go places with your father?"

"No. My father was in World War I and he hardly talks except to himself sometimes."

"Is he shell-shocked?"

"What's that?" I asked.

"Does he get up in the middle of the night and think he's being attacked by the Germans?"

"No. He likes the Germans," I answered.

"I do too," John said.

"Me father thinks he's being attacked by my mother," I volunteered.

"He should take her to Paris. Me parents used to bark at each other all the time until me father took me mother to Paris. When they came back they couldn't wipe the smiles off their faces. Have you ever been to Paris, Walsh?"

"No."

"Go there sometime."

"How can I do that?"

"Maybe I'll loan you the money someday."

"You're jokin'," I said.

"I know I am," he answered.

My mind went to wondering how Paris could have stopped his parents from barking at each other. I thought of asking him for a loan to send Paddy and Molly there but I knew he wouldn't offer a penny.

After a minute or two I noticed a picture of a man on the back page of the paper John was reading. I leaned forward to get a closer look. John then pulled the paper away.

"What are you lookin' at?"

"The picture."

"What friggin' picture?"

I pointed to the picture of the man in the paper. The man was holding a guitar.

"That man! I just took him his breakfast."

John turned the paper around to get a better look at the photograph. "This fella?"

"Yes. I was just talkin' to him."

"This fella?"

"Yis. Who d'ya think I'm talkin' about?"

"What's his name?" John put the paper down on the table so we could both look at it.

We then said out loud: "Andrés Segovia!"

After work while cycling home to Inchicore I couldn't get the guitar music out of my ears and some of the people I had met out of my mind. The world of the hotel was a universe I had fallen into almost by accident and I was as happy as hell about it. All the waiters wore clean shirts and talked all day long about the people they served. Most of what they had to say about the customers and the hotel guests wouldn't have been allowed in a pub on a Friday night. What they had to say about the management would have condemned them to hell for a thousand years or more. I felt I was working in a carnival where the merry-go-round never stopped and where everything said and done by the waiting staff was a commentary on Irish and world political leaders. Somehow the maids who made the beds and cleaned the rooms and the waiters who served everybody and anybody had an answer to every political and social issue of the day. Even the smell of the hotel was something I looked forward to. There was always the smell of something cooking or the remnants of tobacco burning in a pipe being smoked by the odd characters who used the hotel lobby as a home away from home.

While I pedalled the bicycle the sounds the man made on the guitar were ringing in my ears to the point where I thought I couldn't get rid of them. I worried that I might even get an earache that wouldn't go away. Mr. Segovia, a nice man, up at seven in the morning practising when he could have been sleeping. The sounds he made were very different from the noise and sounds of where I lived. As I cycled down the steep hill past Saint James's Hospital, sometimes referred to as "The Kip", which old people entered to die, the wind blowing into my ears blew away the sights and sounds of the hotel and both were soon replaced in my mind by the time I reached Inchicore.

* * *

When the phone from the hotel kitchen rang I was sitting around the table in the service pantry. One of my work mates, Dessie O'Neill, picked it up. The voice on the other end of the phone was so loud it must have curled the gristle of Dessie's right ear.

"Be quick about serving 507! D'ya hear me?"

Dessie turned back towards Liam Twohig, the other service waiter, and with a shrivelled voice called out, "Her breakfast is on its way up!" He slapped down the phone.

Liam shouted so loud I thought he swallowed the teapot. "The fuckin' bitch! I'll lose me job if I go in there and serve that woman. I'm not servin' her!"

"I won't do it either," Dessie O'Neill shot back.

"You will!" Liam responded.

"I will in me balls," Dessie answered.

Then as quick as a forgivable sin Liam dashed out of the pantry.

Dessie yelled after him. "Don't leave me with this! It's your turn!"

It was too late. Liam was gone.

Dessie gazed over at me. His eyes behind his spectacles were spinning in their sockets like two flies chasing each other. "I'm goin' to report that bastard so I am."

He looked as if he was going to jump out the window when the dumb waiter arrived with the breakfast for room 507.

"I don't want to do this. I don't want to," he moaned.

"What's wrong?"

"I'm not even supposed to be workin' today! I'm not servin' that bitch!"

"Who the hell are ya talkin' about?"

"You'll know about it soon enough."

The phone rang again.

I picked it up.

"Who's this?" the shrill voice on the other end asked.

"Me," I answered.

"Who's me?" the voice yelled.

"Gabriel Walsh. Who's this?" I asked.

I then heard a scream.

"I'm the assistant manager!"

I got frightened and thought I might be fired. "Mornin', Mr. Brown!"

"Forget the good-mornin' blabber! Did you serve 507 yet?"

"I just came in. I haven't had a cup of tea yet."

"Just came in? Where were you?"

"I was a few minutes late."

"Who's up there?"

"Dessie and meself," I answered.

"Where's Twohig?"

"He left."

"Left for where?"

"I think he had to go take a piss."

"Is O'Neill there?"

"Yes."

"Tell him to serve 507 right away."

I looked at Dessie. "Mr. Brown said you're to serve the breakfast right away."

Dessie wasn't happy. "I'm supposed to be on me day off!" he yelled back at me.

Over the phone the assistant manager's voice screamed back. "I'm coming up there and that breakfast better be served! You hear me?"

"I just got in," I answered, half-frightened of losing my job.

"I'm talking to the other two!" Mr. Brown shouted into my ear again and then hung up.

Two floor maids, Mary from Cork and Nuala from Kerry, came rushing into the pantry. Both looked as if they had suffered a seizure.

Nuala was shaking and carrying a batch of clean towels in her arms. "Did ye serve her yet? I'm afraid to start up the vacuum until she's finished with breakfast. I'm not going near her room until she's finished with her grub and the tray has come out of there." She dropped several towels on the floor.

"Divine Jesus of Nazareth, save me from her yells and moans this mornin'!" said Mary as she picked up Nuala's towels and handed them back to her.

"Has her grub come up?" Nuala asked.

"Just this second," Dessie answered.

"It hasn't been served yet," I said.

"Christ in heaven, somebody better be servin' it before she has the manager up here!" Nuala said with the grin of a Kerry goat on her face.

At the same time Dessie was timidly inspecting the breakfast tray. "Everythin's here. Fried kippers. Toast! Marmalade! Tea! Milk and sugar! Napkin! And spotless silver. That woman will be the cause of me crucifixion. I'll piss all over meself before I'll enter that room. Last summer she almost had me sacked for not knowing if her fried eggs were fresh or not." He appeared to be in serious pain.

"Get it to her before we're all sacked and out of a job!" Mary howled as she and Nuala scampered out of the pantry.

"Where the fuck did that Liam go?" Dessie said with an agonised shrill.

"The breakfast will be cold if you keep fightin' and arguin'," I said. "Nobody can be as bad as you're talkin' about."

I then impulsively volunteered.

"I'll serve it," I said.

There was a silence as if Judgment Day had occurred.

Dessie's mouth opened wide. "Thanks, Walsh," he responded with eyes looking up at the ceiling.

I picked up the tray and walked out of the pantry as Dessie blessed himself. A sense of redemption was written all over his face and as I got further away from him I heard him calling, "Thanks, Walsh, and good luck!"

Mary and Nuala followed me along the corridor to Room 507. When they spoke about her, their voices trembled.

"Nothin' is ever right. Your hands and fingernails are dirty and your slip needs starch. There's grease on your apron and soup on your shoes. The bed-sheets are not properly ironed. And that bloody record player she leaves on all day! The screechin' and singin' stuff that comes out of it would give ya an earache. I've never heard anythin' like it in all me life and that's as true as God. I was in cleanin' the bathroom once when she put on that screechy thing."

"What screechy thing, Nuala?"

"The gramophone. What d'ya think I'm talkin' about? I nearly poured meself down the drain listenin'."

"When that bloody noise of hers goes on ye better watch out."

The two floor maids were crackling away like two hens discussing their run-ins with a fox.

"Ah Jaysus, I knew she couldn't stay away long. I wish she'd stay over there in New York with them Americans."

I arrived at Room 507. I held the tray in one hand and gently tapped at the door with my passkey. There was no response. I tapped on the door again. Still no response. I began to think that there was nobody in the room at all.

As I turned to look at Mary and Nuala who were still observing me in the corridor, a voice called out from inside the room: "For God's sake, come in!"

Nuala and Mary scampered into the nearest laundry cupboard. I put my hand to the doorknob, turned it gently and walked in.

The room was dark like an underground cave. Usually a guest expecting breakfast is either sitting up in bed or sitting with the newspaper at the small table by the window. This rainy Dublin morning I couldn't see anybody. Yet as I stood in the middle of the dark hotel room I smelled perfume and could hear a woman's voice singing in a foreign language. Two large travelling trunks were against the wall and were wide open. A mountain of personal belongings, hats, dresses, shoes, scarves, glasses, coats were spilling out of them. I looked across the room and with the aid of a small shaft of light escaping from the pulled curtains I saw a record spinning around on a gramophone. The voice on the record continued to screech out. I didn't know what language it was but I guessed it was Italian. The big bed was empty and the blankets and sheets were hanging over the side. The voice on the record continued to squawk. I stood with the breakfast tray in the middle of the dark room and became more fearful by the heartbeat. I began to question myself as to why I had volunteered to serve this breakfast. The rest of the service staff had warned me about this particular customer but I'd paid little attention to their counsel. This morning in the almost dark room I began to regret I hadn't heeded the advice. The door to the bathroom was open and I assumed Maggie Sheridan was there, so I decided to just put the breakfast tray on the small table next to the bed and make a fast run for it.

I walked as quietly as I could to the far side of the bed.

As I approached the table with the tray, a head came up from the floor at the other side. I almost dropped everything. For a second or two I was frightened out of my wits. It was Margaret Burke Sheridan. The woman everybody in the hotel whined about. My fingers became so glued to the tray I couldn't let go of it. I looked across the unmade bed and saw her staring at me. Her hair was all over her face and it had two or three different colours in it. Her face was snow white and she was holding a lipstick in her right hand. Her bottom lip was very red but the top lip was a different colour. I later learned that she was over sixty but she seemed to me much younger. I stared at her. She looked at me but didn't move. I didn't either. I was afraid to. She remained on the floor looking directly at me.

Finally out of practice and training, I mumbled, "Mornin', ma'am." I didn't think I was heard so I said it again much louder. "Mornin', ma'am! Your breakfast!"

There was a stillness and a silence that seemed to last as long as High Mass on a Sunday. The woman kept looking at me and for a second or two I forgot where I was and even who I was. Had the floor opened up under me I would have been happy to fall through it. As I floated in what I felt to be a mixture of Limbo and Purgatory and not too far from the gates of Hell, I heard her voice.

"Good morning, lad," she said.

To my happy surprise her face was calm and peaceful-looking. Something in her voice was reassuring, even kind. I was feeling like I was before I entered the room. Pain, fear and confusion left me like flames leaping up a chimney and all of the odd and strange things I had heard about this woman on the floor in front of me disappeared. I gripped the breakfast tray but it quickly crossed my mind that she might not want it on the table. Maybe she has her breakfast on the floor every morning, I thought. Maybe that's why everybody believes she's a nut case?

The record on the machine stopped. I stood in total silence for what seemed a lifetime. I then walked around to where she was sitting, still half under the bed, and looked down at her. Her long blonde hair was partly covering her eyes and I wasn't sure she could even see me. She didn't seem to want to move. I wondered to myself if she liked sitting on the floor in the dark. I stood awkwardly over her, still holding the breakfast tray. I had an impulse to tell her to get up but I didn't. My mind then raced to thinking that she had hurt herself and couldn't get up but she showed no signs of being hurt or wanting any kind of assistance. She made no effort to move and I finally became convinced she wanted to eat on the floor.

"Would you like your breakfast there on the floor, ma'am?" I asked.

"Here? On the floor?" she answered.

"Yes, ma'am."

She began to laugh. I felt foolish and was convinced that I had fallen into some strange trap this dreary rainy morning.

"I'm sorry, ma'am," I said with a trembling voice.

The woman was still on the floor, laughing at me. All positive feelings had now deserted me. I stood in fear and thought about dropping everything and making a run for it.

Maggie then got up from the floor. She then turned and faced me.

"Put it on the table, please." She was still holding the lipstick tube in her hand. "I dropped this silly thing and had to go under the bed for it," she said as she lifted the silver top on the fried kippers' plate. "Smells good!" She reached over to the toast rack, picked up a slice and took a bite out of it. "Nice and warm, I hate cold toast."

* * *

Soon I had got used to Maggie and the way she carried on since I'd first served her. She talked about her life in opera and the places she had visited and sung in. When she talked to me I felt like a statue. I either stood or sat in front of her while she reminisced about songs, opera, Ireland and the world and just about everything I had never heard of. If she wasn't blabbering on about Michael Collins and de Valera and how the two main figures in the Irish Uprising didn't get along with each other, she was talking about herself being alone and not having a family. She identified with Mr. de Valera because, as she repeated over and over, he didn't really have a happy childhood. I was tempted to say that was the case with everyone I knew in Ireland.

One particular day Maggie was fussing with her old dresses and hats. She then stopped abruptly.

"I was tailor-made for opera. The characters I sing are always in such pain I feel like I'm a member of the same family: sisters of pain, rejection and unfulfilment. The greater the pain, the higher the note I reach. This terrible life-long search to be part of somebody else's life has given me pneumonia more times than I can count. I know I wasn't the only one but what use was that to me? I don't know why God made pain so important in a person's life. What's the use if it's all pain? What's the use if you can't learn to rub two happy thoughts together and know how to repeat it whenever you want? Jesus, when I look back at the early days in the convent and the faces of the other orphans and the thoughts that must have been in their little minds! What did they think at all? And they prayed all day to be thankful for being miserable and lonely and frustrated and angry and bitter. Some of them were even suicidal. I remember a few girls jumped out the window because they couldn't stand being alive any longer. How in the name of the Divine Jesus did any of us ever manage to smile or laugh or wake up the next day? I don't know. I don't.

"And the country, Ireland itself, was something like an orphan if you ask me. What did it know about the people born there? What? I don't know if it knew an awful lot. I seriously don't. It had been beaten and battered by England for centuries. When it got out on its own it was turned over to the Church. We had a leader in Ireland who should have been a priest instead of a politician. I'm not saying that I'm not a Catholic or that I don't believe. I do, I do. When you have nothing and no chance of anything in life it's easy to believe. Well, let me put it this way, if you don't believe in something, what's left? The nuns only had what they were given. I suppose I was lucky to have them. I think they saved a lot of girls in those days.

"All that time I spent in Italy singing my heart out. I had a lot of good times too, I suppose. I'm not saying I didn't. There was that mad aristocrat; he said he was an aristocrat anyway. I allowed him to take me over and I let him use me until I felt more worthless than I can remember. I gave everything up for him. I was hoping and hoping he would hold me up but he didn't. He held me every so often then he let go of me and I fell flat. He was married and religious at the same time. I knew deep down he would never leave his wife. I must have been insane to even imagine it for a second. What was I thinking? I knew hardly anything. I was too needy. That's what I was. Needy! Lost and needy! I couldn't sing any more after that. Sometimes I couldn't even breathe. I was an artist. At least I thought I was. Then again what in the name of God is an artist? Sometimes I think it's some kind of crucifixion or some religious torment. For half my life I couldn't even stand up. Back and forth from Rome to Dublin! To London and Italy! All the operas and I got so soaked in singing women of pain."

I got the feeling that she had forgotten that I was in the room. She quickly turned as if she had just discovered me there.

"Oh, yes, take the tray out, please. Thank you."

I picked up the breakfast tray and, somewhat embarrassed, walked out of her room.

* * *

When I entered her room early every morning Maggie Sheridan was either asleep or resting her eyes. She might have been attempting to delay the beginning of the new day. I sensed she liked the night because it was silent and less likely to make demands. Night for her appeared to be a place where time paused and in its shadow neither age nor fear nor ambition mattered. The world was not awake or looking at her. In the darkness of her closed eyes she could reach back to La Scala and relive the roles she played. Mimi in *La Bohème*. Iris in Mascagni's *Iris*. Maddalena di Coigny in *Andrea Chénier*. Cho Cho San in *Madama Butterfly*. Manon in *Manon Lescaut*.

I got into the routine of opening the curtains for her when she woke up. After I gave her the weather report she asked me so many questions about opera I felt I had sawdust in my head.

Some mornings before she'd even look at her breakfast tray, she'd stare out the window and talk to herself as if I wasn't in the room.

"Sister Agnes was the most loving person. God rest her merciful soul! If anyone deserves a place in heaven it's Sister Agnes. She took her vows seriously. The most unselfish human being ever on the face of this earth. If it hadn't been for her, God knows where I'd be today." She stopped talking to herself and turned back to me with a smile. "Were you listening to me?"

She asked the question as if she hadn't remembered that I was there in front of her and as if she couldn't help herself from falling into some strange part of her own past.

"Yes, ma'am, a little bit. I'm sorry."

She picked up the teapot. When she started to pour the tea I turned to walk out of the room but just as I got to the door I heard her voice calling out. "Wait! Wait!"

I stopped dead in my tracks.

She then let out a happy kind of moan. "God, I miss Italy! I miss it in my bones sometimes. Passionate they are over there. I was so determined to live there for the rest of my life. Why did I ever leave a place where I was so adored?"

I didn't know if I should even try to answer her. I wasn't sure if she was talking to herself.

"I'm off to New York soon. I'm not gone on that place, mind you. You'd shiver to death there in the winter. Do you hear me?"

"Yis, ma'am."

"*Yes*! Not *yis*. Yes! Yes! Say 'yes' the way it's supposed to be said. Don't mumble and don't be afraid to open your mouth. Speak out and speak up."

"Yes, ma'am."

When she felt she'd frightened me she quickly changed the subject.

"You've never been to the opera, have you?"

"No, ma'am."

"Pity, pity. The nuns brought opera to me. Well, one did anyway. I was orphaned when I was . . . oh . . . never mind. I only knew the nuns after I lost my parents. Those poor unfortunate women were entrusted with my life. They were to show me love. The poor nuns . . ." She fell silent. It was as if she didn't want to remember what her words were evoking.

She then got up from the bed, walked to the record player and put on a different record.

"This is Floria Tosca!" she called out.

I stood and watched her sing along with the voice on the record player.

"You wouldn't know Puccini from Verdi, would you now? In the name of God, how would you know? What kind of schooling could you have got anyway? I don't suppose you had much of a chance in any case, had you now? Can you hear this? You've no sense as to what I'm talking about, do you?"

"No, ma'am. I don't."

"How could you? You only know about going to the pictures and imitating all those Americans who sing on the wireless. If you've nothing to say, don't say it."

I was shaking in my shoes and didn't know if I should turn and leave the room or not.

"What's your name?"

"Gabriel," I answered.

"Gabriel?"

"Yes, ma'am."

"Gabriel what?"

"Walsh. Gabriel Walsh, ma'am."

"My breakfast wasn't left lying about this morning, was it?"

"No, ma'am. I brought it right away."

"You did?"

"Yes."

"What time do you come to work?"

"Six o'clock, ma'am."

"That's early."

"Yes, ma'am."

"What does your father do?"

"Nothin'."

"Nothing? No job?"

"No, ma'am. He used to be in the British Army."

"Poor man." She then reached for a piece of toast on the plate in front of her and purposely mumbled loud enough for me to hear. "Life, it's confusing when you don't understand it and it's lonely when you do."

What she meant by that I wasn't sure and with nothing else to say I turned and retreated from the room.

* * *

Mrs. Ruth Houghton Axe, a small and slightly rotund woman, tapped on the door and entered Maggie's room. I had just returned to retrieve the breakfast tray.

Mrs. Axe had a smile on her face and looked exceptionally well dressed, wearing an expensive-looking two-piece suit.

"Good morning, Margarita! Good morning!" she said as if she was addressing both Miss Sheridan and me at the same time.

I was holding the breakfast tray and was about to exit the room.

"The phones in the hotel are out of order this morning. So I couldn't ring. Sorry!" Mrs. Axe said gleefully.

"Yes, yes!" Miss Sheridan responded with a joy in her voice I had not previously heard. "Have you heard from Emerson?" she added without missing a beat.

I stood awkwardly and looked towards Miss Sheridan as if to get permission to leave but she made a signal with her hand which I interpreted was for me to stay exactly where I was.

Mrs. Axe then walked towards the window and looked out towards Stephen's Green.

"Emerson?" she said.

"Yes."

"He called last night. Not happy that I extended my stay. I told him I'd be back on the weekend."

In one of her rambling monologues Miss Sheridan had previously told me Emerson Axe was a descendant of the ninth Attorney General of the United States and a master chess player as well as a fencing champion when he was at Harvard. The couple headed a large investment house in New York City and lived in a real castle in Tarrytown near New York. Miss Sheridan had spent many years with the Axes touring Europe and America, attending opera festivals and operatic contests. Sometimes she served as a judge in certain parts of Europe and as often as not Mr. and Mrs. Axe would accompany her on such artistic adventures. Most of the time they were in New York and all three of them rarely missed an opera season at the Metropolitan Opera house there. La Margarita, as Mrs. Axe called Miss Sheridan, spent most winters in the huge castle that overlooked the Hudson River. The castle stood on top of a hill surrounded by sixty acres.

"How is Emerson?" Miss Sheridan asked.

"Oh, the truth about Emerson is he's got more patience than understanding. I on the other hand have more understanding than patience. If you were to ask me which of the two concepts I prefer, I'd have to say the person with the patience is better off."

"You don't say so, for God's sakes!" Miss Sheridan responded as she looked over at me.

"You know why I think that, Margarita? If you don't know, I'll tell you."

"Please do."

"I'll try anyway. The person with patience doesn't need understanding. He or she can just as easily be contented waiting for things or someone to change. Whereas the person with only understanding, I'm afraid to say, gets frustrated and even angry."

"What's wrong with that?" Miss Sheridan asked.

"Well, it's my way of thinking that, if you only understand without having patience, you're very likely to end up alone.

And annoyed at everything most of the time. I'm glad Emerson has patience. I really am."

"Husbands are that way, I suppose," Miss Sheridan said as she walked across the floor and entered the bathroom.

"Mine is anyway. But he's not too happy about my trip," Mrs. Axe called after her with a laugh.

I moved towards the door. Just as I did Miss Sheridan stuck her head out of the bathroom door and signalled again for me to stay where I was. I went back and put the tray down. My arms were aching. Mrs. Axe remained at the window observing the grey Dublin morning. She then turned back to me as if she knew me.

"What's the weather today?" she asked.

"Prepare for sunshine," I said.

"Is that true?"

"I never think about it, to be honest with ya." I was about to pick up the breakfast tray again when a yell came from the bathroom.

"Say *you*. Not *ya* if you please!"

Mrs. Axe laughed out loud.

Miss Sheridan's voice bellowed out again from the bathroom. "Gabriel has five sisters and three brothers but he's as much of an orphan as I am if you ask me!"

"Is that so?" Mrs. Axe asked as she turned around as if to get a better look at me.

"Can't you tell by looking at him, Ruth?"

Feeling a bit tortured, I turned with the breakfast tray and was about to leave the room when Miss Sheridan came out of the bathroom.

"Do you know how Gabriel got the job here?"

"No."

I was now more embarrassed than ever before.

"He was walking by the hotel one day when he smelled the food cooking. He asked the hall porter if he could work here. Can you imagine? What was it? Chicken? Roast beef? He was drawn in because of the odour that was pouring out onto the street. He smelled the food cooking and his nose brought him in to ask for a job! It must have been coming up from the grate on Kildare Street. I've often walked into the whiffs myself."

"Is that true, Gabriel?" Mrs. Axe asked me, holding back a laugh.

"Didn't you tell me you'd never had chicken in your house, Gabriel?" said Miss Sheridan.

"I did."

Mrs. Axe laughed a bit louder. "You smelled the chicken and you got the job?"

"Ah, somethin' like that, ma'am."

"If he doesn't watch out he'll end up like half of the poor fellows who walk around Dublin with weak legs and flat feet," Miss Sheridan said.

"Who are you talking about, Maggie?" Mrs. Axe asked.

"The waiters who work in this hotel! Haven't you seen them?"

"I haven't noticed. They appear to be very nice."

"Gosh, I wish I could say they were as nice as some of the waiters I've met in other parts of the world."

"You only say that because they're Irish and you're Irish, Maggie."

"I only say it because a lot of them are Dubliners who make fun of everyone they meet. They judge and complain as if they're paying their own wages. Country people are not as fast with the gab if you ask me. God almighty, they don't know how well off they are here! Years ago half the servant girls who worked in Dublin came up from the countryside.

They were treated so harshly many of them became nuns and spent the rest of their lives in a convent. More than a few entered the convent for other reasons as well. Maybe it was better than marrying a –" She stopped and looked at me. "I take that back. I'm only joking. They were all unfortunate. Gabriel, what do we call the Dubliners? What are they called by country people like myself from Castlebar, County Mayo?"

"Jackeens," I answered.

"Jackeens is right. That's the name!" She laughed as if she was remembering something very personal. "*Jackeens!*" she said again, only louder as if to underline the word. "They got the name because during the Troubles most Dubliners didn't want to break with the English Crown. The English flag, the Union Jack as it is called, was a comfortable symbol for the Dublin people. Being wrapped in the Union Jack was important in those days. It might have been, if you ask me. It might have been. Ruth, this lad here, his own father signed up with the English army when he was still wet behind the ears and the same age. Off he went to France and nearly had his head blown off as well as a few other things. But what was he to do at the time? I don't know and I suppose I'll never know. Do you know what I'm attempting to say, Ruth, my dear and beloved friend, American that you are?"

Mrs. Axe clapped her hands as if applauding Maggie's performance. "Yes! Yes! Maggie from Mayo! You might have a point but if I don't eat soon you might have to bury me in this country."

Both women laughed out loud and I sensed the time had at last come for me to leave the room. I firmly gripped the breakfast tray, turned and walked out the door.

* * *

The next morning when I came to retrieve Maggie's breakfast tray I discovered she wasn't in her room. It was the first time she had not been there when I came back to collect the tray. As on every other morning, the light was still on in the bathroom and an opera of some sort was playing on her record player. The breakfast tray was on the side table near the window and only half the breakfast was eaten. I was half-tempted to look under the bed in case Maggie had gone looking for something she might have dropped. Maybe by hiding under the bed, I thought to myself, she is playing a part from one of the operas she has appeared in when she was younger. After instantly dismissing my errant imagination, I decided to grab the tray and leave the room. As I walked towards the door it opened in front of me. I lost my balance and the contents of the breakfast tray went crashing to the floor.

As I instinctively bent down to gather the items, I was immediately assisted by Maggie.

"A good thing I'm not hungry this morning, isn't it?" she said as she placed the teapot on the tray.

I didn't have a chance to apologise before Fifth Floor Mary came rushing to the door. "Are ye all right there?" she said as she got down on her hands and knees and began wiping everything with a large hand-towel.

As Mary was tidying up the mess Maggie put her hand to her shoulder. "Go back to Kerry, Mary! Everything's fine! Come back later when I'm out for the day."

Mary secured her glasses on her nose and departed in a hurry.

As I was about to leave with the tray, Maggie called to me. "I left to go to early Mass this morning. The priest, who is a close friend of mine, was saying his last Mass here. He's off to America. A parish in New Jersey! I don't go to church as often I should. I confess to him every so often and he's been generous with absolution. Should you ever leave Ireland, Gabriel, make sure you remember everything the Holy Church taught you." She then went to her record player and turned it off. "I leave this thing on most of time so that Mary from Kerry doesn't come in and rummage about in my things."

I took that as a signal to leave the room.

* * *

On Grafton Street outside Bewley's coffee shop I saw her reflection in the window. A big black hat with a feather sticking out of it appeared and descended on the window like a large bird coming out of the sky. She was standing behind me, holding the arm of another woman. I felt a mixture of shock and embarrassment and wondered if she'd recognise me out of my waiter's outfit. Without the breakfast tray I felt naked. I closed my eyes and hoped she hadn't seen me. I didn't know what to say or do or which way to turn. I bent my head down and tried to sneak away. As I stepped away from the other onlookers who were also admiring the big coffee machine and the man in white making the coffee, I heard my name.

"Gabriel!" Her voice was clear and unmistakable.

I was spotted. It was embarrassing. I turned around to face Miss Sheridan and Mrs. Axe. "Goodness gracious!" she said, looking pleasantly surprised.

"Pleased to meet you again, Gabriel," Mrs. Axe said with an even broader smile.

Both women seemed to be enjoying their time on Grafton Street.

"Your day off?" Mrs. Axe asked me.

"Yes, ma'am. I'm off every second Saturday."

"That's why we had cold tea and toast this morning, Ruth," Margaret Sheridan said with half a laugh in her voice.

"Mine wasn't so bad," Mrs. Axe said. "You live around here, Gabriel?" she added with the curiosity of a tourist.

"About three miles away," I said.

"He lives up near Kilmainham Gaol," Miss Sheridan said.

"Kilmainham Gaol?"

"Now I only said he lives near it. Not in it!"

"I'm sure he doesn't live in it!" Mrs. Axe said, laughing almost out loud.

"It was where they put the patriots and tortured and killed them," Miss Sheridan volunteered.

As I turned to move away from Bewley's window, Miss Sheridan put her hand to my jacket collar. "Doesn't your poor mother have a needle and thread?" she asked, as she looked me over.

"It's just a bit worn," Mrs. Axe said, doing her best to hold back a laugh. "He looks fine if you ask me!"

Miss Sheridan wouldn't let go. "My God, how can you possibly walk straight in those shoes?" she asked me, tapping the toe of my foot with hers.

I wanted to fall back into Bewley's window and be ground up with the coffee beans that were rolling about in the grinder.

"That shirt you're wearing must have belonged to your grandfather, Gabriel. Am I right about that?"

The shirt I was wearing had belonged to someone but I didn't know who. Most likely it had a few owners before me. My mother picked it up in the Iveagh market on Francis Street a week earlier. The Iveagh market opposite the Tivo cinema was a huge open arena where, among other things, the clothes from Dublin's dead were sold third hand. Sometimes the smell of death lingered in the clothing.

"Goodbye, ma'am," I said and turned to go.

But as I walked on the women walked with me.

The doors of the shops on Grafton Street were beautifully painted and the displays in the windows offered glimpses into a world of fantasy without charging admission. To be noticed on Grafton Street was almost as important as being seen at Mass on a Sunday morning. The street smelled expensive. The latest fashions – clothes, jewellery and shoes – were on display in the shop windows. Some of the shops had uniformed doormen who were quick to open the doors when customers were entering or exiting the premises. They also signalled to anyone who looked poor to keep walking.

About a minute or two later Miss Sheridan and Mrs. Axe stopped to look in the window of a men's clothing store.

"Go inside," Mrs. Axe said.

I didn't know what she meant.

"Go!" Miss Sheridan said as she pushed me towards the interior of the shop.

I had never been in such a place.

They went about the task of outfitting me from head to toe. Rack after rack of clothing was brought in from the back room of the shop to find what Miss Sheridan and Mrs. Axe thought suited me. After about forty-five minutes of testing and fitting, standing and sitting, I was transformed from what can only be described as a tattered scarecrow into a person who might have been born with a silver spoon in his mouth. My feet were measured for new shoes and my legs were fitted to the trousers I was being poured into. Something about the smell of new clothes and the way they looked and felt on me made me forget where I was. Had the clothes been a set of wings I couldn't have felt any higher.

After stumbling over at least six ways of saying thank-you, I said goodbye to Mrs. Axe and Margaret Sheridan.

With my old clothes in a large brown-paper bag, I walked further down Grafton Street until I came to the entrance of Trinity College – the old bastion of education that had been planted there four hundred years ago. It was a place where Catholics didn't go. I stopped and looked at the students entering and exiting the place. For years I'd wondered what was inside the gates of the place. I had always been afraid to even look in. I had heard or read that the Protestant Queen Elizabeth the First of England built it and only rich Protestants were allowed to go there and it was no place for Catholics. The Catholic Church wouldn't allow any Catholic to go there anyway. If you were a working-class Catholic you weren't supposed to even notice it when you walked by. It was one of those strange things that we were brought up with. "Don't look at that big Protestant hole when you're taking the bus at College Green." It was very much like a sin. Whatever it was, it had only to do with Protestants – off limits to Catholics for so long most didn't believe it actually existed even though it was the most obvious building in all of Dublin. Trinity College was a world within a world. Word was that the fellas who were in there wore grey suits with white collars. Protestant ministers, who drank, smoked and were married as well. I stopped at the entrance with my new suit and walked in. While walking past a wastepaper basket I dropped the brown-paper bag with my old clothes into it. Nobody paid any attention to me. I walked around the yard holding my new overcoat on my arm. I was in the middle of the place related to some part of the Protestant Hell. I didn't see anyone walking about with cloven feet. Young people wearing coloured scarves and expensive clothes were dashing every which way. Some were riding bicycles. Someone asked me where the library and the science department were. I looked at two girls walking across the yard and I noticed them looking back at me. I wanted to talk to them but I was afraid they'd discover me. I walked all around the campus until I was back again at the front gate. I felt so good I decided to walk home and half of Dublin, if they wanted to, could look at me in my new clothes.

I liked my new suit so much I sometimes slept in it. One day, after holding on to it as if it was my skin, I decided not to wear it to work. Afterwards when I went looking for it in the bedroom my mother told me she had pawned it and bought food to feed the rest of the family for a week. Sitting at the dinner table that night I watched the rest of my family chewing away on boiled bacon and cabbage. When the plates were licked clean my father apologised to me and thanked me for the meal. My mother promised to get the suit out of the pawnshop before my seventeenth birthday. I knew she wouldn't be able to afford it if I lived to be ninety. I assured her I'd make enough money in the Shelbourne to redeem the suit myself.

◄○►

And then everything changed.

Two weeks later Miss Sheridan entered the tea lounge. She walked to the table next to the big window, sat down and within a second called to me. I crossed the room and stood in front of her.

"Did you say anything to your mother or father about what we discussed?" she asked.

"I mentioned it."

"What did they say?"

"Nothing."

"Nothing?"

"Nobody paid any attention. That's the way it is in my house."

Miss Sheridan turned her head towards the window and then looked back at me. "Sit and never mind about your job. I'll talk to the manager. Sit."

I sat down on the chair in front of her.

"I don't suppose you've ever been to Mayo?" Her voice became sad and soft when she mentioned her home county. "I remember when I first went to London. You've never been there, have you?"

"No, ma'am."

"When I was younger I spent a lot of time in London. Covent Garden."

The way I heard it was 'Convent Garden'.

"That's a magnificent –" She paused. "You wouldn't know much about Covent Garden, would you?"

"No, ma'am."

"I didn't think you would. How could you?"

"You were in a convent for nuns?"

Miss Sheridan laughed. "Heavens no! Very few nuns there! Very few! Actually there is an opera about nuns. The Carmelites! *Les Dialogues des Carmelites!* A young girl who wants to escape the reality of death joins a convent in France. Of course there's no escaping that. Heaven knows I've identified with that character more than once. Young people shouldn't have to be thinking about such things." She stopped again and took a deep breath. I got the feeling she had wandered into talking about something she wasn't comfortable with.

At the same time Quinn came back from his break. He saw me sitting and called out, "Walsh? Get up out a that!" He then approached me. "What're ya sittin' there for?" he asked in disbelief. "You're still workin'."

Miss Sheridan snapped her fingers at him. "Get me a pot of tea, please," she said in very firm voice, more to get rid of him than anything else.

Quinn made an about-face and retreated to the kitchen.

Miss Sheridan then handed me a thick envelope. "Have your mother and father look all this over and get back to me."

I took the papers from her and attempted to stand up.

"Sit!"

I sat down again.

"Is everything clear to you now? You know about getting your passport and all that other paper stuff, don't you?"

"Yes," I said.

"Don't do anything foolish now. For Heaven's sakes please don't do anything that would embarrass me. I've asked Ruth to do this favour. I think you'll be pleased. And tell your mother not to worry."

"Yes, ma'am."

Quinn arrived with the tea.

Miss Sheridan put her hand to the teapot. "Oh, I meant to ask you for toast as well. Would you get some for me, please?"

Quinn withdrew to the kitchen. Miss Sheridan laughed out loud.

"When you go home inform your parents again about all this," she said to me.

She poured her tea and began to drink. Then Quinn arrived with the order of toast. He also put the bill in front of her.

She picked the bill up and looked it over. "Put this on my account, would you? And don't ask me to sign for it. You know who I am. God knows I've been here often enough to own the place."

Quinn walked away with bill in hand.

Ignoring the toast, Miss Sheridan took a few more sips of tea.

"I'll talk to you in the morning," she then said.

She stood up and walked away.

My eyes were still on her as she left the room.

Quinn approached me. "What was goin' on there? Sittin' down havin' tea with a customer? You'll be sacked."

I remained seated and picked up the envelope Miss Sheridan had given me.

"What's in that?" Quinn asked me.

I looked inside the envelope. I knew my parents wouldn't be able to make head or tail of the documents inside.

"I think I'm going to be leavin' this job," I said.

Quinn looked at me. "Where will ya go?"

"First I have to tell my mother and father, and then I'll tell you."

But I didn't tell them that day, nor the next. Then the third day, when I still hadn't produced any results, Maggie and Mrs. Axe took the documents back from me and asked me to bring my mother to the Shelbourne to sign them there.

* * *

My two younger brothers Larry and Ger were on their knees, bent over a chair with their chins in their hands, praying along with my mother, when I came home from work that evening.

My mother prayed: *"Holy Mary, Mother of God, pray for us sinners now and at the hour of our death, amen."*

My brothers took the cue and continued. *"Hail Mary, full of grace, the Lord is with Thee, blessed art Thou amongst women, and blessed is the fruit of Thy womb, Jesus."*

I walked to the kitchen and poured myself a cup of tea. Two hens were pecking away outside the kitchen door. I wondered to myself if they knew how to say the rosary.

My mother called to me, "Aren't you goin' to kneel down and say the rosary?"

I couldn't find it in my mind or body at that hour to kneel down on the cold floor.

"I'm too tired, Ma. I've been workin' all day. I was up too early this mornin' and I can't even think straight."

"You won't pray for an ounce of luck!"

I poured myself another cup of tea.

"*Glory be to the Father and to the Son and to the Holy Ghost, amen.*"

My mother knows God is looking forward to seeing her, I thought. He'll call out her name! 'Molly MacDonald Walsh, you're one of the very best women in Ireland. You've done everything the way you were supposed to and you've prayed night and day and you've made your children pray night and day and I've a big book that has every prayer listed that you ever said and every prayer that your children and mother and father said. Everything is listed here and you haven't missed praying on one holy day. That man you married isn't as good a repenter as yourself, but I know you've done your best to show him the way. Every angel here since the beginning of goodness is singing hymns for you and all the holy people like you.'

Molly got up off her knees and sat down on the chair in front of the fireplace. "Go to bed, you two!" she yelled at my two younger brothers.

Larry and Ger went leaping up the staircase to the bedroom.

"Where's Daddy?" I asked.

"He's upstairs asleep where he always is. Nothin' can wake him. I wish to God he'd find a bit of work."

213

I went up the stairs, sneaked into the small bedroom and saw the shape of my father lying in bed with the bed-sheet covering his head. An old photograph of his parents hung on the wall across from his bed. In the picture my grandparents were very well dressed. My grandfather had a watch attached to a gold chain in his vest pocket. He wore a stiff white shirt collar and tie. He looked well off and content. My grandmother, standing next to him with her hand on his arm, looked handsome and happy as well. Her appearance was very un-Irish. Her dark eyes and black curly hair made her appear Spanish. She wasn't the typical fair-skinned Irish girl. The old photo of my grandparents seemed not only locked in time but in a state of serenity and happiness. I couldn't understand it. How could two members of my family be in the same place at the same time and be happy and smiling? The faded photograph apparently served as a constant reminder to my father that he had come from a class above the woman he married.

A minute or so later my father sensed I was standing in the room and pulled the sheet from his head and got out of the bed. I was surprised to see that he was fully dressed. I walked out of the room and went back downstairs. Almost immediately Paddy came down, holding up his trousers with one hand. He looked me over as he walked to the back door. I was expecting him to growl at me, but he didn't.

"What happened to you?" he said as he passed me.

"Nothin' happened to me," I answered.

He then made his way to the toilet in the back yard.

For some inexplicable reason my mother had fallen silent. It was as if she was waiting for some heavenly reward for having just said the rosary. But she always gave me the feeling that she didn't trust silence and after about ten seconds of it she turned to me.

"He'll never be dead while you're alive."

I was going to reply or defend myself in some way but I was distracted by hearing the hens cackling outside in the back yard. It seemed that they too wanted to be part of whatever was going on inside the house. I sat quietly sipping on my tea.

My father had vanished into the outhouse. It was the only place where there was a bit of privacy. Everybody at one time or another retreated to the crapper. I read most of my comic books there. It also had a lock on the door. I often stayed in the latrine longer than I should have, just to be away from what went on in the house. The toilet had no light or heat but it was quiet and peaceful. In the past it was a good place to hide when Father Devine dropped by or when my mother wanted me to join in and say the rosary. Our neighbours' outhouse was attached to ours. Only a thin wall separated the toilets back to back. Many times when I was sitting quietly reading my comic books I'd hear my neighbours behind me using the toilet. When they talked to themselves I'd hear that as well.

My mother turned back to me. "Were ya workin' late?" she asked me.

"No. I went to visit Rita."

"How is she?"

"Good."

"That Steven brings home a good wage. His poor mother nearly lost her mind when he married me daughter. She didn't even want her to sleep with him on the first night of their marriage! Talk about a mother's love! That went beyond the beyond. D'ya know about that?"

I was about to answer when my sister Phyllis came in. She looked at me sitting at the table and made a noise with her mouth. It wasn't a word but a sound of some kind. I think my new suit bothered her. She then made her way across the room and was about to go out to the toilet in the back when my mother called to her.

"Your father's out there!"

Phyllis turned around, made a few more sounds of disgust and walked up the stairs to her bedroom without saying a word.

From the window I could see my father standing outside in the yard. He was looking down at the hens and delaying his return to the house. I imagined for a minute that he was thinking of jumping over the wall and leaving us and the house for good. My mother turned and looked out and saw him also. His back was to her.

After a minute or two more he returned and faced me in the centre of the room.

"Ya know, I still think ya robbed them clothes you're wearin'," he said.

I knew he was joking by the smile on his face.

"Shut up and leave him alone!" my mother yelled. "You've got the bloody runs again – that's all that moves you nowadays."

I looked at my mother, hoping she'd sense that I didn't want to hear her complain again about my father. I had heard everything that was to be said about him a hundred times and I didn't want to hear any more.

My father then made his way back up the stairs without saying a word.

"I'll never understand that man at all," my mother mumbled under her breath.

"What man?" I asked, thinking she was referring to somebody in the newspaper.

"What man? Your father!" she called out, making sure she was heard all the way up in the bedroom. "Why does he sleep half his life away?"

I didn't answer. I could feel the tension growing.

"He wouldn't get out of the bed when I started the rosary. He heard me and he kept lyin' up there. The man's got no faith if you ask me."

At that point I saw my father's head stick out from the top of the stairs.

"Faith? Good Christ! I've an overdose of faith!"

My mother retreated to the newspaper but she continued to talk back. "I've seen you sleep through Christmas morning and not get up for Mass."

"We'd nothin' to eat. What was there to get up for?"

"Didn't Father Devine give us a turkey? Didn't he?"

"Turkey? The damn smelly bird was so blue it must have died from mortal sin. It smelled even worse after you cooked it. Didn't you have to throw it out?"

My mother seemed caught. She remembered the blue turkey that Father Divine gave her that Christmas. I remembered it as well. The smell of it cooking made us all sick. When it was put on the table it was blue and green and smelly. My mother packed it into a brown-paper bag and left it outside in the back yard.

My sister Phyllis yelled from her bedroom, "Will you two stop fighting? Stop it! You're always fighting. Everybody on the street knows what goes on in this house. Can't you stop for once?"

My father then called down to me, "You'd be better off in the British army, Gabriel!"

Quietness returned. Paddy was back in bed with his head covered. Molly sat in front of the fireplace and warmed her hands. I got up from the table, walked to the old gramophone near the front door and put on one of our two screechy and cracked records.

"You may talk and sing and boast about your Fenians and your clans,

And how the boys from County Cork beat up the Black and Tans . . ."

My mother turned from the fireplace. "In the name of Jesus, turn that thing off! You'll wake up half the street!"

The record came to a halt of its own accord. I hadn't wound it up enough to play the entire record.

All was quiet and silent again. My mother remained at the fireplace reading the newspaper. I sat back down at the table.

"I have to talk to you about somethin', Ma," I said.

"What is it, son?" she answered without taking her eyes off the paper.

"It's about me."

"What about you, son?" She was glued to the newspaper. The fire was still strong and she spread herself out as much as she could in front of it.

"I have to ask you somethin'."

"What d'ya want to ask me?"

"Didn't I tell you about Margaret Burke Sheridan?"

"What about her?"

"I had a long talk with her and her friend the other night."

"What friend?"

"Mrs. Axe. She's American and Margaret Sheridan's best friend."

"Is that what kept you from comin' home and sayin' the rosary?"

"They asked me to go for tea."

"Tea? Are you not sick of tea? Don't you drink your fill of that in the hotel?"

"Yes."

"What did ya eat?"

"Chicken."

"Chicken?"

"Yes."

"Who bought it?"

"Mrs. Axe."

"Mrs. Axe? Who's that?"

"Miss Sheridan's friend."

"An' she bought you chicken?"

"I had potatoes as well. And peas."

"Is that what you want to tell me? You had chicken that somebody bought for you? Is that it? You'd a mouthful of peas as well and a gob of potatoes on top? Is that what I'm supposed to be listenin' to?"

"No."

"Well, leave me alone then."

"They asked me somethin' and I said yes."

"What in God's name are you talkin' about'?"

"They asked me if I wanted to leave my job at the hotel."

"In the name of Jesus, don't tell me that!" My mother looked terrified at the prospect. "After all this time without a bit of work? Remember what happened when you had that nice little job at Jury's hotel? That was one of the nicest jobs for a young fella in Dublin. You were tricked out of that one. Don't for the love of the Virgin Mary leave your job at the Shelbourne! It's only gettin' back on your feet you are. Leave your poor little lovely job? I hope you told them you wouldn't?"

"I told them I would."

"What? What are you sayin' to me? Are you out of your mind? What will you do for a bit of employment if you leave the job? Have you any idea where you'd get another bit of employment? Weren't you traipsin' around for months before you got the job at the Shelbourne? Gabriel, don't start up actin' like your father!"

"Leave him out of it!" I shouted back.

"Close your gob and don't talk back to me like that. I only mentioned it because you've a nice job."

"I wouldn't have to be bothered with a job here because I'd go to America."

"What?"

"I could go to America."

"America? What are ya talkin' about?"

"I'm talkin' about goin' to America."

"Like your bloody father was in Borneo and India and all them places? You're thinkin' of joinin' up in some bloody foreign army or what? You're out of your head if you ask me. Them days in the British army are gone. Remember, son, you've got a job now. You're workin'."

"I'd leave my job."

"That nice clean job you have? Are you daft?"

"If I was in America I wouldn't be daft, would I?"

"How can you go to America in the first place?"

"Margaret Sheridan and Mrs. Axe said they'd help me – if you went along with it."

"Me? I'm just your poor old mother. What can I do?"

"You'd have to agree and sign the papers."

"Papers? What friggin'papers are ya blabberin' about?"

"I'm too young to sign them myself. I need you or my father to sign them."

"You're pullin' me leg now, son, that is what you're doin'. All this codology that goes on because you've a few pennies in your pocket. Leave your poor mother alone."

"Mrs. Axe said I could go if it was all right with you."

"All right with me? How would I know what to do about that?"

"Miss Sheridan wants to meet you and talk about it."

"Talk and meet me? Who y'talkin' about?"

"Miss Sheridan."

"Margaret Burke Sheridan?"

"Yes. Will you do it?"

"Do what?"

"Will you meet her and tell her it's okay for me to go?"

"Go? Go? Go where?"

"Can't ya listen to me for a minute! I've been talkin' the tongue out of my mouth. I said America a hundred friggin' times. America!"

"You want to leave home?"

"I want to go to New York."

"New York?"

"That's where Mrs. Axe lives."

"Mrs. Axe? Who in Christ's name is that?"

"Didn't I tell you before?"

"Ya didn't. If ya did I don't remember."

"She's a friend of Maggie Sheridan and she's a friend of mine now."

"You know her as well?"

"I've known her since she came over to visit Miss Sheridan. I served them their breakfast for weeks. Mrs. Axe is an important woman."

"Important? Important? Who told you that?"

"Margaret Sheridan."

"Are you daft? Are you out of your head?"

"I'm serious. I want to go. I want to go. Will you come and meet Miss Sheridan and Mrs. Axe?"

"Me? Your mother?"

"Yes."

"I'm just a poor old woman! What are you askin' me to do a thing like that for? I only go to Mass and the turf depot to put a bit of heat into the fireplace for all of you. And him upstairs as well."

"You're my mother!"

"You have a father too! I'll wake him up now."

"No. Don't. Let him sleep."

"That's all he does for Jaysus's sakes! He'll be asleep when the bells of Hell are chiming for him and mark me words he won't hear them!"

"Can't you come and meet them tomorrow?"

"Where could I meet them?"

"At the hotel."

By now I was beginning to get tired with the back and forth blather with my mother. She didn't seem to want to know or hear what I was trying to get across to her.

After twenty seconds or so, she spoke again.

"I don't want to see a son of mine go so far away."

I almost fell off the chair I was sitting on.

"I'm not signin' papers," my mother said, without looking back at me, in a very calm voice that made me believe she had heard every word I said. "At the hotel?" she asked calmly.

"Yes, Ma, at the hotel: the place where I've been workin' for the last twelve months."

She raised her head and looked up at the holy statue on the mantelpiece above her and began to talk to it. "The Shelbourne Hotel? Me? You want me to meet Margaret Sheridan at the Shelbourne Hotel?"

I thought she was waiting for the statue to answer her back. My mother remained silent until I finally realised she was waiting for me to respond.

"Can you?" I asked with as much love and affection I could muster.

With a loud voice my mother turned back towards me. "*No, I will not*!" she bellowed.

I thought I had fallen under a bus or something when she said that. I was frightened and nervous and angry at the same time. "You have to, Ma, you have to!"

My mother's voice was now firm and resolved. "I'm not meetin' anyone at the Shelbourne Hotel. No, I'm not. I'm just a poor old woman. What d'ya mean askin' me the likes of that!"

"I want to leave here, Mother. D'you hear me? I'm goin' to go away. I want to go. You have to sign the papers for me!"

My mother then got down on her knees in front of the fireplace and started praying: "*Our Father who art in Heaven, hallowed be Thy name. Thy kingdom come. Thy will be done on Earth as it is in Heaven . . .*"

I lost my temper and screamed so loud the flames in the fireplace blew in a different direction. "*Will ya stop prayin'?*" I yelled.

Molly got up off her knees and banged her hand down heavy on the wooden table where I was sitting. "I won't! I won't! I'll say me prayers and ask God for forgiveness!" she yelled back at me.

At that point my father appeared at the head of the stairs. He was as angry as I had ever seen him. He wasn't happy with his sleep being disturbed and he hated loud voices from as far back as I could remember.

"What in the name of Christ is goin' on? Can't ya close your bloody traps for once? Can't ya?"

I was taken aback to hear him complain out loud. I hadn't heard him raise his voice in years.

My mother turned towards him. "You come down here and talk to your son! Come down now and do what any decent father would do! Tell him we won't sign no papers!"

My father walked down the stairs and stood next to the fireplace and stared into the burning coal as if he was contemplating jumping into the fire.

Paddy Walsh carried with him an air of futility and he appeared to be living more on instinct than on any kind of promise. A quietness of movement and an almost constant silence accompanied him throughout the course of his day. Like a mouse living under a floorboard or under the staircase he cherished bits and pieces of small comforts that came his way, such as his walks into the city and his time in Stephen's Green where he would sit on a bench, stretch out his legs, light up a self-rolled cigarette and stare at the ducks swimming around in the pond.

As he stared into the fireplace I imagined he was thinking he was sitting on his favourite bench in Stephen's Green, away from all family matters. To my surprise he turned to me with the warmest and tenderest look on his face. For a second or two I thought he had vanished into his own childhood.

"What papers are ya talkin' about, son?" he asked me.

"To go to America. Maggie Sheridan is arranging it."

He then stood up and walked closer to me. I could see he hadn't shaved in at least a few days. His detached shirt collar was half-attached to his striped shirt. He stood in his stocking feet. He then to my great surprise began to sing in a calm low voice:

"It's a long way to Tipperary; it's a long way to go!
It's a long way to Tipperary to the sweetest girl I know!"

He appeared to be celebrating. I hadn't seen him look so happy in years. As he looked at me I sensed he was happy for me. I was doing something he was happy about. He then stepped past my mother and went into the kitchen with a smile on his face and poured himself a cup of tea. He came back into the living room and sat down at the fireplace.

My mother watched him like a hawk. It was as if she was seeing him all over again. Her expression had changed and she not only appeared more relaxed she actually looked, at least in my eyes, younger. With the exception of when she was praying or at Mass, I had never seen her look so peaceful and calm. It was a place she had not inhabited for a very long time. It was as if night had come early and she had changed back to the world of silence and darkness where she could feel the touch of his back against hers. She observed my father as if he was somebody she knew a long time ago. Maybe when he was younger he broke out in song when things were bad. Maybe this is what attracted her to him in the first place.

While he sipped on his tea, he sang in a whispering voice. He didn't at all appear to be bothered by anything. It seemed he was happy for me, even if it was only for a moment. Maybe he had broken down and come out of himself this evening when he sensed that I was going to break away from the cage or the prison he felt himself and his family to be in. He sang and mumbled song after song as if he was meeting a challenge in a soldierly way.

My mother was taken off guard. Something about her looked happy and excited as well. Did something happen that made her look forward to being back in bed with him again this very night? Did she forget all about her journey and sacrifices that were to take her to Heaven? Did the thought of lying down again with my father erase any of her day-time thinking? Her eyes were no longer glancing with despair. Was it because the circle of our lives had been broken? Had my plans to leave home and country changed the sense of futility that we had all lived in for so long?

My father sat down in front of the fireplace and sang away.

"Ah when the war was on we'd rashers in the pan,
Now that's it all over we've only bread and jam!
Oh right you are, right you are!
Right you are, me jolly good soldier, right you are!"

He then faced me with a fresh look of confidence. "Gabriel, remember, I was all over the bloody globe. We taught the Jerries a few things, let me tell ya! Bombs, bullets, bayonets every damn thing they threw at us – mustard gas, the bloody lot. Ah, the poor bastards. All of them! All of us!" He snapped his suspenders and added, "What time do you want me to meet them on Thursday?"

My mother called out, "You're lettin' him go? Is that it?"

"He wants to." He looked at me again. "Don't you?"

"Yes," I said.

"I'll meet them tomorrow or whenever ya want me to," he said. "I'll sign the papers and you can go whenever you want."

I felt my blood boiling over and I didn't know what to do with my own feelings so I walked upstairs to the bedroom.

As I readied myself for bed I heard my mother downstairs in the living room talking again. "You needn't go, Paddy. I'll do it. I'll do it. I'll wear somethin' decent and I'll go with him."

A few seconds later I heard the old gramophone playing the only other record in the house. It was a bit hard to separate the words from the scratching on the record but it played nevertheless.

"I love you like I've never loved before,
Since first I saw you on the village green . . ."

The record stopped. There was a silence downstairs. It was unusual, strange, but it was beautiful. I fell asleep.

* * *

After looking in every cupboard and behind every holy picture in the house my mother remembered that she had long ago deposited her corset under the mattress on her bed. In a flurry of enthusiasm she lifted up the mattress and between it and the half-rotten bedsprings she pulled out what she said was her long-lost corset. The corset was a strange-looking garment that might have been pink in colour years earlier but now looked like a slice of bread a week old. Following a brief inspection of the silky and faded garment my mother sat down on the bed and held it close to her chest. The look on her face said she had found some long-lost part of herself. She kissed the faded material and mumbled a few inaudible words. I couldn't tell if the words were prayers or some kind of greeting but whatever they were it was clear that my mother was happier than I had seen her in a long time.

As I was about to ask why she was smiling, she called out, "Too many children!"

I wasn't sure if she was talking to me or to the old corset. She stood up from the bed and raised her voice. "That's what caused me belly to stick out like this – too many children!"

Without saying another word she walked out of the bedroom and made her way down the small flight of stairs. I followed her.

In no more than a second or two my mother was out of her working apron and standing in front of a mirror with the corset in hand. It had been quite some time since I had seen her out of her working apron. I might have been seven years old at the time. When I looked at her now standing in front of the mirror with the old corset I was embarrassed and frightened. Added to the image of my mother losing her mind was the old brownish silky slip she was wearing. It could only be described as a crucifixion cloth. Following a very short inspection in the mirror, my mother began the task of wrapping the corset around her body, or as far as I could tell, imprisoning her body in it. The corset was something like a horse-halter with straps, buckles and laces hanging from it. Her stockings which she had tied above her knees with twine had holes in them. Her shoes had broken laces as well.

After a prolonged struggle with the corset, she struggled into a black dress.

She finally turned towards me with a contented look on her face. By now she looked like a loose sack of coal.

"I'll go to Mass in Clarendon Street. It's near Saint Stephen's Green," she said.

"Can you wear something different?" I asked as she tightened the piece of twine that held up one of her stockings.

"Are ya ashamed of your poor old mother? Is that it? Is that it? You're ashamed of your own mother and the way I dress. Isn't that so?"

"I was hoping you'd wear something different, that's all I'm asking. And you don't have to be wearing them stockings with the twine holding them up either."

"I'll wear what I like. If you don't want me to go with ya, I won't."

"Don't you have another dress?" I asked in as warm and encouraging a voice as I could muster.

"I do have another dress and you know where it is? D'ya know?"

"No."

"It's in the pawnshop. I had to pawn it to put a bit of coal in the fireplace last time you were all freezin' here. You don't remember that, do you?"

"No."

"Well, me dress is in the pawnshop and I've no money to get it out. If your father had a bit of employment it would be a different matter. And why in the name of God isn't he here with you right now? He's the one who should be goin' to this meeting. Ya can talk all ya want and be ashamed all ya want but I'm still your mother and that's the way God made it. You mingle with all them toffs at the hotel but you're still me son and don't you forget it."

"I'm only asking you to take a look at yourself in the mirror and see that the dress doesn't fit you. That's all I'm asking. You look like you can't breathe."

My mother was silent again. She continued to twist her body of many shapes into the old dress. "This used to fit me. I wore it at your brother's funeral, God rest his soul."

"Where'd you get it?"

"The dress?"

"Yes."

"It belonged to Mrs. Burn's sister who went off to become a nun in Africa. After spreading the Holy Word of God she died over there without ever coming back. God rest her soul as well." My mother quickly made the Sign of the Cross and pressed her gums together. I then noticed that she didn't have her false teeth in her mouth. A billow of panic came over me. The sight of my mother without her false teeth made me forget about how peculiar she looked in the black dress. I gaped around the room at all the holy pictures. Saint Francis of Assisi. Saint Joseph. Saint Bridget. Saint Patrick with his big shepherd's stick. The Blessed Virgin standing on a globe of the world in her bare feet and a nice long blue dress. The Sacred Heart of Jesus with his open wounds and bleeding heart. A picture of the Pope was looking on as well. They were all looking down at my mother and me. For a second or two I wondered if they knew where my mother's false teeth were. I was tempted to kneel down and pray to all of them at once and ask them if they'd seen the teeth. Sometimes my mother left her teeth in front of the holy pictures when she knelt on the floor to say the rosary. Other times she wrapped her rosary beads around the teeth and left them under the picture of the Sacred Heart. They weren't in her mouth lately because we hadn't had meat to eat in more than two weeks. Where are they? I silently cried to myself. I was going to pray to Saint Francis of Assisi but I didn't know what prayer to offer up to him. He was beatified and canonised and famous for helping feed birds and rabbits and was the saint of Poverty. He wouldn't help me find them because he wasn't in favour of anybody being too comfortable. He might have been happy to know that my mother lost her false teeth. He gave up his own privileged life to lead a life of poverty. He'd tell me to go out and find a bird with a broken wing or something. Saint Patrick would have told me not to worry because we were all Christians anyway and we'd be allowed into Heaven with or without teeth. My house was filled with pictures of saints but none of them from Dublin and I didn't think they'd know or care much about what went on here. The picture of the Sacred Heart of Jesus would be the only one who could help me find the teeth.

I became so terrified of my mother leaving the house without her teeth I began to mutter, "Jesus, help me find the teeth! Please help me, God! Tell me where my mother's false teeth are and I'll pray for two months without stopping. I'll go to Mass and Communion for the next six years!" I was shaking and mumbling at the same time.

My mother noticed me walking about the room. "What are ya lookin' for?"

I was afraid to tell her. I didn't want her to know that I was worried about her not having her false teeth as well as wearing the old dress she was still struggling with. I walked out into the small kitchen, thinking she might have taken her teeth out there when she was toiling over the stove. I looked everywhere. I looked in the sink. I looked in the oven.

"What's the matter with you, Gabriel?" she called.

"Do you have your things?"

"What things?" she answered back with a conquering grin on her face after finally managing to become one with the dress. "Me teeth?"

"Yes."

"I don't have any teeth," she said, surprising me with her lack of concern.

"I mean your false teeth."

She went over to the fireplace, took the top off the black kettle, put her hand into it and retrieved her false teeth.

"What were you doin'? Cookin' them?" I asked.

"I was cleanin' them. You never know when we'll get a bit of steak or roast beef and I'll need them." Then she added mockingly, "That'll be the day. Won't it, son?"

"What were you trying to do? Boil the teeth?"

"The black kettle is the best place for them when they're not in me mouth."

She then walked over to the mirror next to the statue of the Sacred Heart, mumbled a few words and placed the teeth in her mouth. I then noticed that the zipper at the back of her dress was broken. My mother reached back to get a grip on it but as she pulled the thing tore away from the dress.

"Ah lovin' Jesus! Will ya look what's happened to me now?" she yelled.

I watched in silent horror and wondered what she was going to do about the broken zipper. The saints were still looking down at us but there was no sign of help. After a second or two my mother walked to the mantelpiece and found a safety pin.

"Will ya pin me dress at the back?" she asked me.

She handed me the safety pin and I wanted to stick it in my head. I stood behind her, attempting to pin the back of her dress as she adjusted the false teeth in her mouth.

"Ma?"

"What is it, son?"

"I don't think the dress fits you."

"Never mind if it fits me or not. I don't care. It's all I've got. If you don't want me to wear it, I won't go. Go out and find your father. See what he has to wear. The arse is fallin' out of his trousers and he hasn't a decent shoe to put on his foot. Go on now and find him if you want." She walked away from me before I had a chance to close the pin that was now sticking out at the back of her neck and dress. She stood in the middle of the room, looking like an old lost goose. As she contemplated her reflection in the nearby mirror, she climbed out of the dress and began to untie the laces on the corset that was under it. As she untied, her belly began to appear more and more. It got bigger and bigger each time she loosened one of the laces on the corset.

I felt my life was about to end. I walked up to her as she continued to uncase herself. "Please, Mother, do you have to wear that thing?"

She yelled back at me, "I wore this before you were born. It fitted me when I was a young girl. Long before I met your father." She now stood half-wrapped in the corset. String and straps were hanging in every direction.

I impulsively grabbed one of the strings that was hanging down at the back of the corset and yelled, "Wear somethin' else! I can't stand it! I can't stand lookin' at you dressed up in that thing!"

My mother turned to me with one hand holding in her protruding belly and the other holding onto the corset. "I'll wear what I like. Don't you want them people to see where you come from? I'm your poor mother and this is me. I won't go anywhere if you carry on."

I stepped away from her and sat down on the old armchair and closed my eyes. I tried to look back at the sixteen years of my life with her to see or even imagine her to be any different than she was this day, standing in front of me in her old and tattered clothes. I was tired and exhausted from arguing and began to accept that I had almost no influence over my mother. She would say what she wanted and do what she wanted and she'd wear what she wanted. Wanting her to look and behave like someone different was not going to happen. I now had to accept fully that this was my mother, in all her rags, twines and false teeth. The old dress and the worn-out shoes and the stockings with holes in them was my mother. This had always been my mother even if I never wanted to believe or accept it. She was from another time and she would neither change nor let go of her past. While I sat back in the armchair searching for some kind of warm emotional connection, the sound of my mother's voice brought me back to the present reality.

"Will ya stop actin' like Paddy Walsh and put the kettle on for a cup of tea!"

The mention of my father meant that my mother was losing her patience with me and perhaps herself as well. Why she always resorted to using my father's full name was a bit of a mystery to me. I think in some ways it kept her distanced from him.

I went into the tiny kitchen, filled the pot with water and placed it on the gas stove. I then got two cups and saucers from the wooden cupboard and put them on the table my mother was sitting at in the front room. As I put the cup and saucer in front of her she looked up at me but didn't say a word. Having run out of anything else to say I started to walk about the room.

"What are ya lookin' for now?" my mother calmly asked.

"I left my coat here last night and it's gone."

She smiled. "I took it upstairs. It was cold last night in case you don't remember."

I ran up the stairs in a hurry and found my coat spread across the bed I slept in.

* * *

In less than half an hour my mother and I got off the bus and headed up Grafton Street. Grafton Street, a five-minute walk from the Shelbourne Hotel. It was also just around the corner from the Mansion House, the home of Dublin's Lord Mayor. My mother seemed to be off in her own world as she slowly walked alongside me along the glamorous street with its shop windows full of luxurious displays, its uniformed doormen, its well-heeled clientele. I didn't want to disturb her or complain but I felt I had to.

"You're walkin' very slow, Ma."

"Ah, leave me alone and don't you be bothered with telling me how to walk. Go on. Walk ahead of me if you want," she said, pulling at the old corset she'd insisted on wearing.

"If you could walk a bit faster, Ma?" I said impatiently.

"In the name of God will ya leave me alone! I'm doin' me best! I'm thinkin' I'll have to go somewhere else before I go to the hotel."

"Where?" For a moment or two I thought my mother was going to run away from me. The fear that we weren't that close to each other again surfaced in my mind and I couldn't keep my teeth from rattling. "What are you talkin' about, Ma?"

My mother didn't answer but she increased her pace considerably.

When we got to Clarendon Street, a side lane off Grafton Street, my mother decided she had to stop at the nearby church to say a few prayers. I was hoping she'd walk past the church but she didn't. She stopped and blessed herself.

"I want to go in here and light a candle for you, son."

I was getting closer to fainting. I worried that once she entered the church she might stay there all day praying to every saint she had known since childhood. Clarendon Street had twice as many statues and paintings of Jesus and his apostles as any church in Dublin. It was also my mother's favourite church to do the Stations of the Cross. She even knew the cleaning women who swept the floor and polished the marble on the altar. If she got into a conversation with any one of them I knew we'd be late for our appointment. I kept my mouth shut and entered the church with her.

Inside the church my mother Molly instantly blessed herself and knelt down in subservience. After a few minutes she got up from her kneeling position and walked from painting to painting of Jesus carrying his cross to Calvary. It was something she had done every day of her life since at least the age of seven. At each depiction of Jesus my mother made the Sign of the Cross and mumbled a few prayers to herself. She talked and prayed to the paintings as if they were human. She then moved to the image of Jesus where the blood was dripping from his head. A terrible expression of pain came upon her face. It was as if the man in the picture had come alive and had recognised my mother. This was the man she knew most. The way Jesus shouldered the cross mesmerised my mother. The admiration expressed in her eyes seemed liberating. The suffering and the depiction of torture seemed reassuring to her as she stared upwards.

I remained seated in the back row while my mother walked up to the altar to light a candle. After dropping a few pennies into the collection box she took a small white candle and lit it from one that was still holding a flame. The flickering light from the candle reflected off the brown painted robes of Saint Francis of Assisi. My mother looked up into the painted eyes of the saint and called out something that sounded half-hymn and half-lament. I had never experienced so directly the sense of concentration and commitment she had for the Church and its saints and statues. It was as though she knew them personally and talked to them as if they were old friends who knew everything about her life. I realised there and then that being my mother was only part of her existence. She had another family. They had blue, purple and golden robes and they were made of stone. She believed, lived and belonged in this world of devotion. Christ with the thorns on his head and the blood dripping down his face was an image she identified with. The burden of carrying the cross on his shoulder was a reminder and an inspiration to her. I had not known the depth or meaning of the religion I was born into.

I had been schooled in the religion of pain and self-denial. If I hurt my knees after falling on the ground or if my lip bled from bumping into a table or a chair I'd try to convince myself that I didn't feel the pain. When I walked around in my bare feet in the cold during winter I'd believe that the saints in Heaven were watching me and cheering me on. When it came to having thoughts in my head, particularly sensual or pleasurable ones, simple and innocent as they might be, I'd slap my forehead to chase and frighten them away. But today when I saw my mother in the chapel I felt that there was something to my religion that I had not been taught. I sensed a strange peace while observing her losing all sense of her physical self. She seemed more at home in this house of worship than she did in our own little house in Inchicore. She was at peace. As she moved from each image and statue of the saints and Jesus she talked as if they were all friends meeting again. In some ways I was proud and envious at the same time. I felt a tinge of jealousy towards the statues and the religious paintings.

After making the Sign of the Cross my mother turned away from the altar and walked down the aisle again towards me.

"You're blessed now, Gabriel," she said with a warm smile on her face. She felt better and for the first time in a very long time I began to relax.

* * *

As we stood outside the front door of the Shelbourne Hotel, Molly without notice abruptly turned and ran across the street. I wanted to faint and watched in wonderment and confusion. My mother had left me again at the time I wanted to leave her the most. I watched her make her way through the traffic as she held her hat on her head with one hand and pointed her way with the other in the direction of Stephen's Green. When she got to the other side of the street she walked into the Green. I followed her but she kept walking until she stopped and sat down on a bench in front of the duck pond. She was staring straight out across the park, not looking at anything in particular. I sat down next to her and kept my eyes on the ducks swimming about in the pond. I was afraid to open my mouth in case she'd argue with me. I was even more afraid that she'd jump up from the bench and leave me there alone.

The complicated feelings I had for my mother ran through my veins faster than the blood in them. I thought of the countless times she and I had sat silently side by side throughout my life. In my early childhood she gave me strange looks that made me feel she didn't really know me. At least half the time I thought she was thinking I had done something bad or wrong. There were times when I wished I *had* done something that annoyed her or made her angry. I was willing to confess to anything. Even to things I didn't do or have any part in. I felt if I was accused of having dropped one of the many holy statues in the house or of making a scratch in her mahogany crucifix that was nailed on the inside of the kitchen door, I'd at least be able to talk to her and she'd get to know me better. Sometimes, sitting by the fireplace, she'd look at me as if to ask me what I was doing sitting next to her. But, for the most part, whenever I sat next to her around the fireplace or at the dinner table she appeared not to notice me. Sometimes I thought it was because she didn't have enough wood or coal to heap on the fire or enough food to feed the whole family. Or maybe because there wasn't enough paraffin oil left in the dented tin can to put in the lamps that lighted the house, or any coins to insert into the gas meter to keep the gaslight on so that we could all see each other's faces around the table at night and have boiled potatoes for dinner and stale fried bread for breakfast. But deep down I sensed there was something awry in our relationship.

I don't know how many times I tried to get her attention and tell her about myself – such as when I sewed buttons on my trousers or stitched a hole in the pocket of my jacket or brought home the odd turnip and head of cabbage that rolled off the vegetable cart on the street. Whenever I attempted to declare my presence to her I was ignored and my small accomplishments were dismissed. Occasionally I witnessed my mother complimenting my brothers and sisters and placing an affectionate hand on their heads as if she was blessing and anointing them as her own. At times I would purposefully sit close to her and hope she'd place her hand on my head and make a connection that made me feel I belonged to her and that our small house and the world outside were safe places to live in. But she never did. There were times when I even thought that I was an invisible person and didn't exist at all. When she sensed that I wanted to make contact with her she'd begin humming a song she knew in her childhood. Singing songs from her youth was a habit she had whenever she felt angry or annoyed at my father. The songs more than likely took her back to a time when she was young, free, innocent and single. Certainly a time before she met my father and got married. The most frequent thing she ever said to me, and she said it repeatedly was: "You're just like him! You're the spitting image of your father!" Of her ten children – I was the seventh – biology and timing dictated that I was the child who most resembled my father. Apparently I not only looked like him, I evidently – and unbeknownst to myself – behaved like him as well. Unwittingly I kept alive for my mother what she considered to be the biggest regret and mistake of her life: her marriage. As far as she was concerned I was too much like the man she married and my existence and presence appeared to impede her evolving retreat from him. Whatever the dynamics of it all, I had always felt I was born into enemy territory.

We sat there on the bench together without a word, both of us staring ahead at the duck pond. At last I ventured to look at her. She had an expression on her face as if the Sacrament of Communion was stuck to the roof of her mouth. I didn't recognise her. I thought she was leaving the world, with everybody and me in it. Her face was so expressionless I got frightened.

I called out, "Ma?"

In a second she was changed again. She had come back from somewhere holy and religious. The devotion she had for the Church had conquered her and it wasn't going to let her go. She started to pray again. "Dear Father above, come down and take me from here. I'm not able for it any more. I'm not able for it!" This day like every other day of her life she was surrendering to the reality of her existence and appeared not to be present in front of me at all. After what might have been the longest minute in the history of my life she spoke again.

"I'm not goin' in that place. I'm too poor a woman. Don't ask me, son. Don't ask me. I'm too poor a woman."

I didn't answer. I couldn't answer. I began to cry. The meeting at the hotel was the most important time of my sixteen-year-old life and I was beginning to think it wasn't going to happen. It appeared the world was about to fall in on me at the moment I wanted it to change the most.

"Go over, son, and ask the ladies if they'd mind comin' over here. Would ya do that? Would ya do that for me?"

I stopped sobbing for a moment or two and began to seek a way to make my mother comfortable.

"Ma, can't you just come over just for a minute?"

"I'm sorry, son. I'm sorry. Look at me. Look at the ould dress I'm wearing. I'd be better off sittin' here," she said, wiping away the tears from her eyes. She then started to talk without looking directly at me. "I'm sorry, son. I'm sorry! I couldn't go into the hotel with what I'm wearin'. Look at me. Look how I look."

By this time I had forgotten about the old dress and the twine holding up her stockings. Her face seemed open and clear and her eyes were actually sparkling. She didn't look poor any more. The old hat on her head actually looked good on her. It had a small bird's feather sticking out of it and it even looked fashionable. I saw for the first time why my father had married her.

"You look fine, Ma. Why don't you come over to the hotel and we can get the meeting over with. Nobody's going to say a word one way or the other about anything."

She leaned back and looked directly at me. "I'd be better off sittin' here, son," she said again.

I placed my hand on top of her head to comfort her. "I'll ask them to come over here."

"You don't mind, son?"

"No, Ma. Wait here."

I walked across the street to the hotel.

Mrs. Axe and Maggie Sheridan were sitting in the tea lounge. Maggie stood up as if she was prompted by a moment in some tragic opera.

"Well, well, well," she mumbled rapidly and theatrically. She took advantage of any and every moment to display her larger-than-life personality.

Sitting next to her Mrs. Axe broke into a laugh as if she was enjoying Maggie's performance. Margaret Sheridan and Ruth Axe were naturally complementary. I'd never seen them not smiling when they were in each other's company. Maggie and I had a different kind of relationship. In my own pain, sadness and loneliness she felt some kind of kinship and redemption. My silent pain might have been loud to her. At

241

least it surfaced in my eyes and manner no matter how much I ignored or attempted to deny its existence. I didn't acknowledge loneliness as something strange or unnatural. It was as much a part of me as the colour of my eyes. Loneliness in the Walsh family seemed to be inherited. Maggie Sheridan knew and understood it. Her life forged this kind of ability to express and share something that only pain and loneliness can allow and design. I lived in my own clouds and shadows and only somebody who had travelled that road more and longer than I had could understand it.

As I stood in front of the two women I blurted out in as nervous a voice as I ever remembered having, "My mother won't come in!"

"What's the matter?" Mrs. Axe asked.

"I don't know. She came to the front door but she wouldn't come in. I think she's afraid."

"Afraid of what?"

"She's just afraid. She's not used to places like this. She feels bad or something."

"Poor woman! I know exactly what she's going through. Where is she now?" Maggie responded.

I quickly answered. "She's across the street in Stephen's Green."

Mrs. Axe stood up and walked to the window. "I think we should go over there to her," she said.

"I absolutely agree, Ruth. Why don't we?" Miss Sheridan got up from her chair and started walking towards the lobby.

When we got to the park bench my mother was sitting as still as any of the statues in the park and was staring at the ducks swimming about in the pond. I looked down at her.

"Ma. We're here. This is my ma," I said to the ladies. "Ma, this is Miss Sheridan and Mrs. Axe."

My mother turned her eyes away from the pond and made eye contact with the two women. For a moment or two it seemed like no one knew what to say.

Then Mrs. Axe broke the silence.

"Well, finally we meet," she said with her usual warm smile. "I hope we didn't keep you waiting too long."

In full voice my mother answered, "Not at all, ma'am. I wasn't feeling well. I'm sorry I couldn't step into the hotel to meet you, ma'am."

"Ah, it's a lot better out here in the fresh air," Mrs. Axe responded with an encouraging tone in her voice. She and Maggie then sat down next to Molly.

"So you're Gabriel's mother?" Mrs. Axe reached out and held my mother's hand as if to reassure her that everything was okay.

Miss Sheridan was carrying a small bouquet of flowers and a photo album. The flowers she handed to my mother. "For you, Mrs. Walsh."

My mother looked the two elegantly dressed women over. "Are ya goin' to take him to America?" she asked with a tinge of nervous laughter in her voice.

Mrs. Axe and Miss Sheridan joined her and encouraged the laughter. I sensed the ice melting and sat down on the garden railing next to the bench.

"You always wanted to go to America, son, didn't ya?" my mother said as she looked towards me.

"I think it wouldn't do him any harm if he got the chance to go to America," Miss Sheridan responded. "Mrs. Axe will make sure that everything will be fine with him." She then showed a few photos of herself to my mother. "This is me. I don't suppose you ever heard of me. Anyway, why should you? I'm from Mayo."

"Me son's been talkin' about you from mornin' till night, ma'am."

"I hope he said nice things," Mrs. Axe quickly said.

"Oh, he did! He'd only say nice things, ma'am!"

"I'm sorry we didn't meet you sooner, Mrs. Walsh," said Miss Sheridan. "It's really my fault. You should have more time to consider everything. I've been running back and forth and I hardly know where I am these days. I promise you Gabriel will not be disappointed if he decides to go to New York."

My mother then looked at me with tears in her eyes. By the way she was biting her lower lip I knew she was holding back a lot of pain.

"D'ya want to go, son? Are ya sure about it now? Tell your mother the truth! You want to leave home?" She leaned over the bench as if to emphasise the importance of the question, not just for herself but for me as well. She then stretched out her arm and placed her hand on mine. Her fingers and skin were all worn-out looking. Her fingernails had little black specks of dirt under them.

I took her hand in mine. I realised then that I hadn't been this close to my mother in years and the experience of holding her hand was something I wasn't used to. My mother's hands had been her energy and her wings all her life. She depended on them like no other part of her body. What she wasn't able to achieve with her mind or even with her prayers she could accomplish with her hands. All her life she scrubbed, cleaned and washed everything in front of her with them. The front steps of Hume Street Hospital had been washed and scrubbed by my mother's hands when she was just a young girl. Her hands had held each other in prayer as she believed that she would find peace and complete happiness when they could no longer be joined and held together in prayer. They were so over-used and depended on, they looked like they had never been cared for or held affectionately.

As I continued to hold onto my mother's hand I became afraid to look at her. I felt I would back off and run away crying and even frightened. As I struggled to hold back my feelings, my mother's voice broke into my thoughts.

"You want to leave home, son? Tell me now."

"Yes. I do."

"You're sure of that, son?"

"Yes, I am. I am."

My mother turned to Maggie and Mrs. Axe. "What will he do there, ma'am?"

"He'll work a bit and study also," said Mrs. Axe. "He's smart. I won't let him be idle. I'll make sure he's happy. I'll make him write to you as well. You'll write to your mother, won't you, Gabriel?"

"I will," I said.

"I'll make sure he does," Miss Sheridan added supportively, obviously wanting to reassure my mother. "America is not the end of the world any more. I'm back and forth myself several times a year."

About that exact moment everybody stopped talking. The silence was awkward and I sensed that nobody wanted to ask the next important question without some kind of encouragement. I began to think they were all waiting for me to say something.

"Will you sign the papers, Ma?" I asked.

Mrs. Axe took the papers out of her briefcase and handed them to Molly. My mother looked them over but, because she wasn't used to looking at any kind of documentation, she retreated somewhat nervously. She really didn't know what she was looking at or what to read. After what seemed like a forever pause, she turned back to Mrs. Axe.

"Where am I to sign, ma'am?" she asked.

Mrs. Axe pointed to a line on the form. My mother made a wide scribble and in a second her name was signed. She repeated the effort in another few places pointed out by Mrs. Axe. Mrs. Axe now had the permission to be my legal guardian when I got to America.

Mrs. Axe gave my mother a hug.

Miss Sheridan leaned in and kissed my mother on the top of her head. She then sang out in an aria-like voice: *"Shouldn't we all go get a cup of tea or something?"*

"Good idea, Maggie. Let's go to the Russell," Mrs. Axe said and got up from the bench.

The four of us then walked across Stephen's Green in the direction of Harcourt Street.

By the time we got to the front door of the Russell Hotel my mother had become more relaxed. When she sat down in the armchair in the tea lounge she was even smiling.

She turned to me. "Remember, Gabriel, son. You only learned your religion. I earned mine."

For a moment or two there was a silence around the table. It was obvious that Maggie and Mrs. Axe heard what my mother had said to me. Yet somehow it appeared as if she was talking to them. Perhaps telling them something about herself – or me for that matter. In seconds Miss Sheridan had taken a bundle of photographs out of her handbag and was pointing to photos of herself in various operatic roles.

"Here I am. Aida. La Scala. Look here – here I am at Covent Garden – Madama Butterfly. I won't tell you the wonderful things Puccini said about me because you've probably never heard of him anyway." She hummed a few bars of "*Un Bel Di*" and to humour my mother she showed her photo after photo of various parts she played in the many operas she'd appeared in at an earlier time in her life. Some of them looked funny to my mother and she laughed out loud. Maggie and my mother seemed to connect to each other. I got the feeling that Maggie knew my mother more and better than I did. She seemed to identify with her on some level. Maggie from Mayo and Molly from Carlow were not unlike sisters who had travelled different roads early in their lives. Maggie had no children and Molly might have had too many. Maggie had seen the world and Molly hadn't. Maggie had lived a good part of her life in the fantasy world of opera and, at least in her recent past, her deepest reality was when she performed on the stage. Molly's life seemed to be trapped in a never-ending opera in which she was the tragic heroine, with no end or intermissions. Today both Maggie and Molly were enjoying themselves like I had never seen before.

My mother's eyes lit up and she began to sing alongside Maggie. They were the oddest of duets. My mother was singing like a lark: "*Ah, why did he part and break the heart of his girl from Donegal!*"

Mrs. Axe said, "Don't forget *Carmen*, Maggie!"

Maggie instantly broke into the famous aria from *Carmen*.

My mother was beside herself. "Ah God help us all!" she said and rested.

Maggie then took from her photo collection a more private and personal photograph. She showed it to my mother. It was a photograph of a very lonely and sad-looking teenage girl. Maggie looked no more than fifteen years of age in the photo.

"Me. Maggie from Mayo. If it hadn't been for a nun at the convent I'd still be in Castlebar. God, I think I was the loneliest person on earth in those days. Jesus, I shiver when I think about it. I don't know what it is about life or about any of us that live here under God's watchful eye but if you get cursed and painted with the stripe of loneliness you might as well jump off O'Connell's Bridge."

"Don't forget to mention Marconi, Maggie," Mrs. Axe quickly interjected.

"Marconi? Yes. Mr. Marconi. When he was married to that lovely Galway woman he sent me to Italy for voice training. He gave me the real push in life. God knows I couldn't afford it. Nobody in Ireland had any money in those days."

My mother handed the photographs back to Miss Sheridan. "Lovely, ma'am, lovely pictures. To be truthful I have read a bit about you once or twice in the paper some years ago."

Miss Sheridan smiled. She was pleased. "You did?"

"Yes, ma'am. You're a friend of Dev's? Is that true?"

Maggie leaned back in her seat as if she was about to take centre stage and sing another aria. "Éamon de Valera? I know him well. Another lonely man, if you ask me. No father in his life and only his poor mother to take care of him. She brought him up well, if you ask me. All the things he did for Ireland! Talking back to Churchill when this poor country was hardly more than a stable for horses. Mr. Churchill wanted to drive us all into the sea because we broke the back of the Empire. He was a fine man in his own right but he didn't really know the Irish character. In my estimation he underestimated de Valera." Maggie then turned towards my mother. "If you ever need a bit of assistance from Dev, let me know."

"Yes, call up the President and tell him Maggie sent you," Mrs. Axe said laughingly.

"I'm very serious, Ruth," Miss Sheridan said quickly and defensively. "I know the man well and I've been in his corner most of my life."

My mother then joined in. "If I'd known how nice you two ladies were I'd a worn a decent dress today."

"I asked you to wear a different dress, Ma," I quickly put in.

"Ah, I know you did. But if I'd a known sooner I'd a taken me dress out of the pawnshop and wore it." Pleasure had taken hold of Molly and she was not shy in expressing her feelings. She'd even changed the way her hat was on her head. She'd moved it and made it look more open and fun-like.

"Gabriel will send you a dress from New York, won't you, Gabriel?" Mrs. Axe said with a sense of instruction in her voice.

"I hope he does, I hope he does."

"He'll send you many things, Mrs. Walsh," said Miss Sheridan. "I'll make sure he keeps up with you and lets you know everything."

My mother looked at me again. This time she stared at me longer than I had ever remembered her looking at me. I had to turn away from her eyes.

"Remember, Gabriel, you were always the first up for Mass. Not like the rest of the fellas on the street. He was so good at goin' to Mass I used to call him the Little Archbishop. The spittin' image of his father. His father will never be dead as long as Gabriel's alive. The spittin' image of Paddy, missus!"

"Paddy?"

"Me husband's name, ma'am."

I was hoping my mother wouldn't go on talking, but she did.

"Paddy hasn't worked in a month of Sunda's. He's a changed man since I first married him. I can tell you that, missus."

The two elegant women were then treated to a run-down on Paddy Walsh.

A few minutes later, my mother stood up. "Well, ma'am, have I done all you want of me?"

Mrs. Axe stood and, reaching over to my mother, hugged her tightly. "Yes. You have. You've been wonderful. I am delighted we met, be it late, short or whatever. And don't worry about Gabriel. He'll be fine, just fine. Won't you, Gabriel?"

I shook my head and held my mother's hand. I knew she wasn't feeling as strong as she was pretending. When I looked at her I could only see sadness in her eyes. Was her whole life meant to be such a struggle, I wondered to myself. Was there ever a time when she felt happy or content? She seemed unsure, even lost, and I felt sorry for both of us. I felt like I was choking on some mysterious feeling that had finally awakened between my mother and me. When I looked over at her I couldn't talk. I was afraid I'd say something that would make me want to stay. Molly looked at me with the same kind of confusion in her eyes. I wanted to tell her I loved and cared for her.

She eventually put her hand on my face. "I'm goin' to say a few prayers, Gabriel."

Miss Sheridan stood up and gave my mother a big hug. "God bless you," she said.

Molly turned from the table and walked out of the hotel. I stood pained, confused and even frightened. All of a sudden I felt I had now abandoned my mother and I wanted to grab hold of her and hug her and not let her go. For a few moments I wanted to confess to her that I was only teasing and testing her. I even wanted to admit that I was only playing a game and it was not a real situation I was in. Part of me wished the whole thing would go away. I wanted to erase the idea of leaving home from my mind. For as long as I could remember I'd wanted to leave home but as the impending reality became apparent my nerves began to shake my whole body. Whatever confidence I thought I had was leaking from all parts of me and, as my mother walked further away from me, I wanted to scream and tell her to come back and hold my hand and not to leave me standing alone with Miss Sheridan and Mrs. Axe.

As my mother walked further and further away from me, I felt deprived of breath and even had thoughts that I had finally hurt her in the worse way that I could, for what I thought she had done to me. I had felt abandoned and ignored by her since childhood and now I was exercising the opportunity to get some kind of revenge.

For years and years my mother used to humiliate me and everyone else in the family with her clothes and talk. We all wanted to run away from her when we met her on the street. She was always an embarrassment. But the struggle of surviving with so many children and with so little money was monumental. Her only means of remaining halfway sane was her religion. It encouraged her to accept the life of a martyr of some description. The deeper she fell into the struggle the more sacred she felt she was. Yet today she had found it in herself to put her love for me above everything else. Probably the hardest thing she had ever done in her life.

On the day that made it official that I was to be gone from her, I accepted the fact that she loved me. It was an unfamiliar feeling and I wasn't sure or confident enough to know that I could remain standing on my own two feet as Molly walked further and further away from me. I felt as if I was going to break down into little pieces of myself. For most of my years on earth I had wished and wanted to escape from where I lived and who I lived with. Since I lost my brother Nicholas I felt I had lost all connection to every other member of my family. There was a void and a division between us and it seemed to grow wider as we all grew older. What was now inside my head was a new uncertainty. A part of me was beginning to resist what I wished and dreamed for and somewhere in my mind I was trying to hold back from travelling into a future that was unknown and vague. The past was now reaching out to me as if to keep me from drowning altogether. A feeling ran through my blood and veins and it seemed out of control.

All of a sudden I wanted everybody I ever knew to pray for me. I was even wishing I could go to Mass and receive Communion and attend the Boys' Sodality and have the priest hear my Confession. I would promise not to sin again and I knew I would be pure and honest if I could still be a part of what I was planning on leaving behind. As I shivered with insecurity I began to wish that I could be with my old schoolmaster and the priest who slapped me when I was very young. The memory and familiarity of Confession and Communion would embrace and protect me from the uncertainty of my future.

I had not felt or sensed the bond that I was always seeking with my mother until the moment she agreed to part with me. As she walked into the distance she stopped, turned and looked back at me. I then began to cry and cry and thought of running away from the confused thoughts that were streaming through my head. The familiarity of loneliness was dominant. It was the strongest power I knew. Because of it I would embrace the pain that was always present in my family and in my home, as if it too was a close family member. Agony was not far away or out of my reach and at this hour it was becoming my closest companion. I was beginning to think that I didn't know what I really wanted and felt entangled in a web of guilt. Today my past was rendering me more isolated than ever before.

--<o>--

Mrs. Axe departed for America and Maggie remained alone at the hotel. I went there to say goodbye to a few friends I had worked with and was told by a workmate that Maggie was having dinner in the restaurant. I knew she was scheduled to depart for New York very soon, so I went to the dining room to let her know of my progress regarding my own eventual departure and to say goodbye to her.

It was early evening and the dining room was practically empty. Two waiters, in their formal serving outfits of black-tailed suits and white bow ties, stood at each end of the room like two lost penguins on a floating iceberg. As soon as I stepped into the room, Maggie, apparently at the end of her meal, saw me and beckoned to me with a curled finger. Because she was alone, the booth she was sitting in seemed to wrap around her like a big pair of brown leather wings. She was wearing one of her wide-brimmed hats that resembled an upside-down bird's nest. Part of her long blonde hair was hanging above one of her ears and she looked like she had got dressed up without inspecting herself in a mirror. This might have been because she had no place to go and nobody to meet. I had never, whenever I entered her room and served her breakfast, observed her inspecting her reflection in a mirror. She might not have wanted to see herself as she was in the present. In the past she was hailed as a prima donna and adored by thousands of people, particularly in Italy and Ireland. The Pope at one time even wanted to bestow her with the title of 'Countess' which she refused because of her affection for Irish history and all things Irish. Aristocracy of any kind didn't fit into Maggie's way of thinking. She always seemed to be attached to some kind of rebellion, be it her determination to carry on with her career since childhood or resistance against her vocal teachers in the past who advised her to slow down and relearn the intricacies of how to use her voice. County Mayo and Ireland in general were a constant in her life. Her years in Italy had formed her into a woman of the world with international and famous acquaintances. She was however known to be always carrying Ireland around with her as if it was part of her physical body or the definition of what she considered to be her soul. When Maggie spoke English it was with an Italian flair but an emotional sentiment that was uniquely Irish. If she felt she wasn't being listened to or understood she'd wave her hands in a demanding manner as though she was acting and singing in a Puccini or Verdi opera. Her speech and words were essentially half arias. With the exception of walking about Stephen's Green with her past and photo album under her arm, she rarely ventured outside the hotel. Several times since I'd known her she would be visited by a priest or an elderly nun she had known earlier in life. The few visitors she had more often than not came to praise her past and honour her for her achievements.

This early evening, sitting alone in the restaurant booth, she looked like a single passenger in a waiting room about to be transported to an unknown destination. Where she wanted to go, she might not have known herself. Maggie looked surprised when she saw me and smiled as I approached her.

With a tinge of self-consciousness I sat at the edge of the booth. I didn't know whether to say hello or goodbye and feared somewhat that she might chastise me for remaining silent. The two waiters noticed me as I sat down and wagged their heads with a sense that they approved of me being there but, knowing Maggie as they did, they did not dare approach the table. By now just about everybody I had worked with had heard I was soon to leave for America. In a precise and almost perfect gesture Maggie lifted the white linen napkin to her mouth and dabbed her lips with it. For a moment I thought she was showing me or telling me how to use a napkin. Always upon meeting her she was inclined to correct my speech or instruct me on how to behave, but never for a moment did I believe she meant to do anything other than be positive and helpful.

"You're here to say goodbye to everybody?" she said without looking directly at me.

"I am, but I didn't know you were having dinner," I responded, hoping I'd said the right thing.

She began to laugh. "Life's not always about having breakfast," she said.

I laughed as well. I knew what she was saying and I definitely related to it.

"I'm away from here on Thursday. It took me two days to pack that trunk of mine. Everything I own on this earth is packed into it."

I didn't know what to say. I knew what she meant about the huge trunk that occupied the centre of her room. The thing was so big one could easily have slept it in. The labels pasted on it reflected Maggie's travelling lifestyle. The name of every country in Europe as well as the United States was a map of her uprooted and nomadic life. When the image of the large trunk left my mind it dawned on me to tell her how much my mother had enjoyed meeting her and Mrs. Axe. I had only got out about five words when she waved her hand at me.

"Don't! Don't! Your poor unfortunate mother! God bless her! She's had a tough life. She's the backbone of Ireland if you ask me."

I didn't know how to express agreement with her so I kept quiet.

"You are in many ways very fortunate, Gabriel. I, on the other hand, got so caught up with this damn animal called art I found I could never satisfy it or be satisfied by it. No matter what I said or did or sang. No matter how much I trained and practised. I was always reaching out and up and stretching my guts and heart out, trying to appease some little echo that said I could have a better tone or a more perfect way of caressing a note when I opened my mouth to sing. Of course I don't sing any more. Sometimes I imagine I do, but I don't. I really can't, but don't tell anyone that. The truth is half the time I just wanted to puke it all out of me and drop it on the floor like a cow scuttering in a field after eating too much grass." She reached for the glass of water on the table and refreshed her throat. She looked directly at me and asked me a question I didn't know how to answer. "What do you say to that?"

I was shy about being put on the spot. As I listened to Maggie I felt myself floating about the room in an odd kind of Limbo. I thought I was in some kind of dream or something. I looked about the restaurant and observed the familiarity of it. Numerous times I had carried dishes and walked in and out of the place. I could still hear the voices of some of the waiters I worked with. I had met all kinds of people who sat and ate here every day. Sitting in a booth with Maggie Sheridan at the beginning of dinner hour made me feel insecure and it was not a place I had ever imagined myself being in.

Maggie sensed I was feeling awkward and had retreated into myself. As if to wake me up she began to talk again. "Anyway that's how I feel sometimes! I'm not telling you a lie. My problem is everything is stuck and living in my veins and throat and I can't puke it out when I want to be alone with myself. I'm never able to be by myself. I was always glued to this wish of wanting to make my voice the best part of my existence and that is a fatal flaw if I ever had one or heard of one." She paused, looked in her purse that was on the table in front of her and took out her room key. She held it tightly in her right hand, and then continued. "I suppose that's what being an artist is." After a moment she stood up, wiped her lips again with the linen napkin and dropped it on the table. "Gabriel, be good now and mind yourself. I'm going upstairs to finish packing and I hate it."

She slowly walked out of the restaurant. When she passed from view I noticed the red lipstick marks on the napkin and wondered how the hotel laundry would react to it when it was delivered for cleaning.

* * *

Early on the morning of my departure I lay awake and imagined my father and mother lying asleep in their sagging bed. The bedspring had yet again been repaired with strands of rope and wire but the centre of the spring and mattress still almost touched the floor. I imagined them sleeping back to back. Did they know what each other looked like, I wondered? Neither seemed to want to acknowledge the life they lived together. They were attached by some mixture of pain and pleasure and didn't know how to separate. Pain was such a silent darkness you could depend on it more than the weather. Paddy and Molly walked in different directions and often passed each other on the street without saying hello or 'How are you?' It was as if they didn't want to acknowledge or accept the fact that they knew each other. Both of them lived with an unspoken sense of regret and neither seemed to be able to identify what it was exactly. In spite of the obvious estrangement, night with its absence of light brought my parents back to each other for a brief period of time. In a world of one shade and colour they probably made an effort to soften their mutual resentment. The bed apparently was the only place they could be together without wanting to kill each other.

As they lay in their private slumber I sensed a detachment in myself and for a moment or two I believed I didn't exist at all. I wasn't sure where the feeling came from. Was it because of Paddy and Molly? In many ways I didn't know my own mother and father. I felt the same way about my brothers and sisters. In that very cold and early morning I thought again that something was very wrong with the way we lived.

Downstairs in the small cold front room my polished shoes with my new pair of socks awaited my feet. My sister Rita had given the socks to me as a going-away present. The night before, my mother made me a corn-beef sandwich on white bread and left it in the box outside on the windowsill overnight. The cold moist air would keep it from going stale when I took it on my journey. I lay awake in my small slim cot trying to imagine myself getting up, getting dressed and leaving home. There was a bus, a train and a boat out there waiting to take me away. The dark cold winter morning wasn't encouraging me to get out of bed either. As I thought of myself standing on the deck of the big ship that was to sail from Cobh in Cork to New York, I heard my father snoring again and I began to think that maybe he was only pretending to be asleep. Maybe he didn't want to say goodbye and wish me luck. I tightened the blanket on the bed around my body to keep me from shivering.

Nobody in the family except Rita had paid attention when I told them I was going away to America. They might have thought I was making it up.

In many ways my father's indifference was more painful than my mother's obsession with religion. It was easy to react and respond to Molly because it was clear what she was doing and thinking. My father seemed to never be fully present. I knew him more by the smell of his clothes than the sound of his voice. His clothes smelled of tobacco and dampness. He appeared to live as if nothing took place in his life. I thought to myself that a wife and children were things that happened to my father when he lost his way or didn't know what he was doing and the responsibilities of children were a punishment that he silently resented. Maybe it had more to do with not knowing how to like anything or anybody after he came back from the war. Paddy gave the impression that he was constantly amazed when he looked at us. I think he questioned himself about who we were and who he was and how and why we were all related to each other. My father appeared to be always waiting for something or someone in Ireland to reach out to him and tell him he was welcome and that he belonged and was cared for and appreciated. Somehow that simple wish eluded him and he retreated so far into himself that he became practically invisible. For most of the day Paddy went about life, indifferent to the point where he was his one and only companion. Contentment was something he saw in his teacup when he sat down for a cup of tea. As far as my mother was concerned, pleasure was not just a curse but an enemy. Only Heaven was to be looked forward to and the only way to get there was to live a life as wretched, dismal and unhappy as possible. My father left home at about the same age as I was now. I wondered if he ever had second thoughts about it. Did he begrudge my Uncle John his simpler life in Ireland? Did he resent the fact that he was not very welcome when he came back home years earlier? Was it that he had regrets about marrying my mother? Was that the fatal mortal wound to his heart and soul? Was my mother the bane of his existence? Was it that in Ireland he could do very little about his plight? As a soldier he felt empowered to enforce. As a father he felt awkward, perhaps useless. How could he enforce fatherhood? In some respects all of his children were what post-war Ireland was to him: a strange new experience that he knew and cared little about.

As I began to separate myself from my blanket I became more convinced than ever that I would never know what the union of my parents was about.

I couldn't understand why he was still in bed and not in the small room downstairs waiting for me to get up. This was to be the moment that my parents would show they cared. Every other day of her life my mother was the first out of bed. She'd have the fire going and the tea made before anyone else had a chance to complain about the weather. But this late winter morning she was still slumbering next to my father. I wanted to wake them up but I was afraid to. The small room I was sleeping in began to look bigger and the bed my parents slept in seemed to have shrunk. For some reason it didn't appear to be as big as I used to think it was. Maybe it was because I gave up on wondering about Molly and Paddy lying in it. Or maybe I had hoped they'd somehow turn to each other and change, even a little bit. I never saw two strangers so physically close to each other as my mother and father as they lay every night in the old bed like two tired stray dogs that had nothing to eat all day long. If beds could talk they'd say a lot more than walls. The bedspring had burst open a few weeks earlier and my father, perhaps for the fortieth time, knitted wire through it like a tailor sewing a pair of trousers. The chamber-pot, because it had been dropped so many times when my mother went to empty it in the outhouse had chips of its enamel peeled off it – it wasn't pushed completely under the bed. The large black handle on it was still sticking out from under the bed and it was in danger of being turned over when either my mother or father decided to use it. I only remember this happening once in my lifetime. It was when my father, after coming home from a funeral of one of his army buddies, had too much to drink. That night he woke up in his sleep singing soldier songs from World War I. My mother called him a "good for nothin'". In his retreat to get away from her that night Paddy stepped on the handle of the pot and it tipped over. My mother then leaped out of the bed and ran to the kitchen for a bucket and a handful of old rags to wipe up the mess.

I quietly got out of bed, crawled into my trousers and tiptoed out of the bedroom. When I stepped onto the stairway I made sure not to lean too heavily on the creaky stairs. I didn't want my two brothers and sisters to think I was waking them up so that they could say goodbye to me. Downstairs I put on the shirt I had placed in front of the fireplace the night before. The fading embers from the previous night's fire kept the chill out of it. I put my hands under the cold-water tap and sprinkled water on my face. The water was icy but I wasn't surprised. In less than a few seconds I had the new pair of socks on my feet. It was one of the rare times in my life that I had ever worn anything new and I took my time with the ceremony. Within minutes I was fully dressed. I opened the back-yard door and stepped out into the dark cold rainy morning for my corn-beef sandwich. The sandwich had been wrapped in old newspaper and I noticed that the print had come off on the bread. I took a bite out of it anyway and put the rest of it into my jacket pocket. I went back into the house and sat down on the chair in front of the fireplace and stared at my old suitcase that was held together by a long piece of twine. It looked like it had been around the globe at least twice before.

I looked around the house and noticed every little thing: the curtains, statues, chairs, and the dish that my mother put the pig's cheek on. The cups I drank my tea out of. I was looking forward to leaving but now when it was all a reality I wasn't sure. The little house and the small rooms didn't look so bad after all. Pictures and statues which I hadn't paid much attention to before were now looking warm and friendly. Even the statue of the Infant of Prague looked like it was related to me. The Sacred Heart of Jesus with his bleeding heart looked like a real person who had lived in the house ever since I could remember. I began to think they might be lonely and miss me when I departed. I was thinking of apologising for leaving.

I sat in the semi-darkness and wondered if I should wake up the rest of my family and remind them I was going away and might not be back ever again. If I made a noise somebody would wake up and come down and say goodbye to me. I put a spoon in a teacup and began tapping the inside of the cup. There was no response from anyone upstairs. I stopped the activity after about a minute. Everything around me was so dark I could hardly see myself. All was still and silent. I stood alone and I began to feel frightened. I was even afraid to reach down and pick up the suitcase. My wish to leave home was now terrifying me. If the weather was bad, which it was, I'd have an excuse for not leaving. I'd be able to tell anyone and everyone who asked that the weather kept me from leaving.

I opened the front door. The street was dark and the curtains in the windows of the small red-brick houses were fully drawn. It was even too early for Mrs. Mack to open her window. The street was wet but the rain had stopped and the sky appeared to be turning brighter. I stood outside the door and hoped the rain would come again and that the wind would blow and thunder and lightning would appear and wake everybody up so that they would know I couldn't travel in such bad weather. The longer I stood outside my house wishing for bad weather the clearer the sky became.

I stepped back into my house and sat again in front of the fireplace and waited for somebody to get up and tell me not to leave. My impatience grew. I walked up the staircase again and leaned heavily on the wooden steps and made them squeak and creak. When I got to the top of the landing there was the same stillness and the musical snore of my father. I coughed as if I was sick and suffering from pneumonia. I turned and jumped back down the stairs, hoping somebody would tell me to be quiet.

Down in the front room I was again wrapped in silence and loneliness. I stood in front of the mantelpiece and touched the photograph of my brother Nicholas and wondered what he would say if he knew I was leaving home without anyone in my family saying goodbye to me. If he was home he would tell me not to leave. He would tell me he wanted me to stay and play with him and be part of his life. Nicholas would cry if I told him I was leaving home. He'd beg me to stay. I opened and closed the door a few times, assuming somebody upstairs would think I had left the house and they'd rush down to tell me not to leave. Even with the banging of the door nobody got up.

In the hallway my eyes focused on the old gramophone. One of our two records was in place on the turntable. Fast and furious I wound the machine up. The record started to squeak and squawk and made a terrible noise that would wake the dead. "*I love you like I've never loved before . . .*" I let it squawk a while then stopped it. Did it wake anybody up? I listened. No. All was silent. I looked up the stairs hoping I'd see somebody, anybody, walking towards me. But I didn't. I saw the empty staircase looking down at me. No one was getting up. Not even to use the piss-pot. I felt I was at my own funeral. When my mother and my father, my brothers and sisters, wake up they'll find me gone, I thought. It was as if I hadn't lived in this little house at all.

Doing my best not to cry out loud, with each passing minute I began to accept that it was too late for me and my mother and father and the rest of the family to put together what had always seemed broken. I was one of ten children and I began to accept the fact that I was alone. I was alone then and I was alone now. Back before I reached my fifth birthday my mother once told me she was going to give me away. She said she would give me to the beggar man who showed up on our street once a week begging for money. For a very long time, until perhaps I was seven years old and had made my First Communion, the thought of the beggar man taking me away frightened me more than anything I could imagine. It was rumoured on the street that the beggar man had no home and no family and lived under a bush in a field a few miles outside of Dublin. Whenever my mother threatened to give me away I fell into a deep state of fear and cried until she reassured me that she wasn't really going to part with me. Even the shrill sound of the Banshee crying in the middle of a dark rainy winter's night, foretelling a death in the neighbourhood, didn't frighten me as much. The Banshee, I was told and it seemed to be accepted by everyone in Ireland at the time, was an old ghost-like woman with long dark hair that covered her entire body. The Banshee appeared or settled near a house that had a sick family member. In the middle of the night the Banshee cried and continuously combed her hair. It was believed that when the Banshee finished combing her hair the person she had come to cry over died.

I reached for the old suitcase and decided I had no choice but to leave. I opened the front door, placed my suitcase outside, looked back into the living room, pulled the front door shut and walked away from my home. Before I got to the corner I stopped and sat down on the suitcase.

Then, as if out of a cloud, the milkman and his horse and cart walked past me. "You're up early," he said as he placed his bottles of milk in front of the doors.

I was dying to talk to somebody, anybody, so I called after him. "I'm goin' away."

He didn't seem a bit surprised. "Where ya off ta?" he asked matter-of-factly.

"New York," I called to him. "I'm leavin' here."

"Ya want to take me with ya? You want to know how long I've been doin' this?" The man had been delivering the milk for as long as I could remember. He then called to me as I walked away from him. "Ya don't owe me any money by any chance, now do ya?"

For a second or two I thought he was serious.

He then quickly reassured me. "Ah I'm only jokin'. Listen to me, have a great time over there with the Yanks. I've a few relatives in Boston. If ya bump into any of 'em tell them to send me the fare and I'll be off meself."

He went on about his job and I was glad to have had contact with somebody on the lonely street so early in the morning. When the milkman's horse and cart turned the corner and went to another street I walked on, then stopped again to see if anyone in my family had remembered me. I looked up the street and it was empty.

Then, as I turned to go, I heard my mother's voice: "Gabriel? Gabriel?"

I looked back. She was running towards me. I was too frightened and confused to run towards her so I waited for her to catch up with me. As she approached I pretended to be strong and in control. When she caught up with me I couldn't look her straight in the eyes and tell her I might never see her again so I walked alongside her in silence, pretending I was happy to leave and looking forward to where I was going.

"I'll be over in America by this time next week, Ma. I'll send you a picture of me when I'm there. Miss Sheridan said the first thing I'm goin' to learn to do is drive a car. She said Mrs. Axe has about three or four cars and I can drive one of them."

My mother didn't react to what I was saying. I continued talking as fast as I could just to keep myself from breaking down.

"The ship I'm goin' on is half the size of Inchicore. You could fit two or three Shelbourne Hotels in it. The thing is so big it can't even come into the harbour in Cork. That's the truth, Ma."

We walked around the corner as the first bus of the day was approaching. The bus conductor was happy to have company so early in the morning.

"Good morning," he said as my mother and I found our seats at the back.

"Mornin', sir," Molly said with her reverence for anyone wearing a uniform.

He then slapped the bell, signalling the driver to depart. My mother sat quietly and passively next to me. The bus had just been washed and smelled of disinfectant and was sparkling clean. I looked out the window at the neighbourhood. The unseasonable morning light made it look more pleasant than I had ever before imagined.

As the bus rolled further away from Inchicore, my mother finally turned and faced me.

"Son, I want you to know I did me best with ya. I did me best. What more could I do with nothin' in the home? A few ha'pence and a few shillin' to feed a family on. Who could do it? Me whole body is filled with rheumatism from scrubbin' the cold marble floors of Hume Street Hospital. I did that for years when you were just a very young fella. I can hardly move me legs or me fingers from soakin' them in the water. Only God knows the pain I'm in. Divine Jesus knows how much pain I've known. Respectful Heart of Jesus, smile on me and help me in me pain. I don't know how to hold onto meself any more. I don't. Me prayers are the only thing I have left. Dear God, help me with the pain I carry around with me." My mother began to cry out loud.

I was hoping other people getting on the bus wouldn't see or hear us. I didn't want anybody to know that I was frightened and not able to hide or hold back the tears that were welling up in my eyes. I turned my face but I couldn't hold the tears back any longer.

"I'm sorry, Ma, I'm sorry."

My mother took out her rosary beads and wrapped them around her fingers. As she looked out the bus window, tears came to her eyes. "You remember your brother Nicholas, don't you, Gabriel?"

"Yes."

"He was a lovely boy but God called him and sure that's God's way. I still have a few locks of his hair. I took them the day he was laid out on the slab in Hume Street morgue. He had a smile on his face that day. I think he was happy that he was going to Heaven. Ah, but he was so young! Only a twelve-year-old! May God have mercy on his soul! I know he's up in Heaven with our Heavenly Father. That's the one bit of consolation I have, Gabriel. You know he's lookin' down at us even this mornin', son! Sure you know that, Gabriel, don't you? I'll meet me poor son Nicholas again some day. Please God, in any case." Tears were streaming down my mother's face. "The two of you spent half your childhood in that chip shop. Angelo Fusco the Italian man who owned it was as nice a man as you could find anywhere." My mother put her hand on the top of my head and looked directly at me again and as always I became self-conscious. "You're the spittin' image of your father. The spittin' image! He'll never be dead while you're alive."

It was difficult for me to look at her without thinking she was seeing Paddy. I reminded her of something she either loved or hated in him. I didn't know what it was but it was something she had lost or something she wished she had never found.

"There are times, son, when I look back on me life and wonder why I've never been able to live a life off me knees. If I'm not kneelin' and scrubbin' I'm kneelin' and prayin'. Even when I met your father I was washin' and scrubbin'. The Walshes didn't want any part of me in them days. I don't know what they were always complainin' about but that's the way they were. Who knows what life would have been like had your father and me stayed down in the country instead of runnin' away up here to Dublin? County Kildare wasn't such a bad place if you ask me. No, it wasn't! God help me!" She cried out as if God had no place else to go and nothing better to do than live and work in Inchicore.

After about ten minutes the conductor called out "James's Street!"

When I stepped from the bus I felt I was walking in some kind of dream and was beginning to think that soon I'd wake up from it.

My sister Rita was waiting. She was standing by a pram with her baby in it.

"Are ya wearin' the stockin's I bought for ya?" she asked me.

"I am."

"Ya have another pair, don't ya?"

"I do."

My mother was still sobbing. I was afraid to look at her because I might collapse and not go through with the journey. I was hoping when I got to the train station it was going to be the end of this bad dream. I wasn't able to think about where I was going. Any sense of the future vanished from my thoughts. I looked back to see if my father was behind me. Maybe he woke up and discovered me missing and got the next bus. He didn't. He might have been awake and he might have been too sad or even too afraid to say goodbye to me.

Rita asked, "Where's me daddy?"

My mother blurted out, "He's where he always is. He's in bed."

"Didn't he get up to say goodbye to Gabriel?"

"He didn't!" said my mother. "He was awake. I can assure you of that."

"An' he didn't get up?"

"I think he was asleep," I said.

"He was awake and he was starin' up at the ceilin'," said my mother. "I tell you no lie either."

"Ah, what's the matter with me father?" Rita said and began to cry.

"I think he was asleep," I said again. I didn't want Rita to know or think that our father didn't want to get up and say goodbye to me.

"Maybe he was afraid to get up," said Rita. "Maybe he just couldn't bear it or somethin'. I know me father and I think he gets afraid of things emotional. I bet he's cryin' right now. I know he's thinkin' about you, Gabriel. He's just afraid to let you know how much he cares. That's the way he is. And you're that way too if you want to know the truth. You're just like him. You are. Isn't he, Mother?"

My mother was silent for a moment. "I can't talk any more. I'm not feelin' well. I'm very sad. I shouldn't be lettin' you go, son. I shouldn't. It's a sin of some sort. I'll never be forgiven for lettin' ya go, son. Say a prayer for me when you get to where you're goin'." Then my mother put her hand to my face and kissed me on the cheek. "You're like Paddy. Yes, you are, son. You know what I mean? Don't you, Gabriel? But I think your father just forgot to wake up. He just forgot to wake up."

In the distance I could see the train station. We continued walking.

"How long are you goin' to be on that bloody boat?" Rita asked.

"I think a week." I'd been told it would take six days. This time of year it sometimes took an extra day. Crossing the Atlantic in December was not the best time or season to be travelling. Inside the train station a voice bellowed out, announcing the departure of the train to Cork. My mother and sister grabbed me and held me close. I bit my lower lip hoping I could keep myself from crying, but I couldn't. I broke away from them and boarded the train. When I got inside the carriage I saw my sister banging on the window. She was roaring crying. I thought I was going to pass out. I sat back in my seat, more frightened than I'd ever been in my life.

* * *

A few hours later the sounds of the Cork railroad station broke into my thoughts like a blacksmith hammering a horseshoe. I picked up my suitcase from the floor and stepped out of the train. Many faces and accents of Ireland were gathered in the railway station. Across the platform the smaller shuttle train was about to leave for Cobh which was on Cork Harbour to the east. Crowds of people with suitcases were piling onto it. Others were standing on the platform watching relatives hugging and kissing, crying, holding each other, perhaps for the last time. From Kerry, from Galway, from Tipperary, from all over Ireland men and women of all ages were going in the same direction as I was. Several women held very young babies in their arms and carried bags, suitcases and lots of other personal belongings. Families were breaking up.

The noise of the smaller shuttle train belched out. A man in a heavy black uniform, with a cord of green around his coat collar, called to everybody who was going to America to get on the shuttle. I walked through the crowd and found an open door on the train. The carriage was already crammed. Everyone wanted to be near the window. There was no one outside on the platform for me to see or wave goodbye to. Was my father still asleep? Was he still staring at the ceiling? I sat in a corner that faced the station wall. When the shuttle train began to depart the men and women in the carriage began to cry. Some stuck their heads out the window and yelled back to family and friends. I think I was the only passenger looking at the floor.

After disembarking from the shuttle train in Cobh we were herded onto a tender type of boat. It was windy and raining and everybody going to America got very wet. The tender pulled out from Cobh and sailed towards the *S.S. America*, out in the harbour. The ship was too massive to anchor at the dockside in Cobh. Everybody was eerily quiet. Only the sound of the tender's engine pushing and sloshing through the water could be heard. Faces turned to each other but seemed afraid to express the sadness of leaving. The tender continued its sputtering journey and seemed like a little duck swimming towards a big island. Most of the passengers had tears in their eyes but made no effort to wipe them away. The wind itself appeared to show a respect for the crying emigrants and left the watery beads on the faces undisturbed. As we drew closer and closer to the ship I was stunned at how big it was. The *S.S. America* was so massive it seemed to hold the anxious and impatient ocean still. The symbol of the future stood like a massive hungry Leviathan ready and even anxious to swallow us. In minutes two huge side doors on the ship opened and ladders and gangways appeared. A voice from the upper deck bellowed out instructions on how to approach and board the huge liner. The tender came to a halt alongside the massive boat. The heat from the flood-lights on the ship made a vapour from the chilly ocean water and it created a giant halo that made the marriage of the tender and ship rival any Benediction or religious service I had ever attended. The co-ordinated overture of clattering chains and ladders being lowered, mixed with calls and commands from the ship's crew, equalled what I thought might happen on Judgment Day when all who rose from the dead and qualified for salvation were called to the gates of Heaven.

In seconds and as if a magic celestial wand had been waved, people came to life again. I sensed for myself, and I believed for everybody else who stood around me, that the break had occurred. It was fast loud and clear and shrouded in fog and mist and watery air. My "past' went into some indefinable Limbo where even prayers couldn't reach it. The wish to leave home was manifesting itself clearer than ever before. I was now not indecisive or hesitant. Everybody grabbed their suitcases and got on board. In spite of the cold windy weather people in front and behind me were enveloped in excitement and were talking aloud.

"Where ya off ta?"

"Chicago, Chicago."

"I'm goin' to Philadelphia," another said out loud for everybody to hear.

"You know anybody in Brooklyn?" somebody said to somebody else.

Everybody seemed to be talking to one another even though they had probably never met before. All were related by their wishes for the future.

A woman with very red cheeks was talking out loud to a small group who had gathered around her. "I know everybody in Brooklyn," she said.

"They all know you too, Rosy!"

I walked along the deck a bit further and stood behind a slow-moving line. A man with two suitcases was in front of me. After a few seconds he sensed I was behind him, turned his head and asked in a very thick Cork accent, "Where you goin' ta?"

Before I had a chance to answer him several people called out at once.

"Chicago!"

"Brooklyn!"

"Philadelphia!"

A moment of silence followed. Somebody in the back of the line called out: "California, here I come!" There was loud laughter.

Just as suddenly the line to the cabins began to move a bit faster. Everybody seemed to be in a forced happy mood. Maybe there was no other way to be. Strangers talked to each other, knowing that they all had the impending journey in common. I made my way to the cabin I was assigned. When I entered a big man was sitting on the bed next to the porthole. I said hello and I began to unpack my suitcase. I wasn't bringing much: a second-hand pair of shoes, two of my brother's shirts and a pullover that had been repaired by my mother six months earlier. I wondered why I'd taken so much time to pack so little.

"I'm from Skibbereen," the man sitting on the bed said as he looked at me. The sound of his voice saved me. The man had a head of silver hair. "This is a sad day for me. I've just been back home for the last time. All me relatives are dead and I just sold the family farm."

He asked me if I'd ever been to West Cork.

"I'm from Dublin," I told him.

He fell silent and I noticed he had tears in his eyes.

"Are you alright?" I asked him.

He turned to me with tears streaming down his face. "I'm just tired and sad and what I think and say to meself doesn't make any sense to anybody any more. If I told anybody what I was thinking they'd want me to go see a doctor." He then managed to smile. "Who y'with?"

"I'm on my own."

"By yourself?"

"Yes."

"Where you goin'?"

"New York."

"Where you from agin?"

"Inchicore."

"Where's that?"

"Dublin."

"Dublin? A Dublin jackeen, are ya?" He laughed and stood up. "A good night's sleep will change everything." He then walked out of the cabin.

After putting my suitcase away I followed him onto the deck. It was a cold wet December day. Outside the big Corkman was staring out towards the sea. He seemed to be even sadder than before. When he noticed me standing next to him he slowly turned and walked back towards the cabin.

"I'm goin' in to lie down," the man from West Cork said to me as he went.

I remained standing and looking at the vast spread of ocean in front of me. Some lights went dark and the sounds and noises of the ship began to recede into a seemingly satisfied stillness. Standing alone on the deck I tried to convince myself that all was great in my life. I had broken away from my home and family and for the first time in a long time I sensed I was in a different place where I could only reach my past by closing my eyes. With very little knowledge of where I was going I got caught up in a flood of thoughts and began to feel like I was drowning in the baptism of suspense where images replaced words and thoughts had no beginnings or ends.

* * *

Eight days later and after what seemed like a lifetime of sea-sickness, the ship passed the Statue of Liberty. The cold December air didn't prevent most of the travellers from gawking at the huge statue. I stood among many of my fellow passengers and thought that I was in a dream of some kind. My fantasy image of America was now as real as the fierce wind that blew across my face. In many ways I didn't know where I was or even how I got there. It had something to do with what some of the waiters at the hotel called a crazy opera singer and my serving her breakfast under her bed. Maybe it had to do with the relationship of my parents and the big old bed they slept in. I sensed now that I'd never hear my father snore again or see him roll his cigarettes or hear him sing his soldier songs from World War I. And I knew for sure that the voice of my mother berating him for being a common labourer would not be ringing in my ears any more. The faces in my mind of screaming priests at Mass and the Communion wafers that slid down my throat began to fade as the big ship sailed further into New York Harbour. The need to seek a different future was slowly being answered by this awkward moment on the ship's deck.

An hour or so later we pulled into the harbour on the Upper West Side. I stood and observed the speeding back and forth of yellow taxis and about a million motor cars. Loudspeakers were again blaring and directing passengers to form queues for disembarkation. I stood in line with my old suitcase and walked slowly along the deck.

A few minutes later I saw two men in white carrying the man from West Cork on a stretcher. He didn't get up early like the rest of us who travelled with him across the Atlantic. I didn't know if he was alive or dead. He had made it across the ocean and I wondered if he had any way of telling his people, if he had any, that he had returned to America. Before I could think about it too much I was pushed along and directed towards customs.

--◄○►--

I was sitting in the back of a chauffeured black limousine with Maggie Sheridan. Mrs. Axe was seated in the passenger seat next to the driver. I was in a car for the first time in my life. The car appeared to be as big as my bedroom in Inchicore. It sped along the Saw Mill River parkway towards Tarrytown which was about twenty miles north of Manhattan. Maggie kept asking me how my mother was and if she cried when I left. I was so distracted by the scenery outside of the car I didn't really want to talk about Ireland, Dublin or my family. Images I had of America kept floating across my mind. Most of them of course were from the films I had seen in Dublin.

Maggie, in her usual chastising way told me to turn my head and pay attention to what she was saying. When I finally did turn to talk to her she corrected my English and told me to mind my manners.

Mrs. Axe looked back at both of us and laughed.

As the car continued its journey the chauffeur commented that the Tappan Zee Bridge spanning the Hudson River had opened just recently and the event was broadcast on television. Shortly thereafter the driver pulled off the parkway and in seconds drove through two open gates and almost instantly stopped in front of a huge mansion.

Mrs. Axe's home, as Maggie had reminded me in Dublin, was definitely a castle and looked like it was out of another century. As I stared in wonderment, a man approached and opened the car doors. Maggie and Mrs. Axe got out first. Because of the sight and size of the place I was looking at, I hesitated for a moment before putting my feet on the ground of what was to be my new abode.

Maggie turned back. "Get a move on!" she said to me.

I stepped out of the car and obediently followed her. A few seconds later the main door of the castle opened and Mr. Axe, a man small in stature, came out and shook my hand.

"So you're Gabriel," he said.

I inwardly struggled to be self-assured and answered, "Yes."

Maggie, Mrs. Axe and I then entered the mansion. Mr. Axe closed the huge door behind me. I walked across the massive foyer and for the first time in my life I knew that I would challenge and fight the memories that sometimes made me feel I was the loneliest person on earth.

If you enjoyed *Maggie's Breakfast*
you may also enjoy these memoirs
also by Poolbeg

ME DARLIN' DUBLIN'S DEAD AND GONE

Bill Kelly survived a tough childhood in Dublin to become
one of Ireland's foremost journalists, perhaps best known
for his *Sunday Press* soccer column as 'Big Bill' which was
so popular it ran for thirty years.

Here, with the sure touch of a born storyteller, he takes us
back to his tenement boyhood in a time when 'discos,
television, even the wireless were in the realm of science
fiction' and water wings were made from two paraffin-oil
tins and a piece of twine. Then he leads us onward through
his extraordinary and varied life – his Catholic schooling
where the nuns left him 'in no doubt that hell was a terribly
real place and damn few escaped it' – his debut boxing
event as a pro under an assumed name 'for a fiver for three
rounds' – his introduction to journalism in the newsroom
of Radio Éireann in 1946 – his brief career in PR when he
represented the great boxer Jack Doyle – how he
'rescued Kippure' with the Irish Parachute Club – his
boozing sessions with Brendan Behan and so much more.

Big Bill's love of his native city shines through every word
but it is his own exuberant and humorous take on life that
makes this such a memorable read.

BILL KELLY

ISBN 978-1-84223-566-9